# IBM BASIC®
## User's Handbook

# IBM BASIC®
# USER'S HANDBOOK

Weber Systems Inc. Staff

Ballantine Books • New York

**IBM BASIC® User's Handbook**
Copyright © 1982, 1983 by Weber Systems, Inc.

All rights reserved under International and Pan-American Copyright Conventions. Published in the United States by Ballantine Books, a division of Random House, Inc., New York, and simultaneously in Canada by Random House of Canada Limited, Toronto. This is a fully revised edition of **User's Handbook to IBM BASIC®**, originally published by Weber Systems, Inc.

Microsoft BASIC is a trademark of the Microsoft Corporation
Intel 8088 is a trademark of Intel Corporation
CP/M and CBASIC are trademarks of Digital Research Corporation
IBM PC, IBM BASIC, IBM DOS, IBM Monochrome Display/Printer Adapter, IBM Color Graphics Display Adapter, Asynchronous Communications Adapter, and BASIC 1.0, 1.1, and 2.0 are trademarks of IBM Corporation. This book has been neither authorized nor endorsed by IBM Corporation.

Library of Congress Catalog Card Number: 83-91204
ISBN 0-345-31593-6

Manufactured in the United States of America

First Ballantine Books Edition: February 1984
10 9 8 7 6 5 4 3 2 1

# CONTENTS

1. **INTRODUCTION TO IBM BASIC**     11

    IBM BASIC -- Background 11. Programming Languages -- High Level, Machine, and Assembly 12. Compiled vs. Interpreted Language 13. Cassette, Disk, and Advanced BASIC 14. BASIC 1.0, 1.1, and 2.0 14. IBM BASIC -- Overview 15. Start-Up Procedure 15. Cassette BASIC Start-Up 15. Disk and Advanced BASIC Start-Up 16. Immediate and Program Modes 20. Command and Statement Structure 21. Entering a Program 22. Listing a Program 25. Editing 28. Running a Program 34. Saving a Program 35. Loading a Program 36. Multiple Statements 37.

2. **DATA TYPES, VARIABLES, and OPERATORS**     39

    Introduction 39. Data Types 39. Strings 39. Numeric Data 40. Numeric Precision 42. Displaying Numeric Data 44. Variables -- an Overview 45. Variable Names 45. Initial Variable Values 47. Assignment Statements 49. Expressions & Operators 50. Arithmetic Operators 51. Order of Evaluation 52. Mixing Variable Types in Arithmetic Expressions 54. Relational Operators 54. Logical Operators 56. Order of Evaluation -- Overview. 61.

3. **INPUTTING AND OUTPUTTING DATA**     63

    Introduction 63. PRINT 63. WIDTH 67. LPRINT 68. PRINT USING 68. Numeric Formatting Characters -- Pound Sign 71. Decimal Point 72. Plus Sign 73. Comma 74. Dollar Sign

75. Asterisk 76. Exponential Notation 77. Ampersand 78. Backslash 78. Exclamation Point 79. Literal Characters 79. Horizontal Formatting 80. TAB 80. SPC 81. SPACE$ 81. Vertical Formatting 82. Inputting Data 83. INPUT 83. LINE INPUT 84.

4. **IBM BASIC CONDITIONAL, BRANCHING, AND LOOPING STATEMENTS**    87

Introduction 87. Conditional Branches 87. Branching Statements 88. Subroutines and GOSUB 89. Conditional Statements with Branching 90. Looping Statements 92.

5. **TABLES and ARRAYS**    95

Introduction 95. Subscripted Variables 95. Arrays and Tables 95. Dimensioning an Array 97. OPTION BASE 99. Array Data Types 100. DATA & READ 100.

6. **FUNCTIONS & STRING HANDLING**    105

Introduction 105. Built-In Numeric Functions 105. Mathematical Functions 105. User-Defined Functions 110. Strings and String Handling 112. String Concatenation 112. String Handling Functions 113. String/Numeric Data Conversion 116. Variable Table and String Storage 117. Housekeeping and FRE 118.

7. **FILES & FILE HANDLING WITH IBM BASIC**    121

Introduction 121. Files, Records, & Fields 121. File Specifications 123. Directories 124. Tree Structured Directories 126. Directory Paths 127. File Access 128. Sequential and Random Files 128. Opening a Sequential File 130. Writing to a Sequential File 134. Reading from a Sequential File 135. EOF, LOC, & LOF with Sequential Files 139. Random File Access 140. Opening and Closing a Random File 141. Field Variables 142. Writing Data 145. Writing a Record 145. Reading a Record 145. Reading Data 146. LOC & LOF with Random Files 146. File Commands 149. SAVE 149. LOAD 149. RUN 151. KILL 151. NAME 152. MERGE 152. CHAIN 152. FILES 152. File Devices 153.

8. **IBM BASIC GRAPHICS**    155

Introduction 155. Pixels 155. SCREEN 157. Text Mode 159.

Medium Resolution Graphics Mode 161. High Resolution Graphics Mode 164. IBM BASIC Graphics Statements 164. PSET and PRESET 164. LINE 165. CIRCLE 168. PAINT 171. DRAW 174. DRAW Movement Commands 175. M Command 177. B Command 178. N Command 178. C Command 178. A Command 179. TA Command 180. S Command 180. P Command 181. X Command 182. GET and PUT -- Graphics Mode 184. PUT Statement Operators 188. XOR, OR, AND 188. PSET and PRESET 190.

## 9. BASIC REFERENCE GUIDE 193

Introduction 193. ABS 194. ASC 194. ATN 195. AUTO 195. BEEP 197. BLOAD 197. BSAVE 198. CALL 199. CDBL 200. CHAIN 200. CHDIR 201. CHR$ 202. CINT 203. CIRCLE 203. CLEAR 204. CLOSE 205. CLS 205. COLOR 206. COM 209. COMMON 210. CONT 210. COS 211. CSNG 211. CRSLIN 212. CVI, CVS, CVD 212. DATA 212. DATE$ 213. DEF FN 214. DEFDBL, DEFSTR, DEFINT, DEFSNG 216. DEF SEG 217. DEF USR 217. DELETE 218. DIM 219. DRAW 219. EDIT 222. END 222. EOF 223. ERASE 224. ERR, ERL 225. ERROR 225. EXP 226. FIELD 227. FILES 228. FIX 229. FOR... NEXT 230. FRE 231. GET 232. GET (Graphics) 233. GOSUB... RETURN 234. GOTO 235. HEX$ 236. IF 236. INKEY$ 237. INP 238. INPUT 239. INPUT# 240. INPUT$ 241. INSTR 242. INT 243. KEY 244. KEY(a) 246. KILL 247. LEFT$ 248. LEN 248. LET 249. LINE 249. LINE INPUT 251. LINE INPUT# 252. LIST 253. LLIST 254. LOAD 255. LOC 256. LOCATE 257. LOF 258. LOG 259. LPOS 259. LPRINT 260. LPRINT USING 261. LSET, RSET 261. MERGE 262. MID$ 263. MKDIR 265. MKI$, MKS$, MKD$ 265. MOTOR 266. NAME 266. NEW 267. OCT$ 267. ON COM 268. ON ERROR 269. ON GOSUB, ON GOTO 270. ON KEY 271. ON PEN 273. ON PLAY 274. ON STRIG 274. ON TIMER 275. OPEN 276. OPEN COM 278. OPTION BASE 280. OUT 281. PAINT 281. PEEK 283. PEN 283. PLAY 285. PLAY Function 287. PMAP 287. POINT 288. POKE 289. POS 290. PRINT 290. PRINT USING 291. PRINT#, PRINT# USING 292. PSET, PRESET 293. PUT (Files) 293. PUT (Graphics) 294. RANDOMIZE 295. READ 296. REM 297. RENUM 297. RESET 298. RESTORE 299. RESUME 299. RETURN 300. RIGHT$ 301. RMDIR 302. RND 303. RUN 303. SAVE 304. SCREEN (Function) 305. SCREEN (Statement) 306. SGN 308. SIN 308. SOUND 309. SPACE$ 309. SPC 310. SQR 311. STICK 311. STOP 312. STR$ 313.

STRIG 313. STRIG( ) 314. STRING$ 315. SWAP 316. SYSTEM 316. TAB 317. TAN 317. TIME$ 318. TIMER 319. TRON & TROFF 319. USR 320. VAL 321. VARPTR 322. VIEW 322. WAIT 324. WHILE, WEND 325. WIDTH 326. WINDOW 327. WRITE 330. WRITE# 331.

| | |
|---|---:|
| **APPENDIX A. BASIC Reserved Words** | 333 |
| **APPENDIX B. IBM PC Device Names** | 334 |
| **APPENDIX C. IBM BASIC Error Messages** | 335 |
| **APPENDIX D. ASCII Character Codes** | 341 |
| **APPENDIX E. Extended Code for INKEY$** | 344 |
| **APPENDIX F. Keyboard Diagram & Scan Codes** | 345 |
| **INDEX** | 347 |

# INTRODUCTION

*IBM BASIC User's Handbook* is meant to serve as a tutorial as well as an ongoing reference guide to BASIC programming on the IBM PC computer. The latest release of IBM BASIC (version 2.0) is discussed in detail.

A number of examples are included with the text to illustrate the topics being discussed. Terms that may be unfamiliar to the reader are outlined in bold. These will be defined in subsequent paragraphs.

Chapter 1 is intended to serve as an overview of IBM BASIC. The steps necessary to start-up BASIC, enter, edit, and run a program, and save and load that program on a storage device are described.

Chapter 2 describes the various data types, variables, and operators utilized in IBM BASIC.

Chapter 3 discusses the use of PRINT, LRPINT, PRINT USING, and LPRINT USING in IBM BASIC in order to display data on the screen or printer. The use of INPUT and LINE INPUT for inputting data from the keyboard is also discussed.

Chapter 4 describes the various statements available in IBM BASIC for setting up loops, program control branches, and conditional branches.

Tables and arrays are discussed in Chapter 5 as well as the DATA, and READ statements. Chapter 6 includes a description of IBM BASIC's various built-in functions as well as its user-defined function.

Files and file handling are discussed in Chapter 7. The various IBM BASIC file commands are also discussed in this chapter.

IBM BASIC's graphics modes and graphics commands are described in Chapter 8. Chapter 9 serves as a detailed reference guide to IBM BASIC's commands, functions, and statements.

*IBM BASIC User's Handbook* includes six useful appendices. These detail IBM BASIC's reserved words, device names, error messages, ASCII codes, INKEY's extended codes, and keyboard scan codes.

# CHAPTER 1.
# INTRODUCTION TO IBM BASIC

**INTRODUCTION**

In this chapter, we will provide an overview of the background and history of IBM BASIC as well as the operating details you will need to know to begin using IBM BASIC. These include start-up, program entry, statement structure, program editing, program saving, and program loading.

**IBM BASIC -- BACKGROUND**
**History**

BASIC was developed at Dartmouth College in the early 1960's by professors John G. Kemeny and Thomas E. Kurtz. BASIC was designed as a simple, easy-to-use programming language.

Over the years, dozens of different versions of BASIC have been developed. IBM BASIC is a version of Microsoft BASIC, a variation of BASIC widely used with personal computers. Microsoft BASIC was developed in 1975 by William Gates and Paul Allen for the MITS Altair computer. Gates and Allen eventually formed their own firm, Microsoft Corporation, to market their version of BASIC.

Microsoft BASIC became the industry standard in the personal computer field, and Microsoft Corporation went on to develop and/or market a number of other personal computer related items, including MS-DOS, the disk operating system used on the IBM PC.

Since versions of Microsoft BASIC are available on a number of different computers, learning to program the IBM PC in Microsoft BASIC will help you immensely in mastering variations of that language on other personal computers such as those marketed by TRS-80, Apple, and Commodore.

**Programming Languages**
**High-Level, Machine, and Assembly**

BASIC, like COBOL, FORTRAN, and PASCAL, is a **high level programming language.** In fact, BASIC strongly resembles FORTRAN.

With a high-level language, the programmer need not have a knowledge of the **machine language** used by the computer's microprocessor. With machine or **assembly languages,** an in-depth understanding of the computer and microprocessor is required to write programs.

A machine language program uses numbers to communicate instructions to the microprocessor. For example, the hexadecimal number EA will tell the computer to jump to another memory location and resume execution at that memory location.

An assembly language program uses a phrase known as a **mnemonic** to communicate instructions. The mnemonic JMP is used in 8088 assembly to instruct the computer to jump to another memory location and resume execution there.

Moreover, in both machine and assembly languages, the microprocessor must be told where to find the data to be operated on.

With a high-level language such as BASIC, commands are generally specified in English words that can be associated with the operation to be performed. For example, the BASIC command PRINT instructs the computer to display information. Moreover, high-level languages generally do not require that the programmer specify memory addresses.

In conclusion, it is usually much easier to program in a high-level language as opposed to a machine or assembly language.

However, a high-level language (BASIC included), does have some disadvantages as compared to machine or assembly languages. A high-level language generally requires more memory storage and executes more slowly than does a machine or assembly language program. Also, certain programming tasks can be accomplished in machine or assembly language that could not be accomplished with a high-level language.

For the vast majority of IBM PC users, a high-level language is the most efficient means of programming their computer, and IBM BASIC is by far the most widely used of all high level languages on the PC.

**Compiled vs. Interpreted Language**

High-level computer languages are often distinguished as being either **compiled** or **interpreted** languages.

A compiled language program consists of the **source code** and the **compiled code.** The source code consists of the program statements in their original form. For example, the following is a line of source code from a program written in the CBASIC compiled language:

100 INPUT "ENTER TODAY'S DATE:";DATE.1

The source code is processed by a program known as a **compiler** into the compiled code. The compiled code is very similar to the machine language used by the microprocessor. The compiled code is the code actually used when a compiled program is run. A program known as a **run-time monitor** is used to run the compiled program.

An interpreted language consists of only the source code. The source code is translated line-by-line directly into machine language instructions. The Microsoft BASIC language that is standard on the IBM PC is an interpreted language.

One advantage of interpreted languages over compiled languages is that interpreted language programs are more easily developed. When working with interpreted languages, a programmer need only write a program, enter it, run it, and alter it at his own leisure. When working with a compiled language, the source code must be recompiled every time it is edited. This can be frustrating during the program debugging process.

One advantage of compiled languages over interpreted languages is that the execution time is much faster. The compiled code is much closer to the machine language than the source code. Since interpretation is not necessary, execution of compiled code is much faster.

**Cassette, Disk, and Advanced BASIC**

Three separate versions of IBM BASIC are available for the PC; Cassette BASIC, Disk BASIC, and Advanced BASIC.

Cassette BASIC includes the majority of the available IBM BASIC commands. Disk and Advanced BASIC contain all of the capabilities of Cassette BASIC as well as additional commands that allow the usage of diskettes for data and program storage.

Cassette BASIC is available in ROM on any IBM PC. Both Disk and Advanced BASIC require DOS before they can be run, or before any programs written in these versions can be run. Therefore, both Disk and Advanced BASIC can only be used with an IBM PC with at least one disk drive. Moreover, Disk BASIC requires a minimum of 32K of RAM and Advanced BASIC requires 48K of RAM.

All three versions of BASIC have graphics capability and support an extended character set of 256 letters, numbers, special symbols, and international characters. Disk BASIC also supports disk input and output, contains an internal clock for maintaining the system date and time, supports RS-232 communications, and also allows the usage of two additional printers.

**BASIC 1.0, 1.1, and 2.0**

IBM has released three different variations of IBM BASIC. BASIC 1.0 was the earliest release. BASIC 1.1, which followed 1.0, was almost identical. BASIC 2.0 includes a number of new features not available in BASIC 1.0 and 1.1.

In this book, we will attempt to identify commands found only in BASIC 2.0.

## IBM BASIC -- OVERVIEW
### Start-Up Procedure

As we discussed earlier, BASIC is a high-level language which must be interpreted into the microprocessor's native machine language. This is accomplished with a program known as an **interpreter.**

Before you can execute a BASIC program, the interpreter must be active. The Cassette BASIC interpreter, which is stored in ROM, is activated when the PC's power is turned on.

However, if you are using Disk or Advanced BASIC, the procedure is somewhat more involved. Before loading the Disk or Advanced BASIC interpreter (which are actually extensions of the Cassette BASIC interpreter stored in ROM), DOS must be loaded into memory from disk. After DOS has been loaded, the Disk or Advanced interpreter must then be loaded.

### Cassette BASIC Start-Up

If you wish to start Cassette BASIC on an IBM PC without disk drives, merely turn on the power switch. A display similar to Illustration 1-1 will appear on the video screen.

If you wish to load Cassette BASIC on an IBM PC which contains disk drives, be certain that the system (leftmost) drive does not contain a diskette with DOS copied on it. If it does, DOS will automatically be loaded when the computer is turned on.

### Disk and Advanced BASIC Start-Up

Before the Disk or Advanced BASIC interpreters can be loaded, IBM's disk operating system (DOS) must be loaded.

**Illustration 1-1. Cassette BASIC Start-Up Display**

```
The IBM Personal Computer BASIC
Version D 1.00 Copyright IBM Corp. 1981
xxxxx Bytes Free
Ok
___
```

**Illustration 1-2. DOS Start-Up Display**

```
Enter today's date (m-d-y): 6/24/83
The IBM Personal Computer DOS
Version 1.00  Copyright IBM Corp. 1981

A > ___
```

If you purchased your IBM Personal Computer with one or more optional disk drives, you should have received a copy of DOS. Do not use your master copy of DOS for everyday use. Make copies of the master, and use these copies for everyday use.

To start-up DOS, first insert a copy of the DOS diskette in the diskette drive on the left side of the PC. During insertion, the label side of the diskette should be facing up. Keep inserting the diskette until you hear a click. Then, close the lever over the diskette drive.

Next turn on the power to the monitor and printer (if connected), and finally turn on the power to the System Unit. The following message will be displayed:

>    Enter today's date (m-d-y):

Once the date has been entered, the display will resemble that shown in Illustration 1-2.

The prompt (A >) indicates which is your current drive (in this case -- drive A).

Next, type in the following:

>    A > BASIC [ENT]

If the user wishes to start Advanced BASIC rather than Diskette BASIC, he can do so by entering BASICA rather than BASIC. All other procedures are the same.

The Ok is known as the IBM BASIC prompt. This prompt indicates that BASIC commands or programs can be entered.

If you are a beginning programmer, the information in the remainder of this section may seem a bit confusing. If so, skip this section and continue with the next.

When you are loading Disk or Advanced BASIC, additional parameters can be included with the BASIC or BASICA entry. These parameters can be used for the following purposes:

- Set aside storage areas for programs and data.
- Set aside storage area for buffers.
- Instruct BASIC to load and run a program.

---

___ -- underline signifies operator entry.
[ENT] -- signifies pressing the Enter key.

The configuration for the BASIC command with all of its optional parameters is as follows:

> BASIC [A] [*filespec*] [<*input*] [>] [>*output*]
> [/F:*files*] [/S:*bufsize*] [/C:*bufcom*]
> [/M:[*workarea*][,*blockspace*]] [/D]

The optional parameter *filespec* indicates the file specification of a program that is to be automatically loaded and executed by BASIC. If no filename extension is specified, the extension .BAS will be specified. In BASIC 2.0, *filespec* can include a directory path specification.

Generally, data is input into a BASIC program via the keyboard. <*input* (BASIC 2.0 only) allows a BASIC program to receive data from a file specified by the user. For example, the following command line:

> BASIC PROGRAMA < TEXTA

causes data to be read by INPUT, LINE INPUT, INPUT$, and INKEY$ from the file TEXTA.

Generally, a BASIC program outputs data to the screen. >*output* (BASIC 2.0) allows a BASIC program to output data to a file specified by the user. For example, the following command line:

> BASIC PROGRAMB > FILEB

causes data written by the PRINT statement to be output to the file named FILEB.

Any BASIC command line option preceded by a slash (/) is known as a **switch.** Switches are used to specify optional parameters on the BASIC command line.

The optional parameter /F:*files* indicates the maximum number of files that are allowed to be open at one time while a BASIC program is being executed. The maximum number allowed is 15. If this parameter is omitted, the number of files open will default to 3.

Introduction to IBM BASIC 19

In BASIC 2.0, the number of files that can be specified with /F depends upon the value indicated for the FILES parameter in CONFIG.SYS, the DOS configuration file. The default for FILES is 8, of which BASIC uses 4 files by default. This leaves 4 files available for BASIC I/O operations. Therefore, the maximum value for /F when FILES = 8 is /F:4.

The optional parameter /S:*bufsize* assigns the buffer size to be used with random files. The default value for the buffer size is 128. The maximum size that may be used is 32767. For maximum performance, IBM recommends that you use a buffer size of 512 bytes for random file buffer size. Note that the record length parameter used with the OPEN statement may not be greater than the number of bytes specified in /S:*bufsize*.

The optional parameter /C:*bufcom* is used to initialize the area to be reserved for the communications receive buffer. This parameter is not used unless the Asynchronous Communications Adapter is installed on your system. The default value for this parameter is 256 bytes for the receive buffer and 128 bytes for the transmit buffer. IBM recommends that the value /C:1024 be used for high speed lines. If a value of /C:0 is specified, no buffer space will be reserved for communications. In this case, communications support will be disabled when BASIC is loaded.

The optional parameter /M:*workarea* can be used to initialize the maximum amount of memory in bytes that can be used as a work area under BASIC. The maximum value that can be used is 64K. The default value is 64K. This parameter is often used to reserve work area in memory for machine language subroutines.

/M:*blockspace* allows the user to reserve a working area above the BASIC work area in memory for loading BASIC programs. This is only used in BASIC Version 2.0.

*blockspace* is specified in multiples of 16. When *blockspace* is omitted, the default multiplier (4096) is assessed. Therefore, since 4096 x 16 = 65536, 65536 bytes are allocated by default for BASIC's work area. The following parameter:

/M:,2048

would reserve a maximum of 32,768 bytes for BASIC working area (as 2048 x 16 = 32,768). The following command:

/M:32512,2048

would reserve 32,768 bytes for BASIC but would only allow the usage of the lower 32,512 bytes. The remaining 256 bytes would be reserved for program storage.

/D is a switch which instructs BASIC (2.0 only) that ATN, COS, EXP, LOG, SIN, SQR, and TAN are to be used with double precision values. /D requires approximately 3K of additional RAM for the increased storage required for the double precision values.

When specifying these optional parameters (*files, bufsize, bufcom,* and *work area*), a decimal, octal, or hexadecimal number must be used. Octal number entries must be preceded by &O and hexadecimal number entries must be preceded by &H.

**Immediate and Program Modes**

The immediate mode is also known as the direct or the calculator mode. In the immediate mode, most BASIC command entries result in the instructions being executed without delay. For example, if the following immediate mode line was entered, and the Enter key pressed,

PRINT "JIM SMITH"

the following would be displayed on the video screen:

JIM SMITH

In the program or indirect mode, the computer accepts program lines into memory, where they are stored for later execution. This stored program is executed when the appropriate command (generally RUN) is entered.

Illustration 1-3 contains an example of the entry of a program in the program mode and its execution.

**Illustration 1-3. Program Mode Entry & Execution**

```
Ok
10 PRINT "JIM SMITH"
20 PRINT "1220 EUCLID AVE"
30 PRINT "CLEVELAND, OH 44122"
40 END
RUN
JIM SMITH
1220 EUCLID AVE
CLEVELAND, OH 44122
Ok
```

Notice that in the program mode, that each BASIC program line must be preceded with a line number. Line numbers will be discussed in more detail later in this chapter.

**Command and Statement Structure**

In IBM BASIC, instructions being relayed to the interpeter are known as **commands** in the immediate mode and **statements** in the program mode. In practice, the difference between a command and a statement is primarily one of semantics, as both generally use the same structure and keywords.

Both commands and statements begin with a BASIC **keyword** or **reserved word.** The keyword identifies the operation to be undertaken by the BASIC interpreter. For example, in the preceding section, the PRINT command was used to instruct the PC to display information on the screen.

In IBM BASIC, keywords may be entered in either uppercase or lowercase letters. In the examples in this book, we will display keywords as uppercase letters.

A BASIC command or statement generally includes one or more **arguments** or **parameters** following the keyword. In our example, PRINT "JIM SMITH", "JIM SMITH" is the PRINT statement's parameter.

**Entering a Program**

In the preceding section, we touched upon the fundamentals of entering and running a BASIC program on the IBM PC. In this section, we will expand upon that discussion using the example in Illustration 1-4.

BASIC programs are entered as **program lines.** Any text preceded with a number (**line number**) and ended by pressing the Enter key will be regarded as a program line.

The maximum number of characters that may be included in any one line is 255 including Enter. If a line contains more than 255 characters, those extra characters will be dropped, or **truncated,** when Enter is pressed.

Note that in the first 5 lines of illustration 1-4, a program was entered in the command mode and run in the execute mode. After the answer, 5.0, had been displayed, the Ok prompt appeared.

At this point, the original program is stored in RAM, and can be run again if desired. Also, the program being held in RAM can be added to or changed. That is what was done in line number 150 of Illustration 1-4. An additional statement was inserted between statements 100 and 200 in the program being stored in RAM. This revised program can be executed by again entering RUN.

RAM can only hold one program at a time. The NEW command is used to erase the program in memory so as to allow a new program to be entered. Note the use of NEW in Illustration 1-4.

Note in our examples the following features common to the BASIC programs:

Introduction to IBM BASIC 23

**Illustration 1-4. Entering and Running a Program**

```
Ok
100 PRINT 5
200 END
RUN
 5
Ok
150 PRINT -5
RUN
 5
-5
Ok
NEW
Ok
100 PRINT 50
200 END
RUN
 50
Ok
```

1. Each program line must begin with a line number. The computer executes program lines in order from lowest line number to highest line number.

2. The END statement signals the end of a program. When END is executed, the program run will stop and the Ok prompt will be displayed.

It is recommended that consecutive line numbers (i.e. 1, 2, 3, 4, 5, etc.) not be used in a program. By using line numbers which are a fixed multiple (i.e. 100, 200, 300, etc.), additional line numbers can be inserted between existing lines without renumbering the line numbers.

Line numbers need not be entered in any particular order. For example, the user could enter lines 100 and 200 and then enter line 150. The computer will automatically rearrange the lines according to their line numbers.

If the user enters two lines with the same line number, the computer will erase the first line and replace it with the second. This feature allows the user to replace an entire line by merely entering a new line with the same line number.

A new line can be added to a BASIC program by merely entering a line number followed by the desired text and Enter. When Enter is pressed, the line will be saved as part of the BASIC program.

To delete a line in an existing program, merely enter the line number of the line to be deleted followed by Enter. A group of lines can be deleted via the DELETE command, and an entire program can be deleted with the NEW command. These will be discussed in detail in Chapter 9.

Line numbers can be generated automatically using IBM BASIC's AUTO command. When AUTO is entered without any parameters, line numbers will be generated beginning with 10. Each time the Enter key is pressed, a new line number will be generated with an increment of 10. An automatic line number sequence is depicted in Illustration 1-5. Notice that when the Control and Break keys are pressed simultaneously in line 40, automatic line numbering will end.

**Illustration 1-5. Automatic Program Line Numbering**

```
Ok
AUTO
10 PRINT "JIM SMITH"
20 PRINT "1000 EUCLID AVE"
30 PRINT "CLEVELAND, OH 44059"
40 [Ctrl-Break]
Ok
RUN
JIM SMITH
1000 EUCLID AVE
CLEVELAND, OH 44059
Ok
```

AUTO can also be used with optional parameters to begin line numbering with an initial line number other than 10 as well as an increment other than 10. The use of these parameters is discussed in Chapter 9.

IBM BASIC's RENUM command can be used to renumber program lines. If RENUM is executed without any of its optional parameters, the program in memory's first line will be renumbered as line 10. Successive lines will be renumbered in increments of 10. An example of the usage of RENUM is given in Illustration 1-6.

RENUM can also be used with an optional parameter to specify the value to be used for the first new line number. This is again illustrated in Illustration 1-6. Notice that the execution of RENUM 100 causes the initial line number's value to be 100.

A second parameter can be specified with RENUM to indicate the line number in the current program where renumbering is to begin. This is also depicted in Illustration 1-6. Notice that the command RENUM 115,110 causes line renumbering to begin with line 110.

A third parameter can also be included with RENUM to specify the increment to be used in generating new line numbers. In Illustration 1-6, the following command,

RENUM 1000,100,500

causes the line numbers beginning with 100 to be renumbered with an initial value of 1000 and an increment of 500.

**Listing a Program**

LIST is used to display the program stored in RAM on the screen or printer. This display is often referred to as a **program listing.** An example of the use of LIST is given in Illustration 1-6.

If the program being listed is a lengthy one, it may be listed too quickly to be examined. If this is the case, the listing may be

### Illustration 1-6. RENUM Example*

```
Ok
17 PRINT "This program"
27 PRINT "needs new"
41 PRINT "line numbers."
RENUM
Ok
LIST
10 PRINT "This program"
20 PRINT "needs new"
30 PRINT "line numbers."
Ok
RENUM 100
Ok
LIST
100 PRINT "This program"
110 PRINT "needs new"
120 PRINT "line numbers."
Ok
RENUM 115,110
Ok
LIST
100 PRINT "This program"
115 PRINT "needs new"
125 PRINT "line numbers."
Ok
RENUM 1000,100,500
Ok
LIST
1000 PRINT "This program"
1500 "needs new"
2000 PRINT "line numbers."
Ok
```

---

* LIST causes the program in memory to be displayed on the screen.

stopped by pressing the Ctrl* and NumLock keys simultaneously.**. The listing can be restarted by pressing any other character key.

LIST can be used with optional parameters to display only a portion of the program. For example, LIST can be used with a single line number parameter to list only that line. This is shown in Illustration 1-7.

**Illustration 1-7. LIST'ing a Program**

```
Ok
LIST 1000
1000 PRINT "This program"
Ok
LIST 1000-1500
1000 PRINT "This program"
1500 PRINT "needs new"
Ok
LIST -1500
1000 PRINT "This program"
1500 PRINT "needs new"
Ok
LIST 1500-
1500 PRINT "needs new"
2000 PRINT "line numbers."
Ok
```

LIST can also be used to list a range of line numbers. For example, the command LIST 1000-1500 would list all line numbers with values in the range 100 to 200. This is again shown in Illustration 1-7.

LIST can be used to display all line numbers from the beginning

---

* Ctrl is an abbreviation for Control
** When the Ctrl key is pressed simultaneously with a second key, the operation is known as a Control key combination and is generally abbreviated with Ctrl followed by the second key (ex. Ctrl-NumLock).

of the program to a specified line by prefixing that line number with a hyphen and using it as the LIST parameter. For example, the following command:

LIST -1500

would cause all program lines to be listed up to and including line 1500.

If the line number parameter is followed by a hyphen, all program lines after and including the specified line will be listed. This is demonstrated in the final example in Illustration 1-7.

If you wish the listing output to the printer rather than to the screen, you can do so by specifying LLIST rather than LIST.

**Editing an IBM BASIC Program**

Once you have entered a program, you may discover an error and need to change or edit it. One way to make corrections is to retype the entire line that contains the error.

Fortunately, there is a much easier way to edit program lines. The IBM PC's **line editor** or **editor** allows the user to insert, delete, or change text within a program line.

The editing of a program line consists of the following four steps:

1. Display the lines to be edited on the screen if they are not already present.
2. Locate the position where the change is to be made.
3. Enter the change via the keyboard.
4. Send the change to memory by pressing the Enter key.

These four steps are accomplished with a group of special commands such as LIST and EDIT and the editing keys. The majority of these keys are located on the numeric keypad. When the NUMLOCK key is depressed, the numeric keypad can be used for entering numbers. When the NUMLOCK key is not depressed, the numeric keypad keys can be used for editing purposes.

Each editing key has a symbol or group of letters on it, such as ←, →, ↑, ↓, DEL etc. These symbolize that key's editing function. The BASIC program editing keys are summarized in Table 1-1.

Introduction to IBM BASIC   29

### Table 1-1. BASIC Program Editor Keys

| Key | Function |
|---|---|
| Home | This key can be used to move the cursor to the upper lefthand position on the screen. |
| Ctrl-Home | This key combination clears the screen and positions the cursor to the "home" position. |
| ↑ | Moves the cursor up one row (Cursor-Up). |
| ↓ | Moves cursor down by one row (Cursor-Down). |
| ← | Moves cursor one position to the left. If the cursor is positioned to the leftmost position, it will "wrap around" to the rightmost position of the preceding line (Cursor Left). |
| → | Moves cursor one position to the right. If the cursor is in the rightmost position, it will move to the leftmost position of the next line down (Cursor Right). |
| Ctrl → | Moves cursor to the next word. Words are groups of characters which begin with either a letter or a number and are separated from other words by blanks or special characters. Ctrl → is also known as next word. |
| Ctrl ← | This key combination is also known as previous word. It moves the cursor to the previous word. |
| End | Moves the cursor to the end of the logical line. |
| Ctrl-End | Erases from the cursor position to the end of the logical line. |
| Ins | This sets the insert mode. If the insert mode |

**Table 1-1 (cont). BASIC Program Editor Keys**

| | |
|---|---|
| | was off, pressing Ins turns it on. If the insert mode was on, pressing this key turns it on. If the flashing cursor covers the lower half character position, the insert mode is on. The insert mode is also turned off when the user presses any of the cursor movement keys or Enter. |
| Del | This key deletes the characters at the current cursor position. All characters to the right of the deleted character are moved one position to the left to fill the space left empty by the deleted character. |
| Backspace | The Backspace key is identified by ← (like the Cursor left key). However, the Backspace key is located directly to the left of the NUMLOCK key. The Backspace key results in the deletion of the last character typed. In other words, the character to the left of the cursor will be erased. The characters to the right of the one deleted will be moved one position to the right to fill the empty position. |
| ESC | This key will cause the entire line to be erased from the screen when it is pressed anywhere within that line. If the line is a program line, it will not be erased from the program in memory. |
| Ctrl-Break | This key combination causes the program to return to the direct mode. Any changes made to the line being edited will not be saved. |
| →| | The Tab key moves the cursor to the next tab stop. Tab stops occur every eight character positions.<br><br>When the insert mode is on, pressing the |

Introduction to IBM BASIC 31

**Table 1-1 (cont). BASIC Program Editor Keys**

|  | Tab key causes blanks to be inserted from the current cursor position to the next tab stop. |
|---|---|

## Editing Example

The best way to illustrate the editing process is with the use of an example. Suppose that the following program lines had been typed in:

    100  DASA 200,300,400,500,600
    200  READ A, B, C, D, E
    —

The underline in line 3 indicates the position of the cursor.

Our example contains an error; the misspelling of DATA. Also, we wish to insert 100, before 200 in line 100, and also delete ,600 from the end of the same line.

Our first step is to position the cursor at the first error. To correct the error in line 100, we would first press the ↑ key twice and then press the → key 6 times. The cursor would now be positioned as follows:

    100  DA_S_A 200,300,400,500,600
    200  READ A, B, C, D, E

Step 1 of the editing process has now been accomplished. The cursor is positioned over the error. We are now ready to execute Step 2 by typing in the change. In this case, we merely type in T. The T will replace the S. The following will then be displayed:

    100  DATA_ 200,300,400,500,600
    200  READ A, B, C, D, E

We could press Enter at this point to send the change into RAM. However, since we have 2 additional corrections (the insertion of 100, and the deletion of ,600), we will continue editing.

First of all, we will move the cursor two spaces to the right by pressing the → key twice. The display will then appear as follows:

        100 DATA 2̲00,300,400,500,600
        200 READ A, B, C, D, E

At this point, we wish to insert 100, in the DATA list. To do this, we press the Ins (Insert) key and enter the data to be inserted (100,). The new text will be entered at the current cursor position, and all existing text will move to the right. The display will now appear as follows:

        100 DATA 100,2̲00,300,400,500,600
        200 READ A, B, C, D, E

Once the required data has been inserted, the insert mode should be cancelled. This is done by pressing the Ins key once again. We can now make more corrections on the same line.

Another way to cancel the insert mode is to press the Enter key. However, doing so sends the current program line to RAM. Since we have one final correction on the current line, we will turn off the insert mode by pressing the Ins key a second time.

Our final correction is to delete ,600 from line 100. First, the cursor should be positioned under the comma preceding 600 by pressing the → key the required number of times.

We are now ready to delete ,600. This is accomplished by pressing the Del key 4 times. Every time the Del key is pressed, the character at the cursor position is deleted and the remainder of the text in the line is moved one position to the left. After pressing the Del key 4 times, our display appears as follows:

        100 DATA 100,200,300,400,500__
        200 READ A, B, C, D, E

Since the needed corrections have been made, we are now ready to send line 100 to memory. This is accomplished by pressing the Enter key.

In the preceding example, the lines being edited were already displayed on the screen. If the lines to be edited are not displayed, you can display them by executing the LIST or EDIT command.

For example, if the following lines were stored in RAM,

>        100  DATA 100,200,300,400,500
>        200  READ A, B, C, D, E

and the screen was blank with the cursor in the **home** position, the LIST command could be used as shown in Illustration 1-8 to display line 100.

Also, the EDIT command could be used as shown in Illustration 1-9 to display line 100. The EDIT command is explained in more detail in Chaper 9.

**Illustration 1-8. LIST Example**

```
LIST 100
100  DATA 100,200,300,400,500
Ok
___
```

### Illustration 1-9. EDIT Example

```
EDIT 100
100  DATA 100,200,300,400,500
```

**Running a Program**

Once a program is present in memory, the operator can run it. As mentioned previously, a program can be entered into memory via the keyboard or it can be loaded into memory from a storage device such as the floppy disk drive. The procedure for loading programs will be discussed later in this chapter.

The RUN command is used to begin program execution. RUN can be used with or without an optional line number or file specification as its parameter. Because RUN is generally executed without an optional parameter, we will limit our discussion of RUN in this section to its execution without parameters. The usage of RUN with parameters is discussed in Chapter 9.

When the RUN command is entered and the Enter key pressed, program statements entered in the indirect mode (with line numbers) will be executed in order, beginning with the lowest line. An example of the usage of RUN is shown in Illustration 1-10.

Introduction to IBM BASIC 35

**Illustration 1-10. RUN Command**

```
Ok
100 PRINT "THIS IS LINE 1"
200 PRINT "LINE 2 IS BEING EXECUTED"
300 PRINT "LINE 3 IS BEING EXECUTED"
400 PRINT "LINE 4 IS THE FINAL LINE"
500 END
RUN
THIS IS LINE 1
LINE 2 IS BEING EXECUTED
LINE 3 IS BEING EXECUTED
LINE 4 IS THE FINAL LINE
Ok
```

**Saving a Program**

As you may recall from our discussion of program entry, only one BASIC program may be stored in RAM at any one time. When the IBM PC's power is turned off, the contents of RAM are erased and any program stored there will be lost unless it is first stored on a permanent medium such as cassette or diskette.

Before a program can be saved, it must first be assigned a name from one to eight characters in length. This name is known as a **filename.** A filename can also include a suffix of three characters known as a **filename extension.** The filename and filename extension must be separated with a period. A detailed discussion of filenames is included in Chapter 7.

Once you have decided upon a filename for your program, you can save it on diskette or cassette using the SAVE command.

For example, if Cassette BASIC was active, you could save the program in RAM on cassette with the following command:

SAVE "PRGMA"

If either Disk or Advanced BASIC was active, the program would be saved on diskette rather than cassette.

When SAVE is executed, the program remains in RAM where it can be added to, edited, or run if desired.

When the SAVE (and LOAD) commands are specified with Disk and Advanced BASIC, the program file will be saved on the **default** drive. IBM's Disk Operating System specifies drive A as the default drive upon power on. The user can, however, change the default drive to B, C, etc.

If the user wishes to save a program file on a drive other than the default, he can do so by prefixing the filename indicated with SAVE with the letter of the drive where the file is to be saved. For example, the following command,

SAVE "B:PRGM1"

would cause the program in RAM to be saved on the diskette in drive B with the filename PRGM1.

The various device names used in IBM BASIC are listed on page 154. Notice that the cassette also has a device name (CAS1:).

**Loading a Program**

Once a program has been saved on cassette or diskette, it can again be loaded back into memory using the LOAD command. If LOAD is executed under Cassette BASIC, IBM BASIC will search the cassette tape for the indicated file. If either Advanced or Disk BASIC are active, LOAD will search the indicated diskette for the file to be loaded.

An example of a LOAD command is given below:

LOAD "PRGM2"

As with the SAVE command, a device name should be specified in front of the filename if the file to be loaded is not located on the default drive.

Before a program is loaded, any existing program in memory will be erased. Once the program has been loaded into memory, it can be edited or run as any other program would be.

If the file specified with LOAD is not present on the indicated diskette, the following error message will be displayed:

File not found

**Multiple Statements**

In our examples thus far, we have only included one BASIC statement in each program line. In IBM BASIC, multiple statements may be included in a single program line as long as each of the statements are separated with a colon.

The following program uses multiple statements in line 10.

```
10 PRINT "JOHN":PRINT "NELSON"
20 PRINT "ATLANTA"
30 PRINT "GEORGIA"
40 END
RUN
JOHN
NELSON
ATLANTA
GEORGIA
Ok
```

# CHAPTER 2.
# DATA TYPES, VARIABLES,
# and OPERATORS

## INTRODUCTION

In Chapter 1, we gained an overview of IBM BASIC and learned a few of IBM BASIC's fundamental operating details. In Chapter 2, we will begin learning the basic concepts necessary to master IBM BASIC. In this chapter, we will discuss the various types of **data** used in IBM BASIC as well as the various **operations** that can be performed on that data.

## DATA TYPES

The data processed in IBM BASIC can be classified under two special headings; string and numeric. String and numeric data are stored differently in memory by the IBM PC. Also, the various **operators** in IBM BASIC affect string and numeric data in different manners.

### Strings

A **string** can be defined as one or more **ASCII** characters. The various ASCII characters are listed in Appendix D and consist of the digits (0-9), letters of the alphabet, and a number of special symbols.

IBM BASIC also allows a string of zero characters. This is also known as the empty or null string and is used much as a zero is in mathematics.

As you may already have noted from our examples in Chapter 1, when a string is used in an IBM BASIC statement, it must be enclosed within quotation marks. The quotation marks serve to identify the beginning and ending points of the string. They are not a part of the string.

A string enclosed with quotation marks is known as a **string constant**. A **constant** is an actual value used by BASIC during execution. The following are examples of string constants.

> "JOHN SMITH"
> "12197"
> "E97432"
> "BOSTON, MA 01270"
> "213-729-4234"

Notice that numbers can be used within a string constant. Remember, however, that the numbers within a string constant are string rather than numeric data.

One final point that should be kept in mind regarding string constants is that they cannot contain quotation marks. For example, the following string constant:

> "John said, "Goodbye." as he walked away."

would be illegal. Since quotation marks are used to denote the beginning and ending points of a string constant, their inclusion within the string itself would cause difficulties and therefore are not allowed.

In Chapter 7, we will discuss how the CHR$ function can be used to place the ASCII code for quotation marks within a string constant.

**Numeric Data**

**Numeric data** can be defined as information denoted with numbers. Numeric data is stored and operated on in a different manner than string data.

Numeric constants consist of positive and negative numbers. Numeric constants cannot include commas. For example, 10,000 would be an illegal numeric constant.

IBM BASIC further classifies numeric constants as **integers**, **fixed-point** numbers, **floating-point** numbers, **hexadecimal** numbers, and **octal** numbers.

Integers can be defined as the whole numbers in the range between −32768 and 32767 inclusive. Integer numbers do not have a decimal portion.

Fixed-point numbers can be defined as the set of positive and negative real numbers. Fixed-point numbers contain a decimal portion.

Floating-point numbers are represented in exponential notation. A number in exponential notation takes the following format:

$$\pm x E \pm yy$$

Where;

 $\pm$  is an optional plus or minus sign.

 x  can either be an integer or fixed point number. This position of the number is known as the coefficient or mantissa.

 E  stands for exponent. D can also be used instead of E to specify a double-precision* floating point constant.

 yy  is a one or two digit exponent. The exponent gives the number of places that the decimal point must be moved to give its true location. The decimal point is moved to the right with the positive exponents. The decimal point is moved to the left with negative exponents.

---

* Double-precision is explained in the next section.

The following are examples of floating-point numbers and their equivalent notation in fixed-point.

| Floating-Point | Fixed-Point |
|---|---|
| 17E−4 | .0017 |
| 237.9823E−9 | .0000002379823 |
| 173.1E5 | 17310000.0 |

Any number in the range of 10E−38 to 10E+38 can be represented in floating-point form.

Hexadecimal numbers use 16 as a base rather than 10 as in decimal notation. The digits 10, 11, 12, 13, 14, and 15 are represented with the letters A, B, C, D, E, and F respectively. Hexadecimal numbers are prefixed with &H in IBM BASIC. The following are examples of hexadecimal numbers and their equivalent decimal values:

| | |
|---|---|
| &HA4 | 164 |
| 10008&H231 | 561 |
| &HA1A | 2586 |

Octal numbers use 8 as the base. The digits 0 through 7 are used in octal. Octal numbers are prefixed with &O in IBM BASIC. The following are examples of octal numbers and their equivalent decimal values:

| | |
|---|---|
| &O457 | 303 |
| &O12 | 10 |
| &O20 | 16 |

**Numeric Precision**

**Precision** in the context of numeric data can be defined as the number of significant digits used in representing the data. In IBM BASIC, numeric data may be stored as integers, single-precision numbers, or as double-precision numbers. Each of these are stored differently in the PC's memory, so the distinction is important.

Integers are whole numbers in the range −32768 to 32767.

A **single-precision** value consists of a numeric value with a maximum of seven digits. Any additional digits are truncated beginning with the least significant digits. Any of the following that are not integers will be evaluated as single-precision constants:

- a value written with seven or fewer digits.
- a value written in exponential form using E.
- a value with the trailing exclamation point (!).

A **double-precision** value consists of a numeric value with a maximum of seventeen digits. Any additional digits are truncated beginning with the least significant digits. Any of the following will be evaluated as double-precision constants:

- a value written with eight or more digits.
- a value written in exponential form using D rather than E.
- a value with the trailing number sign (#).

The following are examples of integers, single-precision constants, and double-precision constants:

| Integers | Single-Precision Values | Double-Precision Values |
|---|---|---|
| −7978 | 47988 | 37854.98321 |
| 32600 | 37.0 | 1.97# |
| 47 | 1.79E7 | 3.248D−06 |
| 192 | 29! | 4.98372443217 |
| −687 | 1497.832174! | 14.738# |

Note that 47988 is a single-precision constant. This is due to the fact that it lies outside the allowed range for integers (−32768 to 32767). Also, note that 37.0 is not an integer since it contains a decimal point.

Finally, the preceding examples illustrate how a constant can be forced to represent a value that it would normally not represent by adding either the exclamation point (!) or the pound sign as a suffix. For instance, 29 would normally represent an integer, yet 29! indicates a single-precision value. Also, although 1497.832174 indicates a double-precision value, 1497.832174! indicates a single-precision value. Finally, 1.97 normally represents a single-precision value, while 1.97# forces that value into double-precision format.

At this point, you may be wondering why it is necessary to define three degrees of precision for representing numeric constants. The answer lies in the fact that integers require less memory area for storage than do single-precision values, which in turn require less space than double-precision values.

Also, arithmetic operations require less excution time with integers than with single-precision values. Single-precision values require less execution time than double-precision values.

Therefore, by using integer rather than single-precision values or single-precision rather than double-precision values, the programmer will conserve memory and increase execution speed.

Finally, note that a double-precision constant will only be printed with a maximum of 16 digits even though as many as 17 digits can be stored. Also, although a single-precision value can be stored and printed with up to seven digits, only six of those will be accurate. If your program requires accuracy of seven digits, you should use double-precision numeric data.

**Displaying Numeric Data**

You may have already noticed that numbers may be displayed in IBM BASIC in a different form than that in which they were entered. For example, a number entered in fixed-point format may have been converted to floating-point format, the # or ! signs may have been added to the number, or insignificant zeros (ex. 007.97 or 3.0200) may have been dropped.

BASIC stores numbers according to its own conventions. Once a number has been stored, it may be redisplayed in a different form from that in which it was entered.

## VARIABLES-AN OVERVIEW

In the preceding section, we discussed IBM BASIC's different types of data--string and numeric. In the remainder of this book, we will refer to a string constant as a string and a numeric constant as a number.

So far, we have only discussed representing data as a constant. The value of a string or numeric constant such as "JIM HILL" or 27.92 remains the same.

Data can also be represented by using a **variable**. A variable can be defined as an area of memory that is represented with a name. That name is known as the **variable name**. The information stored in the memory area defined by a variable name can vary (hence the name variable) as IBM BASIC commands or statements are executed. The data currently stored in the memory area defined by a variable is known as the variable's **value**.

### Variable Names

IBM BASIC allows variable names of up to 40 characters in length. A variable name must begin with a letter of the alphabet (A-Z) followed by additional letters, digits, or decimal points. Blank spaces are not allowed within a variable name. The following are examples of valid IBM BASIC variable names.

```
        PA4.1    A
        X123     TOTAL.JUNE
        QR37A    Z17
```

A variable name may not duplicate an IBM BASIC reserved word (see Appendix A). However, a variable name may incorporate a reserved word as part of its name.* Therefore, although the following would be invalid variable names:

        NEW                AND                PRINT

the following variable names would be valid:

        NEW.PHONE    DATA.X    PRINTNAME

Variables, like constants, can either be numeric or string. Numeric variables can be integer, single-precision, or double-precision.

A variable type can be declared by using a type identification character. The type identification characters are as follows:

        % = integer
        ! = single-precision
        # = double-precision
        $ = string

For example, the following variable names,

        ANCIENT$      B12!      JACK%

would be declared as string, single-precision, and integer respectively. If a variable type character is not specified, the variable type is assumed to be single-precision.

Variable names can also be declared by the DEFINT, DEFDBL, DEFSTR, or DEFSNG statements.

DEFINT (define-integer), DEFDBL (define double-precision), DEFSTR (define-string), and DEFSNG (define single-precision) define all variables that begin with the letter specified as their

---

* The exception to this rule is FN. A variable name may not begin with FN.

argument. For example, the following statement,

DEFSTR A

would result in all variables beginning with the letter A being defined as string variables.

If variable type declaration statements are used, they should be placed at the beginning of the program before any of the variables being declared are referenced.

The variable type declaration characters (%, !, #, and $) take precedence over the type declaration statements (DEFSNG, DEFINT, etc.).

Remember, just as with constants, if a higher degree of precision is specified for a variable, more memory will be required to store its value and more time will be required to perform operations with the data assigned to the variable.

## Initial Variable Values

Numeric variables are initially assumed to have a value of zero. String variables are initially assumed to be null. Values may be assigned to a variable as the result of a calculation or as the result of an assignment statement (discussed later).

It is illegal to attempt to assign a string value to a numeric variable or vice versa. However, IBM BASIC does allow a single- or double-precision value to be assigned to an integer variable and a double-precision value to be assigned to a single-precision variable.

When such a situation occurs, BASIC will convert the number from one precision to that indicated by the variable. The following rules will be followed when making this conversion.

1. When a higher-precision value is assigned to a lower-precision variable, the value will be rounded, as shown in the following example.

```
Ok
10 A=99872.38412#
20 PRINT A
30 B%=998.38
40 PRINT B%
50 END
RUN
 99872.38
 998
Ok
```

Notice in our preceding example that the double-precision value was rounded when it was assigned to the single-precision variable (A) as well as the integer variable (A%).

2. When a lower precision value is converted to a higher precision, the resulting high precision value will have no greater degree of accuracy than the low precision value.

```
Ok
10  A = 2.08
20  Z# = A
30  PRINT A
40  PRINT Z#
50  END
 2.08
 2.079999923706055
Ok
```

Notice that even though Z# is displayed with a greater number of significant digits than A, its accuracy is limited to that defined by A. If we converted Z# to single precision, it would round to 2.08.

3. When an arithmetic operation is undertaken using operands with differing degrees of precision, those operands with a lesser degree of precision will be converted so as to be equal in precision with the operand utilizing the highest degree of precision.

```
              Ok
              10 C# = 7/3#
              20 PRINT C#
              30 END
              RUN
               2.333333333333333
              Ok
```

## Assignment Statements (LET)

The LET statement is used to assign a value to a variable. LET statements are also known as **assignment** statements.

LET is used with the following configuration:

LET *variable = expression**

Whenever a LET statement is used in a program, the value of the variable on the left side of the equation is replaced with the value appearing on the right.

The reserved word, LET, need not actually be included in a LET statement. Both of the following statements have the same meaning:

```
              100 LET A = 5
              200 A = 5
```

The value assigned to a variable can either be a constant, a variable, or the result of an operation. In the following example, A$ is assigned the string constant "JOHN", B is assigned the numeric constant 27.9, C is assigned the value of B, and D is assigned the value of B multiplied by 2.

---

* In our configuration examples, BASIC reserved words will be depicted in uppercase, regular-face type. Parameters to be entered by the programmer will be depicted in lower-case italics.

```
Ok
10 A$ = "JOHN"
20 B = 27.9
30 C = B
40 D = B * 2
50 PRINT A$
60 PRINT B
70 PRINT C
80 PRINT D
RUN
JOHN
 27.9
 27.9
 55.8
Ok
```

## EXPRESSIONS & OPERATORS

The values of variables and constants are combined to form a new value through the use of **expressions.** The following are examples of expressions.

```
4 + 7
A$ + B$
3 * 1
14 < 21
X AND Y
```

IBM BASIC includes several types of expressions including **arithmetic, relational,** and **Boolean.** In our previous examples, the first three examples were arithmetic expressions, while the fourth and fifth were examples of relational and Boolean expressions respectively. Each of these types of expressions will be discussed in detail in the following sections.

The sign or phrase describing the operation to be undertaken is known as the **operator.** An operator is a symbol or word which represents an action which is to be undertaken on one or more values specified with the operator. These values are known as operands.

Data Types, Variables, and Operators 51

The operators in our previous examples were as follows:

+
+
*
<
AND

**Arithmetic Operators**

Arithmetic operators are used to perform mathematical operations on numeric or string variables. The arithmetic operators are listed in Table 2-1 in their order of evaluation.

**Table 2-1. Arithmetic Operators**

| Symbol | Operation | Example |
|--------|-----------|---------|
| ^ | Exponentiation | A ^ B |
| - | Negation | -A |
| * | Multiplication | A * B |
| / | Floating Point Division | A/B |
| \ | Integer Division | A \ B |
| MOD | Modulo Arithmetic | X MOD Y |
| + | Addition | A + B |
| - | Subtraction | A - B |

The first arithmetic operation specified in Table 2-1 is exponentiation. Exponentiation is the process of raising a number to a specified power. For example, in the following,

$$A^5$$

the numeric variable A would be evaluated as:

$$A * A * A * A * A$$

In IBM BASIC, exponentiation is indicated with the caret symbol, ^ . This symbol is produced by the 6 key with the keyboard in the shift position.

Exponentiation can be used in an arithmetic expression as shown below:

$$7 \wedge 2$$

The preceding expression would evaluate to 49.

The second operation indicated in Table 2-1 is negation. When the – sign precedes a number, the symbol is used to specify that number's sign. This usage is known as negation.

The symbols + and – are used for addition and subtraction respectively. The asterisk (*) is used to indicate multiplication, while the slash (/) is used to indicate division.

Most of the arithmetic operators will already be familiar to you. However, two of them, integer division and Modulo arithmetic, may not be familiar.

In integer division, the operand is rounded to an integer value before the division is performed. The quotient is also truncated to an integer. For example, in the following expression,

$$A = 37.98 \setminus 7.87$$

A would evaluate to 4.

Modulo arithmetic gives the integer value that is the remainder of an integer division operator. In the following expression,

$$A = 10 \text{ MOD } 3$$

A would evaluate to 1.

### Order of Evaluation (Arithmetic Expressions)

All of our preceding examples were **simple expressions.** A simple expression is one which contains just one operator and one or two operands. Simple expressions can be combined to form **compound** expressions. The following are examples of compound expressions:

(A + B) * 7 - 4
(A + B) AND (C + D)
IF A = 1 AND B = 1 THEN C = 1

With compound expressions, it is necessary that the computer knows which operation should be undertaken first. IBM BASIC follows a standard order of evaluation within compound expressions. This order is outlined in Tables 2-1 and 2-2.

In this section, we will discuss the order of evaluation of compound arithmetic expressions. Later in this chapter, we will discuss the order of evaluation of relational and logical operators as well as the overall order of evaluation of arithmetic, relational, and logical operators as a group.

In an expression with more than one arithmetic operator, the operators with higher priority are evaluated first followed by those with lower priority. Evaluation is accomplished from left to right in the expression. The following is an example of the evaluation of the arithmetic operators in an expression.

$$A = 37.1 + 12.9 * 2.1 + 7 - 4 \wedge 2$$
$$= 37.1 + 12.9 * 2.1 + 7 - 16$$
$$= 37.1 + 27.09 + 7 - 16$$
$$= 55.19$$

Parentheses can be used to alter the order of evaluation in arithmetic expressions. Expressions appearing within parentheses have the highest priority in the order of evaluation. For example, the use of parentheses with our preceding example could change the value of the expression.

$$A = (37.1 + 12.9) * 2.1 + (7 - 4) \wedge 2$$
$$= 50.0 * 2.1 + 3 \wedge 2$$
$$= 50.0 * 2.1 + 9$$
$$= 105.0 + 9$$
$$= 114.0$$

## Mixing Variable Types in Arithmetic Expressions

Although certain variable types may be mixed in an IBM expression, it is preferable to use a single variable type throughout each expression. By doing so, execution time will be decreased, memory requirements will be reduced, and the probability for program errors will also be reduced.

An example of mixing different numeric types in the same expression is given below:

$$A = B + 1$$

Both A and B are single-precision numeric variables, while 1 is an integer constant. The integer constant must be converted to a real number (as shown below), before the expression can be evaluated.

$$A = B + 1.0$$

When numeric variables are used in expressions, the variable on the left side of the equal sign is assigned the value of the expression on the right side. The value on the right side of the expression will be converted to the value specified by the numeric variable on the left side. For instance, in the following,

$$A\% = 1.03 + 2.07$$

the value on the left hand side of the expression (3.1) will be converted to the integer 3 so that it agrees with the integer variable A%. If A% were replaced with A, no conversion would have been necessary.

## Relational Operators

Relational operators are used to make a comparison using two operands. The following relational operators are used in IBM BASIC.

## Data Types, Variables, and Operators 55

```
< or LT  →  less than
<= or LE →  less then or equal to
> or GT  →  greater than
>= or GE →  greater than or equal to
= or EQ  →  equal to
<> or NE →  not equal
```

A relational operation evaluates to either true or false. For example, if the constant 1.0 was compared to the constant 2.0 to see whether they were equal, the expression would evaluate to false. In IBM BASIC, a value of –1 represents a condition of true, while a value of 0 represents false.

The only values returned by a comparison in IBM BASIC are –1 (true) or 0 (false). These values can be used as any other integer would be used. The following results are generated by the following relational expressions:

```
5 GT 7    0 (false)
5 GT 3   –1 (true)
7 LE 7   –1 (true)
```

Relational operations are evaluated after the addition and subtraction arithmetic operations. The order of evaluation of the relational operators is given in Table 2-2.

Although different numeric data types may be compared in a relational expression (ex. integer to single-precision), numeric and string data may not be compared.

Relational operations using numeric operations are fairly straightforward. However, relational operations using string values may prove confusing to the first-time computer user. Strings are compared by taking the ASCII value for each character in the string one at a time and comparing the codes.

If the strings are of the same length, then the string containing the first character with a lower code number is the lesser. If the length of the strings are unequal, then the shorter string is the lesser. Blank spaces are counted and have an ASCII value of 32.

**Table 2-2. Order of Evaluation (Relational Operators)**

| Symbol | Operation | Example |
|---|---|---|
| = | Equality | A = B |
| <> or >< | Inequality | A <> B; A >< B |
| < | Less Than | A < B |
| > | Greater Than | A > B |
| <= or =< | Less Than or Equal To | A <= B; A =< B |
| >= or => | Greater Than or Equal To | A >= B; A => B |

The following comparisons between strings would evaluate as true.

```
"ABC" = "ABC"
"ABC " > "ABC"
"aAA" > "AAA"
"Alfred" < "Alfredo"
A$ < Z$ where A$ = "Alfred" and Z$ = "Alfredo"
```

Note that all string constants must be enclosed in quotation marks when used as constants.

**Logical Operators**

Logical or Boolean operators are generally used in IBM BASIC to compare the outcomes of two relational operations. Logical operations themselves return a true or false value which will be used to determine program flow.

The logical operators are NOT (logical complement), AND (conjunction), OR (disjunction), XOR (exclusive or), IMP (implication), and EQV (equivalence). These return results as shown in Illustration 2-1.

A logical operator evaluates an input of one or more operands with true or false values. The logical operator evaluates these true or false values and returns a value of true or false itself. An operand of a logical operator is evaluated as true if it has a non-zero value. (Remember, relational operators return a value of −1 for a true value.) An operand of a logical operator is evaluated as false if it is equal to zero.

The result of a logical operation is also a number which, if non-zero is considered true, and false if it is true.

The following are examples of the use of logical operators in combination with relational operators in decision-making:

```
IF X > 10 OR Y < 0 THEN 900
IF A > 0 AND B > 0 THEN 200 ELSE GOTO 300
ERROR.FLAG% = NOT ERROR.FLAG%
```

In the first example, the result of the logical operation will be true if variable X has a value greater than 10 or if variable Y has a value less than 0. Otherwise, it will be false. If the result of the logical operation is true, the program will branch to line 900. Otherwise, it will continue to the next statement.

In the second example, the result of the logical operation will be true only if the value of both variables A and B are greater than zero. If the result of the logical operation is true, program control will branch to line 200. Otherwise, program control will branch to line 300.

In the final example, the value of ERROR.FLAG% is switched from true to false or vice versa.

Illustration 2-1 contains tables that may prove helpful when evaluating program statements using logical operators in combination with relational operators.

## Illustration 2-1. Logical Operators

### NOT Operation

| T | F | A Operand |
|---|---|---|
| F | T | NOT A |

### OR Operation

| T | T | F | F | A Operand |
|---|---|---|---|---|
| T | F | T | F | B Operand |
| T | T | T | F | A OR B |

### AND Operation

| T | T | F | F | A Operand |
|---|---|---|---|---|
| T | F | T | F | B Operand |
| T | F | F | F | A AND B |

### XOR Operation

| T | T | F | F | A Operand |
|---|---|---|---|---|
| T | F | T | F | B Operand |
| F | T | T | F | A XOR B |

## Data Types, Variables, and Operators

**IMP Operation**

| T | T | F | F | A Operand |
|---|---|---|---|---|
| T | F | T | F | B Operand |
| T | F | T | T | A IMP B |

**EQV Operation**

| T | T | F | F | A Operand |
|---|---|---|---|---|
| T | F | T | F | B Operand |
| T | F | F | T | A EQV B |

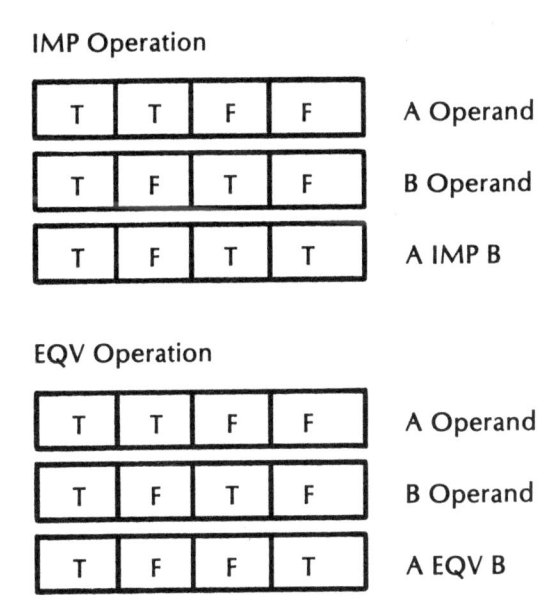

The most commonly used logical operators are NOT, AND, and OR. These are best explained with a simple analogy. Suppose that Steve and Sherry were shopping in the produce department of their grocery store. If they decided to collectively purchase an item if either of them individually wanted that item, they would be acting under the OR logical operator.

Now, suppose that Steve and Sherry decided that they would only purchase an item if they both wanted that item. They would then be acting under the AND logical operation.

Now, suppose that Sherry was angry with Steve. If Sherry decided not to purchase the items that Steve wanted, she would be acting under the NOT logical operation.

Logical operands actually convert their operands to their 16 bit binary equivalents before evaluating them. If an operand is negative, the two's complement is used to form that operand's 16 bit equivalent.

Illustration 2-2 gives examples of the conversion of decimal integers to their 16 bit equivalent.

**Illustration 2-2. Converting Integers to Their 16 Bit Equivalents**

**Positive Integers -- Decimal to Binary**

$87_{10} = 0\ 1\ 0\ 1\ 0\ 1\ 1\ 1_2$
$16_{10} = 0\ 0\ 0\ 1\ 0\ 0\ 0\ 0_2$
$33_{10} = 0\ 0\ 1\ 0\ 0\ 0\ 0\ 1_2$

**Negative Integers -- Two's Complement**

$-87_{10}$
    Step 1. Calculate $87_{10}$ in binary   0 1 0 1 0 1 1 1
    Step 2. Calculate NOT(01010111)  1 0 1 0 1 0 0 0
    Step 3. Add 1 For Final Result      1 0 1 0 1 0 0 1

$-16_{10}$
    Step 1. Calculate $16_{10}$ in binary   0 0 0 1 0 0 0 0
    Step 2. Calculate NOT(00010000)  1 1 1 0 1 1 1 1
    Step 3. Add 1 For Final Result      1 1 1 1 0 0 0 0

$-33_{10}$
    Step 1. Calculate $33_{10}$ in binary   0 0 1 0 0 0 0 1
    Step 2. Calculate NOT(00100001)  1 1 0 1 1 1 1 0
    Step 3. Add 1 For Final Result      1 1 0 1 1 1 1 1

The examples in Illustration 2-3 demonstrate the use of the logical operators with positive and negative integers.

## Illustration 2-3. Logical Operations on Integers

Z=27 AND 9

| 0 | 0 | 0 | 1 | 1 | 0 | 1 | 1 |
|---|---|---|---|---|---|---|---|
| 0 | 0 | 0 | 0 | 1 | 0 | 0 | 1 |
| 0 | 0 | 0 | 0 | 1 | 0 | 0 | 1 |

Operand 1 = $27_{10}$
Operand 2 = $9_{10}$
Z=$27_{10}$ AND $9_{10}$
Z = $9_{10}$

Z = 24 OR -7

| 0 | 0 | 0 | 1 | 1 | 0 | 0 | 0 |
|---|---|---|---|---|---|---|---|
| 1 | 1 | 1 | 1 | 1 | 0 | 0 | 1 |
| 1 | 1 | 1 | 1 | 1 | 0 | 0 | 1 |

Operand 1 = $24_{10}$
Operand 2 = $-7_{10}$
Z = $24_{10}$ OR $-7_{10}$
Z = $-7_{10}$

Z = 9 XOR 33

| 0 | 0 | 0 | 0 | 1 | 0 | 0 | 1 |
|---|---|---|---|---|---|---|---|
| 0 | 0 | 1 | 0 | 0 | 0 | 0 | 1 |
| 0 | 0 | 1 | 0 | 1 | 0 | 0 | 0 |

Operand 1 = $9_{10}$
Operand 2 = $33_{10}$
Z = $9_{10}$ XOR $33_{10}$
Z = $40_{10}$

### Order of Evaluation -- Overview

Earlier in this chapter, we outlined the order of evaluation within an expression with respect to arithmetic operators. Now that we have introduced the concepts of relational and logical operations, we can revise our order of evaluation as follows.

1. Arithmetic Operators
    a. Exponentiation        A ^ B
    b. Negation              −A
    c. Multiplication, Division   A * B, A/B
    d. Integer Division      A \ B
    e. Modulo Arithmetic     A MOD B
    f. Addition, Subtraction A + B, A − B

2. Relational Operators
    a. Equality              A = B
    b. Inequality            A < > B, A > < B
    c. Less Than             A < B
    d. Greater Than          A > B
    e. Less Than or Equal To    A < = B, A = < B
    f. Greater Than or Equal To A > = B, A = > B

3. Logical Operators
    a. NOT
    b. AND
    c. OR
    d. XOR
    e. IMP
    f. EQV

# CHAPTER 3.
# INPUTTING AND OUTPUTTING DATA

## INTRODUCTION

In Chapters 1 and 2, we briefly described the usage of the PRINT statement to output data. In this chapter, we will discuss the usage of PRINT for outputting data to the screen or printer in depth.

We will also discuss the PRINT USING statement as well as some of the various methods used to control the horizontal and vertical format of output.

After we have discussed the methods used in IBM BASIC to output data, we will discuss the IBM statements used to input data into variables. These include INPUT and LINE INPUT.

## PRINT

To this point, we have only used the PRINT statement to output a single constant or variable value to the screen.

The PRINT statement can also be used to output more than one item to the screen. When PRINT is used in this manner, the spacing between the items to be printed can be controlled by separating them with a comma or semicolon. For example, compare the results of the following PRINT statements.

```
Ok
PRINT "BILL" "STEVE" "LARRY"
BILLSTEVELARRY
Ok
PRINT "BILL","STEVE","LARRY"
BILL            STEVE              LARRY
Ok
PRINT "BILL";"STEVE";"LARRY"
BILLSTEVELARRY
```

Notice that in out first example, no delimiter was used to separate the three string constants. These were output as one continuous string.

In the second example, the comma was used to delimit the string constants. When a comma appears in a PRINT statement, the computer is instructed to begin printing the next parameter in the PRINT statement at the beginning of the next print zone. IBM BASIC divides the spacing on a line into a series of print zones. Each print zone contains 14 spaces. In our example above, BILL would begin in column 1 (print zone 1); STEVE in column 15 (print zone 2); and LARRY in column 29 (print zone 3).

Commas are very useful when data is to be output in tabular form. This is illustrated in the following example program.

```
Ok
10 PRINT "Name","ID No.","Pay"
20 PRINT "Jack Williams",3749,"$450.71"
30 PRINT "Ann Timmons",3622,"$811.32"
40 PRINT "Jay Randolph",2511,"$632.97"
50 END
RUN
Name           ID No.    Pay
Jack Williams  3749      $450.71
Ann Timmons    3622      $811.32
Jay Randolph   2511      $632.97
Ok
```

In the third example at the top of this page, the semicolon was used as the delimiter. The semicolon causes each string data item

Inputting and Outputting Data 65

in the PRINT statement to be output immediately adjacent to the preceding item.

When the semicolon is used to delimit numeric items in the PRINT statement, a blank space will be output following the number. Also, positive numbers will be output with a blank space preceding the number and negative numbers will be output with the minus sign preceding the number. This is illustrated in the following example.

```
Ok
10 A = 10
20 B = -20
25 C = 30
30 PRINT A
35 PRINT B
40 PRINT A;B;C;100;"ABCD";-100
50 END
RUN
 10
-20
 10 -20  30  100 ABCD-100
```

Notice from our example that the first PRINT statement in line 30 causes the numeric value stored in A (10) to be output with one blank space preceding it. In the second line of output, since the numeric value being output is negative (-20), the blank space preceding the number is replaced with the minus sign.

In the third line of output, again the first value (10) is preceded with a blank space since it is positive. The second value (-20) is not preceded with a blank space since it is negative. Note that two blank spaces separate the second value output (20) and the third (30). As we previously noted, numeric values are output with a trailing blank space. Since the third value output is positive and is preceded with a blank space, two blank spaces separate these values. The same applies to the spacing between the third and fourth values being output.

Notice that only a single blank space separates the fourth value output (100) and the fifth value output (ABCD). Since ABCD is a string, a blank space will not be output preceding it.

Finally, note that no blank spaces separate the fifth and sixth values. Since the fifth value (ABCD) is a string, it is not followed by a blank space. Moreover, since the sixth value is a negative number (-100), the blank space that would normally precede it is replaced by the minus sign.

When only numbers are being output by PRINT using the semicolon as a delimiter, we need not concern ourselves with inserting blank spaces into the output, as blank spaces are automatically output after each numeric value. This is illustrated in the following example.

```
Ok
PRINT -10;20;6 + 4 * -1;4 ^ 2;0
-10  20  2  16  0
Ok
```

Notice from the preceding expression that when an arithmetic expression is specified in a PRINT statement, that expression's result will be output.

Although we need not concern ourselves with inserting blank spaces into the PRINT statement output when only numeric values are being output, we may need to insert blank spaces in the output when strings or strings and negative numeric values are being output. This is illustrated in the following example.

```
Ok
10  A$ = "The answer is"
20  B$ = "The answer is "
30  A = 20
40  B = -20
50  PRINT A$;A
60  PRINT A$;B
70  PRINT B$;B
80  END
RUN
The answer is 20
The answer is-20
The answer is -20
Ok
```

Notice the inclusion of the blank space between "is" and the ending quotation mark in line 20. By including this space, a blank space appears between "is" and -20 in the final line of output.

Generally, when a PRINT statement has been executed, the cursor or print head will advance to the leftmost position on the next output line. This is known as a carriage return/line feed, which can be abbreviatd as CR/LF.

A CR/LF can be suppressed by ending a PRINT statement with either a comma or a semicolon. When a semicolon is used to end a PRINT statement, the output from the next PRINT statement will be positioned immediately after the data output by its predecessor. This is illustrated in the following example.

```
10 PRINT "Data1";
20 PRINT "Data2";
30 PRINT "Data3";
40 END
RUN
Data1Data2Data3
Ok
```

When a PRINT statement is ended with a comma, subsequent data will be output at the next print zone on the same display line. This is shown in the following example.

```
10 PRINT "Data1",
20 PRINT "Data2",
30 PRINT "Data3"
40 END
RUN
Data1     Data2     Data3
Ok
```

## WIDTH

The WIDTH statement is used to set the width of the screen or printer output line. Generally, the screen output line is set to 80, and the printer output line is set to either 80 or 132. The following program will set the screen output line to 40.

```
10 WIDTH 40
20 PRINT "Data1",
30 PRINT "Data2",
40 PRINT "Data3",
50 PRINT "Data4"
60 END
RUN
```

Data1        Data2
Data3        Data4
Ok

Notice that with a 40 column output width, we only have 2 print zones per line. Also, the characters are output with a height and width twice that of those output at an 80 column width.

## LPRINT

The LPRINT statement functions exactly as does PRINT, except that data is output to the printer rather than the screen. Before executing LPRINT, be certain that your printer is turned on and loaded with paper.

## PRINT USING

The PRINT USING and LPRINT USING statements allow the programmer much greater control over the format of the data being output than do the PRINT and LPRINT statements. The PRINT USING statement is used with the following configuration:

PRINT USING *format string;expressions*

*expressions* are the data items to be output by PRINT USING. Each separate item in *expressions* must be delimited with a comma or semicolon. However, unlike the PRINT statement, these delimiters do not affect the spacing between the characters on the output line.

Inputting and Outputting Data 69

The spacing between the characters in a PRINT USING statement as well as their **format** is defined by the format string. The format string consists of a series of formatting characters. These define which if any special characters, symbols, or punctuation marks are to be included with the data being output. The various formatting characters are summarized in Table 3-1 and will be discussed in the following sections.

The format string reserves an area on the output line where the specified data will be displayed. This area is known as a **field.** The size of the field is defined by the format string. If the data being output does not completely fill the field, blank spaces will be placed in the remaining positions.*

### Table 3-1. PRINT USING Formatting Characters

| Character | Description |
|---|---|
| **String Characters** | |
| ! | specifies that only the first character in the string is to be printed. |
| \ \ | is used to specify the number of characters to be printed from the string. This is the number of characters enclosed within the slashes plus 2. If the backslashes are given with no spaces, then two characters will be printed. If the string is longer than the space allowed by the format, the extra characters will be dropped. If the field specified by the format is larger than the string, spaces will be added to the right of the string. |
| & | specifies a variable length string. When the format field is specified with &, the string will be output in the same manner as it is input. |

---

* The exception to this rule is the use of the asterisk as a formatting character.

## Table 3-1 (cont). PRINT USING Formatting Characters

| Character | Description |
|---|---|
| **Numeric Characters** | |
| # | specifies a digit position. If the number being printed has fewer digits than allowed for by the formatting characters, that number will be right-justified in the formatting field. |
| . | A decimal point may be inserted anywhere in the format field. The decimal point will be included in the output in the same position indicated in the format field. |
| + | A plus sign can be included at the beginning or end of the format string. This formatting character causes the number's sign (+ or -) to be printed in front of or behind the number. |
| - | The minus sign, when included at the end of the format string, will cause negative numbers to be printed with a trailing minus sign. |
| ** | When placed at the beginning of a format field, a double asterisk causes any leading blanks in a numeric field to be filled with asterisks. The positions indicated by ** will be filled with digits if no blank spaces are available. |
| $$ | The double dollar sign results in a dollar sign being printed at the left of the numeric field. The double dollar sign indicates two digit positions, one of which is a position for the dollar sign. |
| **$ | The **$ formatting character combination causes a dollar sign to be printed before the number and any leading blanks to be filled with asterisks. **$ allows for three additional |

Inputting and Outputting Data 71

### Table 3-1 (cont). PRINT USING Formatting Characters

| Character | Description |
|---|---|
|  | digit positions, one of which is the dollar sign. |
| ,. | When a comma appears to the left of the decimal point in a numeric formatting string, the result is that a comma will be printed to the left of every third digit on the left hand side of the decimal point. A comma allows for an additional digit position. |
| ^^^^ | When four carets are placed after the ^^^^ formatting characters which indicate the digits, an exponential format is specified. These four carets allow for the printing of one of the following:<br><br>$E \pm xx$<br>$D \pm xx$<br><br>where x signifies a number. |
| _ | The underline character, when used in the format string, causes the next character to be printed as a literal character. |
| % | A percent character is printed in front of a number when that number is larger than its format field. Also, if rounding causes a number to go beyond its format field, a percent sign will be printed in front of the rounded number. |

## Numeric Formatting Characters -- Pound Sign (#)

The most commonly used numeric formatting character is the pound sign (#). Each # specifies a position for one digit in the output field. The usage of # is depicted in the following example.

```
       10 A = 1
       20 B = 23
       30 C = 456
       40 D = 2711
      *50 E$ = "### "
       60 PRINT USING E$;A,B,C,D
       70 END
       RUN
          1  23  456 %2711
       Ok
```

Notice from our example that when a value does not entirely fill an output field, it will be right-justified in that field. The field's unused spaces will be filled with blanks. Also, notice the inclusion of the percent sign (%) in the final output field. A % sign is printed in front of a number when the data being output is larger than the format field.

**Numeric Formatting Characters -- Decimal Point (.)**

The decimal point (.) may also be included anywhere within the format field. A decimal point will be placed in the output field at the position indicated in the format field.

```
       10 PRINT USING "##.# ";11.9,332.985,4,.9243
       RUN
       11.9 %333.0 4.0 0.9
       Ok
```

The preceding example illustrates the usage of the decimal point in a format field. Our first output (11.9) contains the same number of numeric characters as does the format field and is output as 11.9.

---

\* In our examples in this section, we will include trailing blanks at the end of the format field in order to separate the numeric values being output.

Inputting and Outputting Data 73

The second output (332.985) contains more digits to both the left and right of the decimal point than does the format field. Notice that the decimal portion is rounded so as to fit in the format field. The numeric portion is displayed with the % to indicate that this is larger than that allowed for in the format string.

The third value being output (4) contains neither a decimal point nor a decimal portion. Notice that the inclusion of the decimal point in the format string causes it to be output.

The fourth value (.9243) does not include digits to the left of the decimal point. Notice that a zero is included to the left of the decimal point in the output. Also, the decimal portion is rounded so that it fits within the space allowed by the format string.

**Numeric Formatting Characters -- Plus Sign (+)**

In our examples thus far, we have only output positive values. When negative values are output, the minus sign will be output. However, the minus sign will occupy one of the digit positions specified in the format string.

```
10 PRINT USING "### ";-1,-22,-333
RUN
 -1 -22 %-333
Ok
```

Notice in the preceding example that the format field allowed for enough digit positions for -1 and -22 to be output. However, -333 requires more positions than allowed by the format field and is preceded by the % sign.

This problem can be solved by including the plus sign (+) in the format string. The plus sign causes a positive number to be output with a leading + and a negative number to be output with a leading -. The plus sign also reserves a position in the output field for the sign. Therefore, one of the digit positions specified in the format string will not be required for output of a sign.

```
10 PRINT USING "+### ";1,-27,344,-9282
RUN
 +1 -27 +344 %-9282
Ok
```

Notice in the preceding example that a sign is included with each numeric output.

Generally, the sign is output on the left hand side of a numeric field. However, in certain instances, it may be useful to position the sign to the immediate right of the output. This is generally the case when a monetary value is being output, as the dollar sign is positioned on the left hand side of the output.

The sign can be placed on the right hand side of the output by including the plus sign (+) as the rightmost character of the format string.

```
*10 PRINT USING "$##.##+ ";9.87,13.82,-11.11
RUN
$ 9.87+ $13.82+ $11.11-
Ok
```

We can also use a trailing minus sign (-) in our format string. This causes the minus sign to be output to the immediate right of negative values and a blank space to be output to the immediate right of positive values.

```
10 PRINT USING "$##.##- ";9.42,-77.11,98.71
RUN
$ 9.42  $77.11- $98.71
Ok
```

**Numeric Formatting Characters -- Comma (,)**

Commas may be placed in a format field to force their insertion in the numeric output. Commas that are not included within the

---

\* The use of the dollar sign ($) as a formatting character will be discussed later in this chapter.

numeric output will be output instead as blank spaces.

Commas can be placed anywhere within the format string. Regardless of where the commas are placed in the format string, they will be output in their correct position.

```
10 PRINT USING "###,###,###.## ";798482.47,9874.52,9873476.01
RUN
 798,482.47   9,874.52   9,873,476.01
Ok
10 PRINT USING "#########,,.## ";798482.47,9874.52,9873476.01
RUN
 798,482.47   9,874.52   9,873,476.01
Ok
```

## Numeric Formatting Characters -- Dollar Sign ($)

When a single dollar sign is placed at the beginning of a format string, a dollar sign will be placed in the first position of the output field.

```
    10 PRINT USING "$##,###.## ";98.57,3268.91,9.72
    RUN
    $    98.57  $3,268.91  $     9.72
    Ok
```

Notice in our preceding example that the dollar sign is not positioned immediately in front of the numeric output. By specifying two dollar signs ($$) rather than one at the beginning of the format string, the dollar sign will be placed at the immediate left of the numeric output. This is known as the floating dollar sign.

```
   10 PRINT USING "$$#,###.## ";9.78,329.50,1571.71,99532.47
   RUN
      $9.78    $329.50  $1,571.71  $99,532.47
   Ok
```

Notice that in each of our preceding examples a dollar sign is input to the immediate left of the numeric output. Take special note of the final example. Even though the pound signs (#) in the format string allow only four digit positions to the left of the decimal point, five digits are output. When the floating dollar sign ($$) is specified in a format string, the rightmost dollar sign indicates that another digit can be included in the output field. In other words, it functions like an extra pound sign (#).

Therefore, in our example, the format string ($$#,###.##) allows numbers up to and including 99,999.99 to be output.

### Numeric Formatting Characters -- Asterisk (*)

If the single dollar sign is being used in the format string, the programmer generally will want to fill any digit positions where data is not being output to prevent possible tampering with the check.

By including double asterisks at the far left hand side of the format string, any unused digit positions in the numeric output will be filled with asterisks rather than blanks. Each asterisk allows for the output of an additional numeric character. For example, the format string (**##.##) would allow output of numeric data up to a value of 999.99.

```
10 PRINT USING "**###.##  ";.79,57.2,1092,98787.21,7.1
RUN
****0.79   ***57.20   *1092.00   ****7.10
Ok
```

Notice in our preceding example, that any unused digit positions in the output to the left of the decimal point are filled with asterisks.

If a comma is to be inserted in the output field, be certain that you do not insert the comma between the asterisks in the format string. The comma should be positioned just to the right of the two asterisks.

```
10 PRINT USING "**,##.# ";1009.7,571.3,32.4
RUN
 1,009.7   **571.3   ***32.4
Ok
```

If the dollar sign ($) is included in the format string with asterisks (**), the asterisks should be placed to its left. If the dollar sign precedes the asterisks in the format string, the dollar sign will be positioned at the leftmost position in the numeric output.

```
10 PRINT USING "$**,##.## ";5.26,29.94,127.52,1978.72
RUN
 $****5.26   $***29.94   $**127.52   $1,978.72
Ok
10 PRINT USING "**$,##.## ";5.26,29.94,127.52,1978.72
RUN
 ****$5.26   ***$29.94   **$127.52   $1,978.72
Ok
```

Notice that the comma was placed to the right of the dollar sign in the format string in our second example. The commas may not be placed between the dollar sign and the asterisks (**$).

## Numeric Formatting Characters -- Exponential Notation ( ^^^^ )

When the format string ends with four carets, the numeric value will be output in exponential notation.

When specifying the format string for exponential output, one additional pound sign (#) should be placed to the left of the decimal point. This allows a minus sign (-) to be output to the left of a negative value. A blank space will be output to the left of a positive value. The plus sign (+) can be used in place of the pound sign (#). This would result in the plus sign (+) being output before a positive value and the minus sign (-) being output before a negative value.

10 PRINT USING "+#.## ^^^^ ";7911230000,-.0000032,9000*137
RUN
+7.91D+09   -3.20E-06   +1.23E+06
Ok
10 PRINT USING "##.## ^^^^ ";7911230000,-.0000032,9000*137
RUN
7.91D+09   -3.20E-06   1.23E+06
Ok

The four carets ( ^^^^ ) allow for the four characters used in exponential notation. The first character can either be E, which denotes a single-precision value, or D which denotes a double-precision value. A plus sign (+) indicates that the decimal point is to be moved to the right. A minus sign (-) indicates that it should be moved to the left. The number following the sign indicates the number of places that the decimal points must be moved to evaluate the exponential value.

**String Formatting Characters -- Ampersand (&)**

The ampersand character (&) in a format string indicates that a string of any size can be output. This is also known as a **variable length string field.**

        10 PRINT USING "& ";"A","AA","AAA","AAAA"
        RUN
        A  AA  AAA  AAAA
        Ok

**String Formatting Characters -- Backslash (\)**

The backslash character (\) is used to output a **fixed length string field.** Such a field's size remains constant regardless of the number of string characters being output.

If the string being output contains fewer characters than those allowed by the format field, the output will be right-justified in the output field, and blank spaces will be input in the extra positions.

Inputting and Outputting Data 79

The format field for a fixed length string field consists of two backslashes separated by blank spaces. Each backslash and blank space allows for a character position in the format field.

10 PRINT USING "\ \ ";"A","AA","AAA","AAAA","AAAAB"
RUN
A  AA  AAA  AAAA  AAAA
Ok

Notice from our example that the final string output ("AAAAB") contains more characters than that allowed for by the format string. This results in its rightmost character being truncated.

**String Formatting Characters -- Exclamation Point (!)**

With the backslash character, the smallest fixed length string field that can be output is a two-character field. The exclamation point can be used to output a fixed length field of just one character.

10 PRINT USING "!";"Kenneth","Lawrence","Peters"
RUN
KLP
Ok

**Numeric or String Formatting Characters--**
**Literal Characters**

**Literals** are characters which have no special meaning as formatting characters (ex. 7, A, Z, @). When a literal character is included in a format string, it will be included in the output field exactly as it is specified in the format string.

10 PRINT USING "The winner is &. ";"Joe","Nancy","Phil"
RUN
The winner is Joe.  The winner is Nancy.  The winner is Phil.
Ok

Notice that the decimal point was used in the preceding example as a literal character. The decimal point is only used as a formatting character in a numeric format string.

In certain instances, we might wish to use certain formatting characters such as the pound sign (#), ampersand (&), or exclamation point (!) as literals. This can be accomplished by preceding that character with the underline character (_) in the format string. The underline character is not actually output by the format string, but merely indicates that the following character is to be treated as a literal rather than as a formatting character.

```
10 PRINT USING "& _& & went shopping _! ";"Sue","Jane",
   "Alice","Teresa"
RUN
Sue & Jane went shopping!  Alice & Teresa went shopping!
Ok
```

## HORIZONTAL FORMATTING

The formatting of a row of output can be controlled using PRINT USING. This can be accomplished by positioning the items to be output as desired in the format string.

IBM BASIC also includes several functions that allow the programmer to control the horizontal format of output. These include TAB, SPC, and SPACE$.

### TAB

BASIC allows an item to be printed in any position on the screen or printer with the TAB command. The print position can range from 1 to 255.

```
10  PRINT TAB(10)"10";TAB(200)"200";TAB(210)"210"
RUN
      10                    200   210
Ok
```

Notice that the example caused output to be positioned at columns 10, 40, and 50.

In the preceding paragraph, we mentioned that print positions can range from 1 to 255. These 255 print positions are the result of the fact that a logical line in IBM BASIC can consist of up to 255 characters. The IBM video display can be either set for 40 characters per line or 80 characters per line (with the WIDTH statement as discussed earlier).

When the TAB function is specified with an argument greater than the output device's column width, the number of positions tabbed will be calculated MOD that width. In our example, the column width was 80. With the second TAB argument, 200 MOD 80 results in 40. Therefore, the data specified after TAB(200) will be output beginning in column 40.

TAB can only be used in the PRINT and LPRINT statements. TAB cannot be used in PRINT USING or LPRINT USING.

## SPC

SPC causes the number of spaces specified as its argument to be sent to the display or printer.

```
10 PRINT "JOHN" SPC(10) "FLETCHER"
RUN
JOHN          FLETCHER
Ok
```

In our preceding example, SPC(10) causes the cursor to move 10 positions to the right once JOHN has been output.

SPC can only be used with the PRINT and LPRINT statement, and cannot be used with PRINT USING or LPRINT USING.

## SPACE$

SPACE$ is a built in function which returns a string consisting of the number of blank spaces indicated as its argument.

```
Ok
100 FOR X = 1 TO 3
200 A$ = SPACE$(X)
300 PRINT A$;X
400 NEXT
RUN
 1
  2
   3
Ok
```

SPACE$ can be used within a PRINT USING format string as shown in the following example.

```
*10 A$ = "###" + SPACE$(7) + "&"
 20 PRINT USING A$;127,"Peter"
 30 END
RUN
127       Peter
Ok
```

## VERTICAL FORMATTING

Vertical formatting is generally more important in designing written reports to be output by the printer than in outputting to the screen.

Formatting is generally achieved by sending a control code to the printer via the LPRINT statement and the ASCII function. For instance, the following statement:

LPRINT CHR$(10);

---

\* The use of + to combine strings is known as concatenation and will be discussed in Chapter 6.

would send the line feed character to the IBM printer. Notice the inclusion of the semicolon following the statement. The semicolon prevents a second CR/LF from being executed due to the execution of LPRINT.

Refer to your printer's operating manual to determine which control codes are available.

## INPUTTING DATA

Data can be input into the IBM PC and assigned to a variable while a program is being executed. This can be accomplished with the INPUT and LINE INPUT statements.

### INPUT

When an INPUT statement is executed, the computer will display a question mark and wait for the operator to enter a response. That entry will be assigned to the variable indicated. The entry must be ended by pressing the Enter key. Program execution will then resume.

The values of several variables can be input with a single INPUT statement. These variables may either be numeric or string as shown in the following example:

> 100 INPUT A$,B$,C

When the preceding INPUT statement is executed, the INPUT prompt (?) will be displayed. The operator should then input the data items for variables A$, B$, and C. Each input should be separated by a comma. The Enter key should be pressed after all input entries have been made. An example of a valid entry for the preceding INPUT statement is given below:

> JOHN,SMITH,281

These entries will be assigned to the variables as follows:

$$A\$ = \text{"JOHN"}$$
$$B\$ = \text{"SMITH"}$$
$$C = 281$$

If an incorrect number of entries were made or if a string constant were input for a numeric variable or vice versa, the following message would be displayed,

> ? Redo from start
> ?

and the computer would wait for a valid entry.

It is good programming practice to include a prompt message with the INPUT statement to let the operator know what data the computer is expecting. For example, the following INPUT statement:

   100 INPUT "ENTER COMPANY NAME,NUMBER";A$,B

would result in the following prompt being displayed:

ENTER COMPANY NAME, NUMBER? <u>ACME MFG INC, 27</u> [Ent]

These entries will be assigned to the variables A$ and B as follows:

$$A\$ = \text{"ACME MFG INC"}$$
$$B = 27$$

Notice in our preceding examples that we did not enclose our string entries in response to INPUT prompts within quotation marks. When a string is being entered in response to an INPUT prompt, the quotation marks can be excluded unless the entry includes commas or begins with one or more blank spaces.

## LINE INPUT

The LINE INPUT statement is a variation of the INPUT statement. LINE INPUT allows an entire line (up to 255 characters) to be input to a string variable.

Unlike INPUT, any printing ASCII character (including the blank space and quotation mark) will be accepted by LINE INPUT. Also, unlike INPUT, a question mark will be printed by LINE INPUT. However, a prompt can be included with LINE INPUT just as it can with INPUT.

When LINE INPUT is executed, the program will pause and wait for the user's input. Once the entry has been made and Enter pressed, program execution will proceed and the data entered will be assigned to the string variable specified with LINE INPUT.

# CHAPTER 4.
# IBM BASIC CONDITIONAL, BRANCHING, AND LOOPING STATEMENTS

**INTRODUCTION**

Thus far in our discussion of IBM BASIC, our statements have been executed in sequential order. Several IBM BASIC statements are available which can be used to alter program control. These include:

    GOTO      IF, THEN
    GOSUB    WHILE, WEND
    ON, GOTO  FOR, NEXT
    ON, GOSUB

These statements will be discussed in the following sections.

**Conditional Branches**

One of the most important features of a computer is its ability to make a decision. BASIC uses the IF, THEN, ELSE statement to take advantage of the computer's decision making ability. The IF, THEN, ELSE statement takes the following form:

    IF *expression* THEN *statement* ELSE *statement*

The IF statement sets up a question or a condition. If the answer to that question is true, the *statement* following THEN is executed. If the answer is false, the *statement* following ELSE will be executed.

In the following example, if X is equal to 1, then Y will be set to 1. If X is not equal to 1, Y will be set to 0.

100 IF X = 1 THEN Y = 1 ELSE Y = 0

The IF, THEN, ELSE statement may be shortened to just IF, THEN as shown below:

100 Y = 0
200 IF X = 1 THEN Y = 1

In this example, if X is equal to 1, the statement following THEN will be executed. If X is not equal to 1, program execution will continue with the next program statement (in our example--line 200).

The ON statement can also be used with GOTO or GOSUB to set up a condition which will branch program control. ON, GOTO and ON, GOSUB will be discussed later in this chapter.

**Branching Statements**

Branching statements change the execution pattern of programs from their usual line by line execution in ascending line number order. A branching statement allows program control to be altered to any line number desired. The most commonly used branching statements in BASIC are GOTO and GOSUB.

GOTO takes the following format:

GOTO *line number*

For example, the following program statement,

500 GOTO 999
.
.
999 END

would branch program control at line 500 to line 999.

## Subroutines and GOSUB

Many times you will find that the same set of program instructions are used more than once in a program. Re-entering these instructions throughout the program can be very time consuming. By using **subroutines**, these additional entries will be unnecessary.

A subroutine can be defined as a program which appears within another larger program. The subroutine may be executed as many times as desired.

The execution of subroutines is controlled by the GOSUB and RETURN statements. The format for the GOSUB statement is as follows:

GOSUB *line number*

The computer will begin execution of the subroutine beginning at the *line number* indicated. Statements will continue to be executed in order, until a RETURN statement is encountered. Upon execution of the RETURN statement, the computer will branch out of the subroutine back to the first line following the original GOSUB statement. This is illustrated in the following example.

```
              100 INPUT "ENTER CHECK AMOUNT";A
              200 GOSUB 900
              300 INPUT "ENTER PAYEE'S NAME";B$
              400 LPRINT B$,A
              500 GOTO 100
            ⎛ 900 REM VERIFY ENTRY
            ⎜ 910 E$ = "ENTRIES OVER $1000 ARE NOT
            ⎜     ALLOWED"
Subroutine ⎨ 930 IF A > 1000 THEN PRINT E$:GOTO 100
            ⎜ 940 IF A < 0 THEN GOTO 999
            ⎝ 950 RETURN

              999 END
```

Subroutines can help the programmer organize his program more efficiently. Subroutines also can make writing a program easier. By dividing a lengthy program into a number of smaller subroutines, the complexity of the program will be reduced. Individual subroutines are smaller and, therefore, more easily written. Subroutines are also more easily debugged than a longer program.

**Conditional Statements with Branching**

Branching statements are often used in conjunction with conditional statements. In such a situation, the normal execution of the program is altered depending upon the outcome of the condition set up in an IF or an ON statement. This is shown in the following example.

```
100 INPUT "ENTER THE AMOUNT";A
200 IF A = 0 THEN GOTO 900
300 PRINT A
400 GOTO 100
900 INPUT "ARE YOU FINISHED (Y/N)";A$
910 IF A$ = "N" THEN GOTO 100
920 IF A$ = "Y" THEN 999 ELSE 900
999 END
```

In our preceding example, if the value input for A has a zero value, then the program will branch to line 900 where the operator will be prompted whether he has finished entering data. In line 910, the program will set up a condition where if the input was N, the program will branch to line 100. If the entry was not equal to N, the program will continue to line 920.

In line 920, the program will check to see if the value input was equal to Y. If so, the program will branch to line 999 where it will end. If not, the program will branch to line 900 where the operator will be prompted again for an entry of Y or N.

Note in line 920 that a GOTO statement is not used to precede the line number being branched to. When a line number is indicated following a THEN or ELSE statement, the computer does not require the presence of GOTO, which is assumed.

The ON, GOTO and ON, GOSUB statements are also combinations of a conditional statement and a branching statement. The use of the ON, GOTO statement is illustrated in the following program.

```
10 INPUT A
20 ON A GOTO 40,50
30 GOTO 99
40 PRINT "A = 1":GOTO 99
50 PRINT "A = 2"
99 END
```

If the variable or expression following ON evaluates to 1, program control branches to the first line number specified after GOTO; if 2, to the second; if 3, to the third, etc.

If the variable or expression evaluates to a number greater than the number of line numbers following GOTO, program control will branch to the statement immediately following the ON, GOTO statement. This is also the case if the variable or expression following ON evaluates to zero.

The ON, GOSUB statement is very similar in nature to the ON, GOTO statement. The following statement is an example of an ON, GOSUB statement.

100 ON X GOSUB 1000,2000,3000

If the value of X is 1, the subroutine at line 1000 is executed. If X is 2, the subroutine at line 2000 is executed. If X is 3, the subroutine at line 3000 is executed. If X evaluates to 0 or to a number greater than 3, the statement immediately following the ON, GOSUB statement will be executed.

If ON, GOSUB causes a branch to a subroutine, program control will revert to the line immediately following the ON, GOSUB statement, once the subroutine has been executed.

## Looping Statements

Suppose that you needed to compute the squares of the integers from 1 to 20. One way of doing this is by calculating the square for each individual integer as shown below.

```
100  A = 1 ^ 2
200  PRINT A
300  B = 2 ^ 2
400  PRINT B
500  C = 3 ^ 2
600  PRINT C
       ⋮
```

However, this method is very cumbersome. This problem could be solved much more efficiently through the use of a FOR, NEXT loop as shown below.

```
100  FOR A = 1 TO 20
200  X = A ^ 2
300  PRINT X
400  NEXT A
500  END
```

The sequence of statements from line 100 to 400 is known as a **loop**. When the computer encounters the FOR statement in line 100, the variable A is set to 1. X is then calculated and displayed in lines 200 and 300.

The NEXT statement in line 400 will request the next value for A. Execution returns to line 100 where the value of A is incremented by 1 (to 2) and then compared to the value appearing after TO. Since the value of A is less than that value, the loop will be executed again with the value of A set at 2.

The loop will continue to be executed until A attains a value greater than 20. When this occurs, the statement following the NEXT statement will be executed.

# IBM BASIC Conditional, Branching, and Looping Statements 93

In our preceding example, A is known as an **index variable.** If the optional keyword STEP is not included with the FOR statement, the index variable will be incremented by 1 every time the NEXT statement is executed.

STEP can be included at the end of a FOR statement to change the value by which the index variable is incremented. The integer appearing after STEP is the new increment. For example, if our preceding example were changed as follows,

```
100 FOR A = 1 TO 20 STEP 2
200 X = A ^ 2
300 PRINT X
400 NEXT A
500 END
```

the index variable, A, would be incremented by 2 every time the NEXT statement was executed.

One loop can be placed inside another loop. The innermost loop is known as a **nested** loop. The following program contains a nested loop.

```
050 DIM R(2,3)
100 DATA 10,20,30,40,50,60
200 FOR I = 1 TO 2
300 FOR J = 1 TO 3
400 READ R(I,J)
500 NEXT J
600 NEXT I
```

Our preceding example is used to read data into the numeric array R. Arrays as well as the READ and DATA statements will be discussed in Chapter 5.

One error that you should take care to avoid when using nested loops is to end an outer loop before an inner loop is ended. Also, be certain that every NEXT statement has a matching FOR statement. If the IBM BASIC interpreter cannot match every NEXT statement with a preceding FOR statement, an error will result.

The WHILE, WEND statements also set up a loop. The loop begins with the WHILE statement and ends with WEND. The loop will continue to execute as long as the expression after WHILE evaluates as true (not zero). An example of a WHILE, WEND loop is given below.

```
100 X = 3
200 WHILE X
300 PRINT X
400 X = X - 1
500 WEND
600 END
RUN
 3
 2
 1
Ok
```

As long as X (in line 200) has a non-zero value, the loop will continue to execute. All WHILE statements must have a corresponding WEND statement. If not, the following error will be displayed:

WHILE without WEND

# CHAPTER 5.
# TABLES and ARRAYS

## INTRODUCTION

In Chapter 2, we introduced the concept of variables. A variable is designed to hold a single data item -- either string or numeric. However, some programs require that hundreds or even thousands of variable names be used.

The processing of large quantities of data can be greatly facilitated through the use of arrays and tables in a program.

**Subscripted Variables**

Obviously, the use of thousands of individual variable names could prove extremely cumbersome. To overcome this problem, BASIC allows the use of **subscripted variables.** Subscripted variables are identified with a **subscript,** a number appearing within parentheses immediately after the variable name. An example of a group of subscripted variables is given below:

A(0), A(1), A(2), A(3), A(4),..., A(10)

Note that each subscripted variable is a unique variable. In other words, A(0) differs from A(1), A(2), A(3), A(4), etc.

**Arrays and Tables**

Subscripted variables should be visualized as an **array** (or **table**). In our previous example, the data contained in the array defined by A would consist of a one-dimension array with 11 elements.

```
A(10)
A(9)
A(8)
A(7)
A(6)
A(5)
A(4)
A(3)
A(2)
A(1)
A(0)
```

Arrays can also have two dimensions. Two-dimensional arrays are also known as tables. A table containing 6 rows and 8 columns is depicted below.

**Columns**

|  | 0 | 1 | 2 | 3 | 4 | 5 | 6 | 7 |
|---|---|---|---|---|---|---|---|---|
| 0 | A(0,0) | A(0,1) | A(0,2) | A(0,3) | A(0,4) | A(0,5) | A(0,6) | A(0,7) |
| 1 | A(1,0) | A(1,1) | A(1,2) | A(1,3) | A(1,4) | A(1,5) | A(1,6) | A(1,7) |
| 2 | A(2,0) | A(2,1) | A(2,2) | A(2,3) | A(2,4) | A(2,5) | A(2,6) | A(2,7) |
| 3 | A(3,0) | A(3,1) | A(3,2) | A(3,3) | A(3,4) | A(3,5) | A(3,6) | A(3,7) |
| 4 | A(4,0) | A(4,1) | A(4,2) | A(4,3) | A(4,4) | A(4,5) | A(4,6) | A(4,7) |
| 5 | A(5,0) | A(5,1) | A(5,2) | A(5,3) | A(5,4) | A(5,5) | A(5,6) | A(5,7) |

**Rows**

Notice from our illustration that a position within the table is identified with a subscripted variable. The subscript contains two numbers. The first number identifies the row number and the second identifies the column. For instance, A(1,2) identifies the element located in column two of row one.

Array variables can be assigned values and used with operators as can any other variable. This is illustrated in the following example.

```
10 A(0) = 5
20 A(1) = 6
30 A(2) = 7
40 A(3) = 8
50 A(4) = 9
60 PRINT A(0) * A(1)
70 A(5) = A(2) + A(3) + A(4)
80 PRINT A(5)
90 END
RUN
 30
 24
Ok
```

**Dimensioning an Array**

Before an array variable can be used in a program, an area in memory must be reserved to store its elements. This is known as dimensioning the array and is accomplished with the DIM statement.

The DIM statement defines the maximum subscript value that can be used for an array. For example, the following DIM statement:

DIM A(20)

would define a one-dimension array consisting of twenty-one elements ranging from A(0) to A(20) inclusive.

Two-dimension arrays are dimensioned as follows:

DIM A(4,7)

The preceding DIM statement would dimension an array consisting of five rows with eight columns each. This table was depicted earlier.

Notice that a DIM statement was not included in our example on page 97. When a subscripted variable which has not been previously dimensioned is referenced in a program, the array variable is automatically dimensioned with a maximum subscript value of 10. If we added the following program line to our example:

85 A(11) = 24:PRINT A(11) * A(1)

the following error message would be displayed:

Subscript out of range in 85

This error is generated because an array variable was referenced with a subscript greater than that allowed for.

If the following DIM statement was also inserted in our example program:

5 DIM A(11)

it would execute properly, because A(11) would have been defined by the DIM statement.

Generally, it is a good programming practice to dimension all array variables and to group all DIM statements at the beginning of the program. This prevents an array variable from inadvertently being referenced before it has been dimensioned.

When an array is no longer needed in a program, the DIM statement can be reversed with an ERASE statement. This will free the memory area previously reserved for the array. This is illustrated in the following program.

```
 5 PRINT FRE(0)
10 DIM A(99,99)
20 PRINT FRE(0)
30 ERASE A
40 PRINT FRE(0)
50 END
RUN
 61704
 21690
 61701
Ok
```

In line 5, the number of available bytes in memory are displayed. FRE is a function which displays the available free bytes in memory. FRE is explained in more detail in Chapter 9.

In line 10, the DIM statement reserves an area in memory for a table consisting of 10,000 elements. From line 20, it is evident that the number of free bytes has decreased substantially. This is due to the fact that an area of memory has been reserved for the elements in table A.

In line 30, the ERASE statement reverses the DIM statement and the memory previously required for the elements in table A are freed.

**OPTION BASE**

Many programmers find it a nuisance to begin numbering array elements with a subscript of 0. They find that having A(10) represent the eleventh element in an array named A causes confusion.

The OPTION BASE statement can be used in an array to specify the beginning subscript for all array variables. If the following statement is inserted in a program:

OPTION BASE 1

array subscripts will begin with 1 rather than 0. If OPTION BASE is to be used in a program, it should be placed at its beginning, prior to any DIM statements and before any array variables are referenced.

**Array Data Types**

Arrays can be defined according to the type of data they are to store by specifying the proper variable type in the DIM statement. For example, if an integer variable was used to define an array, that array would store integers. Any attempt to store a string value would result in an error. Any attempt to store a single or double-precision value would result in rounding.

By the same token, an array defined with a string variable will hold string data, an array defined with a single-precision numeric variable will hold single-precision numeric data, etc. The rules for converting numeric data from one precision to another apply to both non-array and array variables.

Notice from our example on page 103 that a different type identifier causes an array variable name to be unique. In other words, A%(3), A#(3), and A(3) each define a separate variable and a separate memory location.

**DATA & READ Statements**

Earlier, we discussed how data could be assigned to a variable with a LET statement as well as how data could be input directly from the keyboard and assigned to a variable with the INPUT statement.

However, neither the LET nor the INPUT statements are practical for assigning data values to the individual variables in a large array or table. DATA and READ statements are much more practical for assigning values to variables in an array. DATA and READ statements can be used for assigning values to any variable -- not just array variables.

A typical DATA statement is shown below.

    100 DATA "WILLIAMS",27,"ST. LOUIS","314-727-1141"

Notice that this DATA statement contains four data items, three of which are string and one which is numeric. In our example, we have enclosed the string data items in quotation marks. However, this was not actually required. In a DATA statement, a string only needs to be enclosed in quotation marks if it contains a comma, a colon, or if its first character is a blank space.

DATA statements are used in tandem with READ statements to assign data values to variables. An example of a READ statement is given below.

    200 READ NAME$,AGE,CITY$,PHONE$

When a READ statement is executed, the computer will first search for a DATA statement. When a DATA statement is found, the values in the DATA statement will be assigned one-by-one to the variables in the READ statement.

If the first DATA statement encountered does not have enough data items to be assigned to all the variables in the READ statement, the next DATA statement will be searched for. The values from this and succeeding DATA statements will continue to be assigned to the variables in the READ statement until all of the variables in the READ statement have been assigned a value.

The computer keeps track of the next DATA statement data item to be used via an internal pointer. When any future READ statements are executed, this pointer will determine which is the next data item to be read into the READ variable.

BASIC includes a statement known as RESTORE, which when executed, sets the DATA item pointer back to the beginning of the DATA statement list. The use of the DATA item pointer and the effect of RESTORE on it is depicted in Illustration 5-1.

### Illustration 5-1. DATA Statement Pointer

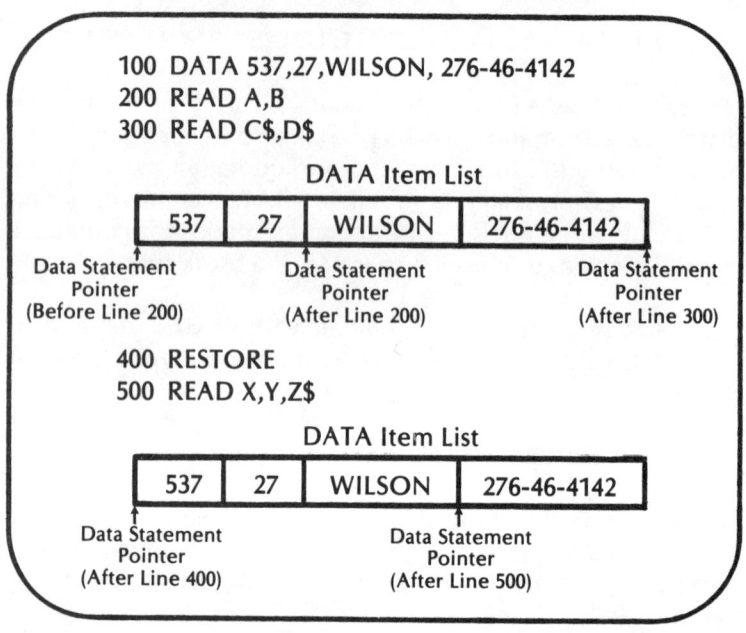

```
100 DATA 537,27,WILSON, 276-46-4142
200 READ A,B
300 READ C$,D$
```

DATA Item List

| 537 | 27 | WILSON | 276-46-4142 |
|---|---|---|---|

↑ Data Statement Pointer (Before Line 200)  ↑ Data Statement Pointer (After Line 200)  ↑ Data Statement Pointer (After Line 300)

```
400 RESTORE
500 READ X,Y,Z$
```

DATA Item List

| 537 | 27 | WILSON | 276-46-4142 |
|---|---|---|---|

↑ Data Statement Pointer (After Line 400)  ↑ Data Statement Pointer (After Line 500)

When not properly used, DATA and READ statements can be the source of program errors. One potential error source occurs when the program attempts to READ more data items than were given in the DATA statements. Such an error would occur in the following program.

```
100 DATA 7,8,11,13,15
200 FOR I = 1 TO 7
300 READ X(I)
400 PRINT X(I)
500 NEXT
600 END
```

In the preceding example, the program would attempt to read 7 data items. However, since the DATA statement only contained 5 data items, the following error message would appear:

Out of data in 300

Another potential source of an error when executing DATA and READ statements are situations where the program attempts to read a numeric data item into a string variable or vice versa. If such an error is encountered, the following error message will be displayed:

Syntax Error

DATA and READ statements are often used in conjunction with FOR, NEXT loops to read large amounts of data into arrays. An example of this use of FOR, NEXT is given below:

```
10 OPTION BASE 1
20 FOR I = 1 TO 3
30 READ A%(I)
40 READ A(I)
50 READ A#(I)
60 READ A$(I)
70 NEXT I
80 FOR X = 1 TO 3
100 PRINT A%(X),A(X),A#(X),A$(X)
110 NEXT X
120 DATA 3,3.34234,4.329029392,JOHN,56,393.0,
         38382900.09,JERRY,390,339.89,3939093.93,
         CRAIG
RUN
 3          3.34234       4.329029392   JOHN
 56         393           38382900.09   JERRY
 390        339.89        3939093.93    CRAIG
Ok
```

An example of the use of the READ and DATA statements in conjunction with a FOR, NEXT loop for the purpose of reading data into a two-dimensional array is given in the program on the following page.

```
 50 OPTION BASE 1
100 DATA 100,200,300,400
200 DATA 500,600,700,800
300 DATA 900,1000,1100,1200
400 DIM A(3,4)
500 FOR I = 1 TO 3
600 FOR J = 1 TO 4
700 READ A(I,J)
750 PRINT A(I,J),
800 NEXT J
900 NEXT I
1000 END
RUN
100         200         300         400         500
600         700         800         900         1000
1100        1200
Ok
```

The preceding program would read data items into the table A( ) as shown in Illustration 5-2.

### Illustration 5-2. A( ) Array Values

|   | 1 | 2 | 3 | 4 |
|---|---|---|---|---|
| 1 | 100 | 200 | 300 | 400 |
| 2 | 500 | 600 | 700 | 800 |
| 3 | 900 | 1000 | 1100 | 1200 |

# CHAPTER 6.
# FUNCTIONS & STRING HANDLING

**INTRODUCTION**

In mathematics, a function is generally defined as a quantity whose value will vary as a result of another quantity. In computing, functions define operations that are performed on strings or numeric values.

In BASIC, a number of functions are already defined by reserved words and are a part of the BASIC interpreter. These are known as **built-in** functions (see Table 6-1). Built-in functions cover a wide range of standard math operations such as absolute value, square root, logarithms, etc. Built-in functions are also available for working with strings, as well as a variety of other operations.

IBM BASIC also allows the programmer to define his or her own functions. These are known as **user-defined** functions. Both built-in and user-defined functions will be discussed in this chapter, as well as in Chapter 9.

**BUILT-IN NUMERIC FUNCTIONS**
**Mathematical Functions**

The majority of the IBM BASIC functions are used in mathematical applications. The availability of these built-in mathematical functions allows for more efficient programs involving mathematical calculations. We will provide an overview of IBM BASIC's math functions in this section. Each individual function will be described in detail in Chapter 9.

### Table 6-1. IBM BASIC Built-In Functions

| | | | |
|---|---|---|---|
| ABS | FRE | MKI$ | SQR |
| ASC | HEX$ | MKS$ | STICK |
| ATN | INP | OCT$ | STR$ |
| CDBL | INPUT$ | PEEK | STRIG |
| CHR$ | INSTR | PEN | STRING$ |
| CINT | INT | POINT | TAB |
| COS | LEFT$ | POS | TAN |
| CSNG | LEN | RIGHT$ | USR |
| CVD | LOC | RND | VAL |
| CVI | LOF | SCREEN | VARPTR |
| CVS | LOG | SGN | VARPTR$ |
| EOF | LPOS | SIN | |
| EXP | MID$ | SPACE$ | |
| FIX | MKD$ | SPC | |

All of the IBM BASIC mathematical functions operate in much the same manner. Each function is defined by a reserved word (ex. SIN for Sine, COS for Cosine, LOG for Logarithm, etc.).

A numeric constant, variable, or expression will appear in parentheses following the reserved word which identifies the function. The function for that numeric value will then be calculated by the computer. The use of several mathematical functions is shown in Illustration 6-1.

IBM BASIC includes the following three trigonometric functions:

> SIN(N) = sine of the angle given in N.
> COS(N) = cosine of the angle given in N.
> TAN(N) = tangent of the angle given in N.

The angle N must be given in terms of radians. One radian is the equivalent of 57.29578 degrees. One degree equals .017453 radians.

**Illustration 6-1. Mathematical Functions**

```
Ok
 100 PRINT SIN(.47)
 200 PRINT COS(.98)
 300 PRINT TAN(.37)
 400 PRINT SQR(49)
 500 PRINT INT(5.79)
 600 PRINT INT(-5.79)
 700 PRINT FIX(7.93)
 800 PRINT FIX(-7.93)
 900 PRINT ABS(-4.7)
1000 PRINT SGN(2.7)
1100 PRINT SGN(-2.7)
1200 END
RUN
 .4528863
 .5570226
 .3878632
 7
 5
-6
 7
-7
 4.7
 1
-1
```

Therefore, the following can be used to calculate a trigonometric function with its argument (X) given in degrees:

SIN(.017453 * X)
COS(.017453 * X)
TAN(.017453 * X)

The other three trigonometric functions, secant, cosecant, and cotangent can be computed by using SIN, COS, and TAN as shown in the following formulas.

$$SEC(X) = 1/COS(X)$$
$$CSC(X) = 1/SIN(X)$$
$$COT(X) = COS(X)/SIN(X)$$

IBM BASIC also includes the arctangent function ATN. This function returns the angle (expressed in radians) whose tangent is given in its argument.

$$ATN(X) = \text{angle in radians whose tangent equals } X$$

The following formula can be used to calculate the angle expressed in degrees (rather than radians) whose tangent is given in X.

$$57.29578 * ATN(X)$$

IBM BASIC also contains functions for calculating logarithms and exponents. The exponential function takes the following form:

$$A = EXP(B)$$

The preceding EXP function is calculated by computing the value of e raised to the B power. e is known as the base of natural logarithms. The value e in IBM BASIC is 2.71828183.

The natural logarithm of a number may be calculated with the LOG function.

$$LOG(X) = \text{natural logarithm of } X$$

Logarithms wth a base other than 10 may be calculated using the following formula:

$$LOG_b(X) = LOG(X)/LOG(b)$$

where b is the base of the logarithm.

## Functions & String Handling 109

IBM BASIC includes the SQR function for determining the square root of its argument.

$$SQR(X) = \text{square root of } X$$

The square root of a number can also be calculated with the exponential arithmetic operator. The following expression,

$$X \wedge (1/2)$$

will calculate the square root of X. The exponential arithmetic operator can also be used to calculate a root other than the square root (ex. cube root) as shown below.

$$X \wedge (1/3)$$

IBM BASIC also includes several functions that can be used in working with numeric values. These include INT, FIX, ABS, SGN, CINT, CSNG, and CDBL.

The INT function returns the integer with the greatest value which is less than or equal to its argument. INT takes the following form:

$$INT(X) = \text{highest integer whose value is less than or equal to } X$$

Illustration 6-1 contains examples of the usage of the INT function.

The FIX function is used to discard the decimal portion of a numeric value. FIX takes the following form.

$$FIX(X) = \text{integer portion of } X$$

Illustration 6-1 contains examples of the usage of the FIX function.

The ABS functon returns the absolute value of its argument. ABS takes the following form.

$$ABS(X) = |x|$$

An example of the use of ABS appears in Illustration 6-1.

The SGN function returns the sign of its argument. An example of the use of SGN appears in Illustration 6-1.

The CINT function is used to convert its argument to an integer. The decimal portion of the argument will be truncated. CINT can only be used with numbers in the range between –32768 and 32767.

The CSNG function is used to convert its argument to a single precision number. The CDBL function is used to convert its argument to a double precision number.

**User-Defined Functions**

In the preceding section, we discussed a number of predefined IBM BASIC functions. IBM BASIC also allows the user to define his own functions. These are known as **user-defined** functions. A user-defined function must be defined with the DEF FN statement before it can be used in the program.

For example, the following DEF FN statement would define a function in which the argument was squared and 1 was then subtracted from the product.

$$100 \ \ DEF \ FNA(X) = X \wedge 2 - 1$$

The name of the function (FNA) appears immediately following the DEF statement. Any valid variable name may be used as a user-defined function name. The following would be a valid function name:

$$FNHEX.TO.DEC\%$$

In our first example, notice the X in parentheses following the function name. This is known as a **dummy argument.** Any valid variable name can be substituted for X as the dummy argument.

## Functions & String Handling 111

When the user-defined function is called in the program, the argument supplied with the function when it is called will be substituted for the dummy argument whenever it appears on the right-hand side of the DEF FN statement. The expression is then evaluated and the value is returned as the value of the function.

```
10 M = 3.9878
20 DEF FNS(X) = COS(X) + SIN(X)
30 PRINT FNS(M)
RUN
-1.4116
Ok
```

The previous example contains a program that has a DEF FN statement at line 20. The function is assigned the name S, and the dummy argument X is used in the function. The operations in the function (COS(X) + SIN(X)) can be as complicated as necessary. At line 30, the S function is called to evaluate the function for the value of the variable M. The function substitutes 3.9878 for the dummy argument X and returns a numeric value that is displayed by the PRINT statement.

Data types for user-defined functions can be specified by using the type declaration statements (DEFSTR, DEFINT, DEFSNG, DEFDBL) or by using the type declaration characters ($, %, !, #).

When a data type is specified for a dummy argument, the data being substituted for that argument will be converted to the same type prior to the substitution.

```
10 M = 3.9878
20 DEF FNS(X%) = COS(X) + SIN(X)
30 PRINT FNS(M)
RUN
 1
Ok
```

When a variable type is specified with the function name, the value returned by the function will be of that type. An error will result if the type conversion cannot be made.

## STRINGS & STRING HANDLING

As a programmer, you will encounter a number of situations where you may need to work with string data. For example, you might want to combine several strings, compare two strings, separate portions of a string, or even convert string data to its numeric equivalent. IBM BASIC allows for all of these.

### String Concatenation

The process of joining together one or more strings is known as **concatenation.** The arithmetic operator for addition (+) is used for string concatenation. However, concatenation is very different from addition. In concatenation, the strings being concatenated are joined to form a new string as shown below.

```
Ok
100 A$ = "JOHN"
200 B$ = "SON"
300 C$ = A$ + B$
400 PRINT C$
500 END
RUN
JOHNSON
Ok
```

Either string constants or variables may be concatenated. Any number of strings may be concatenated as long as the resulting string contains 255 or fewer characters.

The same relational operators are used for comparing strings as are used for comparing numeric data. These include the following:

```
   < or LT  →  less than
  <= or LE  →  less than or equal to
   > or GT  →  greater than
  >= or GE  →  greater than or equal to
   = or EQ  →  equal to
  <> or NE  →  not equal
```

Strings are compared one character at a time beginning with each string's first character. This comparison is made with each character's corresponding ASCII code.

Fortunately, ASCII code comparisons are relatively simple. A comparison of the characters by ASCII codes is almost identical to an alphabetical comparison. A character is less than another with respect to ASCII codes, if that character precedes it in the alphabet. Lowercase letters are always greater than their uppercase counterparts and numbers are always less than letters. Appendix D contains the ASCII character codes.

If two strings with differing lengths are being compared, the longer string is always evaluated as being the greater. In other words, "aaaa" is greater than "aaa".

Like numeric relational operators, string relational operators return a value of 0 if the relation is false and a value of −1 if it is true. Whenever strings are being compared, they must be enclosed within quotation marks.

**String Handling Functions**

IBM BASIC contains a number of string handling functions which allow the user to extract a part of a string or to replace a part of a string with a different string. These functions are LEFT$, MID$, RIGHT$ and LEN.

The LEFT$ function takes the following format:

$$LEFT\$(string, X)$$

where *string* is the string from which characters are to be extracted and *X* is the number of characters to be extracted. The LEFT$ function will extract the leftmost number of characters given in *X* from the string given in *string*.

Illustration 6-2 contains an example of the use of LEFT$.

**Illustration 6-2. LEFT$**

```
Ok
100 A$ = "JOHNSON"
200 B$ = LEFT$(A$,4)
300 PRINT B$
400 END
RUN
JOHN
Ok
```

The RIGHT$ function works exactly like the LEFT$ function except that the rightmost number of characters specified are returned. Illustration 6-3 contains an example of the use of RIGHT$.

**Illustration 6-3. RIGHT$**

```
Ok
100 A$ = "JOHNSON"
200 B$ = RIGHT$(A$,3)
300 PRINT B$
400 END
RUN
SON
Ok
```

The MID$ function can be used to either return a portion of a string or to replace a portion of one string with another string. MID$ takes the following format when used to return a portion of a string:

$$a\$ = MID\$(b\$,x[,y])$$

The string being returned is a$. a$ is being returned from b$. The string being returned will begin with the xth character in b$. The

## Functions & String Handling

number of characters returned from *b$* is specified in *y*. *y* is an optional parameter. If *y* is omitted, all rightmost characters in *b$* will be returned in *a$*. An example of the use of MID$ to return a portion of a string is given in Illustration 6-4.

**Illustration 6-4. MID$ Used to Return a Portion of a String**

```
Ok
100 X$ = "NEW CASTLE"
200 Y$ = MID$(X$,5,4)
300 PRINT Y$
400 END
RUN
CAST
Ok
```

To replace a portion of a given string with another string, use the following format.

$$MID\$(b\$,x[,y]) = a\$$$

The string given in *a$* will replace the characters in *b$* beginning at the xth character in *b$*. *y* is an optional parameter which indicates the number of characters from *a$* which will be used in the replacement. An example of the use of MID$ to replace a portion of a string is given in Illustration 6-5.

**Illustration 6-5. MID$ Used to Replace a Portion of a String**

```
Ok
100 X$ = "NEW CASTLE":Y$ = "MUNSON"
200 MID$(X$,5) = Y$
300 PRINT X$
400 END
RUN
NEW MUNSON
Ok
```

### String/Numeric Data Conversion

Programmers often encounter situations where numeric data must be converted into string data and vice versa. This is often the case where a function is being used which will accept only string or numeric data as its arguments.

The STR$ and VAL functions are used to convert numeric data to its string equivalent and strings to their numeric equivalent respectively. The ASC function is used to convert a single text character to its ASCII numeric equivalent. The CHR$ function converts an ASCII numeric code to an equivalent text character.

Examples of the use of STR$, VAL, CHR$, and ASC are given in Illustration 6-6 and 6-7.

**Illustration 6-6. STR$ and VAL Examples**

```
Ok
100  ZIP = 33578
200  ZIP$ = STR$(ZIP)       :REM ZIP$ = "33578"
300  ZIP2 = 33579
400  ZIP2$ = STR$(ZIP2)
500  ZIP3$ = ZIP$ + ZIP2$   :REM ZIP3$ = "3357833579"
600  ZIP3 = VAL(ZIP3$)      :REM ZIP3 = 3357833579
700  ZIP4 = INT(ZIP3/10000)
800  PRINT ZIP4
900  END
RUN
 335783
Ok
```

### Illustration 6-7. CHR$ and ASC Examples

```
Ok
100 A$ = "GILBERT"
200 A1% = ASC(A$)
300 PRINT A1%
400 X% = 90
500 X$ = CHR$(X%)
600 PRINT X$
700 END
RUN
 71
Z
Ok
```

**Variable Table and String Storage**

IBM BASIC maintains an area in memory in which an entry is maintained for every variable (including array variables) referenced either in a program or in the direct mode. This memory area is known as the **variable table.**

For numeric variables, the value currently assigned to that variable is also stored in the variable table. When that variable's value is changed, the value stored in the variable table will also be changed.

In IBM BASIC, the amount of memory required to store an integer, single precision, or double precision value in the variable table remains constant. An integer variable (including an integer array variable) requires two bytes, a single precision value requires four bytes, and a double precision value requires eight bytes.

On the other hand, the amount of memory required to store a string variable's value can vary depending upon that value. A string variable requires one byte of storage for each character in the string plus an additional three bytes.

Since the memory space required to store a string value can vary, it would be difficult to store these values in the variable table, as that table would have to be continually revised as different values were assigned to string variables. For this reason, IBM BASIC stores string values in a separate memory area known as **string space.**

IBM BASIC stores a value in the variable table which associates the string variable name (in the variable table) with its associated value in string space. This is known as the **descriptor.** The descriptor describes the number of characters currently assigned to the string variable as well as its location in string space.

Descriptors are not limited to referencing string values stored in the string space. Descriptors can reference strings stored anywhere within BASIC's working area -- including file buffers and the program itself. When a string constant is assigned to a string variable in a BASIC program (ex. 10 A$ = "JOHN"), that constant need not be stored in the string space as the descriptor can reference it in the program storage area.

**Housekeeping and FRE**

Areas assigned to strings can become unused because strings in BASIC can have variable lengths. Every time a different value is assigned to a string variable, its length may change. This may cause the space assigned to a string to become partially unused.

When FRE is used with a string argument, a **housekeeping** will be performed before the function returns the number of free bytes. A housekeeping is where BASIC gathers all useful data and frees any areas of string space memory which were once used for strings, but are currently unused.

FRE's primary function is to return the number of unused bytes in memory. Either a string or numeric argument can be specified with FRE. The actual value of the argument is otherwise ignored, and, like the argument for a DEF FN statement, is referred to as a dummy argument.

If the string space is in need of a housekeeping, IBM BASIC will automatically halt program execution and perform one. However, it is a good programming practice to include a FRE function with a numeric argument in a program to test whether sufficient available memory is available for execution, and if not, to perform a housekeeping by executing FRE with a string argument.

# CHAPTER 7.
# FILES & FILE HANDLING WITH IBM BASIC

**INTRODUCTION**

In the preceding chapters, we did not discuss the concepts and programming techniques related to storage of data on cassette tape or floppy diskettes. In this chapter, we will discuss these concepts. We also will discuss how to write programs that make use of these devices.

**Files, Records, and Fields**

Before learning specific concepts which relate to the cassette tape unit and diskette drives, it is essential that the user understand the concepts of **files, records,** and **fields.**

A file can be defined as a collection of related data. Files can be distinguished as being either **program files** or **data files.** A program file consists of a program which has been saved on diskette or cassette tape.

A data file consists of a collection of related information which has been saved on a diskette or cassette tape. Generally, a data file is read from storage by a program or written to storage by a program.

Data files are divided into smaller segments known as records and fields. A field is a single piece of data. Fields are grouped together as a record. These records, in turn, make up the file.

A simple illustration may help you understand the concepts of a data file, record, and field. Take an address book as an example of a data file. This file would contain name, address, and telephone number data for the individuals appearing in the address book. Each individual's name, address, and phone number would represent one record. For example, the following data would make up one record:

Jay Gatsby
1 Shore Lane
West Egg, NY 10565
516-787-2122

Each individual data item within the record (i.e. name, street address, city, state, zip code, telephone number) could be thought of as a field.

A data file is written or read as a series of numeric constants. For example, our address book example might be read as follows.

"Jay Gatsby","1 Shore Lane","West Egg","NY",10565,"516-787-2122"
"Nick Carraway","7 Shore Lane","West Egg","NY",10565,"516-787-2736"

When these data items are read or written, the first field will have been defined as the name, the second as the street address, the third as the city, the fourth as the state, the fifth as the zip code, and the sixth as the telephone number.

Note that the fifth field is numeric, while the others contain string data. Notice that the string data is enclosed in quotation marks.

Finally, note that each data item is separated by a comma. For the computer to be able to distinguish where one data item ends and another begins, these items must be separated with a character known as a **delimiter.** A delimiter might consist of a comma (as in our example), a blank space, a line return character, or a form feed character.

The advantages of using data files with programs is obvious. Data files allow the user to save, alter, and redisplay data as is necessary. For example, using our address book as an example, programs could be written to do the following.

1. Enter changes in an individual's record by reading the file from storage until the desired record is found, inputting the required changes, and rewriting the file back into storage.

2. Displaying an individual's name, address, and telephone information by reading the file from storage until the desired record is found, outputting the field data to the screen, and rewriting the file back into storage.

The use of a data file with a mass storage device is analogous to the use of a file cabinet for storing information in an office.

**File Specifications**

Every file is identified with a **file specification,** which consists of a **filename** and a **device name.**\* The filename identifies the file to be searched for, and the device identifies where the file is to be searched for.

Some examples of file specifications are given below.

>       CAS1:TEXT
>       B:CUSTOMER
>       A:LETTER2.TXT

Every file is identified by a filename which can include up to eight characters. These characters can contain the letters A to Z or numbers 0 to 9. Filenames for files being stored on diskette may also include a **filename extension.** A filename extension consists of a period and three letters which appear immediately after the primary filename.

---

\* In certain instances in BASIC 2.0, a directory path must also be specified. Paths will be discussed later in this chapter.

A filename can be entered with upper or lowercase letters. However, the computer will interpret all lowercase entries as capitals. The following filenames all refer to the same file:

>Vendor.TXT
>VENDOR.txt
>VENDOR.TXT
>vendor.txt

The file specification prefixes the filename with a device name. The device name is the name of the storage device which is to hold the file.

A device name can consist of from 1 to 4 characters followed by the colon. The following are recognized as valid device names in BASIC 2.0.

| | |
|---|---|
| A: | Diskette drive 1 |
| B: | Diskette drive 2 |
| C: | Fixed drive 1 |
| D: | Fixed drive 2 |
| CAS1: | Cassette tape unit |
| COM1: | Async. communications adapter #1 |
| COM2: | Async. communications adapter #2 |
| KYBD: | Keyboard |
| LPT1: | Printer #1 |
| LPT2: | Printer #2 |
| LPT3: | Printer #3 |
| SCRN: | Screen |

The device name need not be specified in the file specification if that device is the default drive. In Cassette BASIC, the default device is CAS1:. In Disk and Advanced BASIC, the default device is A: (for drive 1).

**Directories**

A **directory** is a file which contains information regarding the other files contained on a disk drive.

In BASIC versions 1.0 and 1.1, a single directory was sufficient for a diskette. With the inclusion of fixed disk drives, it became necessary to allow a number of directories, as a fixed disk can hold thousands of files.

BASIC 2.0 allows the user to organize fixed disk files by grouping files in various directory structures.

In BASIC 2.0's Disk and Advanced versions, a **path** to a file can be included with the file specification.

A path consists of a series of directory names, each separated with the backslash character ( \ ). The path is specified per the following configuration:

*device:path*

The *device* name indicates where BASIC is to look for the file. The *path* indicates the path to be followed to find the directory which includes the indicated file.

Paths can be included with the following commands:

| | | |
|---|---|---|
| BLOAD | KILL | OPEN |
| BSAVE | LOAD | RMDIR |
| CHAIN | MERGE | RUN |
| CHDIR | MKDIR | SAVE |
| FILES | NAME | |

If a string constant is used for a path, it must be enclosed within quotation marks. For example, the following specification is valid:

"B:\ MKTA \ RPTB \ ACME"

If a path begins with a backslash, the search begins with the root directory. Otherwise, the search begins with the current directory. If the file to be accessed is not in the current directory, a path leading to the current directory must be specified.

The concepts of root directory, current directory, and tree structured directories are discussed in the next section.

**Tree Structured Directories**

As with floppy diskettes, a single directory is created on a fixed disk when it is formatted. This directory is known as the **root** directory. The root directory can hold either 64 or 112 file entries.

The root directory can contain the names of other directories as well as filenames. These other directories, known as **sub-directories,** are actually files. Sub-directories are not limited in size and can contain any number of files. In fact, sub-directories can include other sub-directories as well as files.

Sub-directories follow the same naming conventions as filenames -- a primary name of 1 to 8 characters and an optional extension of 1 to 3 characters.

Different directories can contain identical filenames or directory names. In other words, each directory can contain file and directory names that appear in other directories as well.

BASIC can identify a default directory just as it can a default device. This default directory is known as the current directory. When a filename is entered without specifying a directory, BASIC will search the default directory.

Upon start up, BASIC will use the root directory as the current directory. The current directory can be either changed or identified via the CHDIR command.

## Directory Paths

BASIC 2.0 requires the following data when it is asked to search for or to create a file:

- Device
- Filename
- Directory Containing File

If the file is in the current directory, the directory need not be identified, because the current directory is used by default.

If the file is not in the current directory, BASIC must be given the **path** of directory names which lead to the desired directory.

The following illustration depicts an example of directory structure.

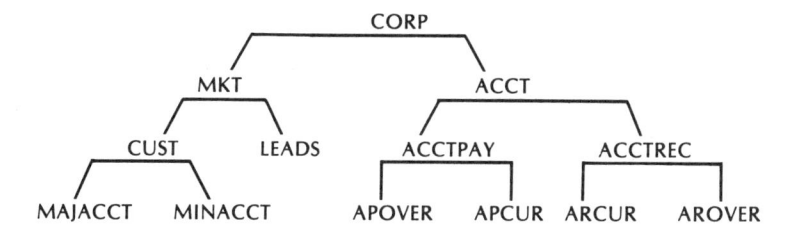

```
                        CORP
                       /    \
                   MKT        ACCT
                  /   \      /    \
              CUST  LEADS  ACCTPAY  ACCTREC
             /   \          |   |    |   |
         MAJACCT MINACCT  APOVER APCUR ARCUR AROVER
```

If we wished to specify the file MAJACCT, we could do so by specifying the file path from the root directory as shown below.

\MKT \ CUST \ MAJACCT

If the current directory was MKT, MAJACCT could be specified as follows:

CUST \ MAJACCT

Sub-directories are identified in DOS DIR or BASIC file listings with two special entries. The first entry contains a period instead of a filename. This indicates that the item being listed is a sub-directory. The second entry contains two periods instead of a filename. This is used to locate the next higher directory which defines the sub-directory. This directory is known as the sub-directory's **parent** directory. For example, in the illustration on the preceding page, the parent of the sub-directory CUST is MKT.

## FILE ACCESS

File access refers to the processes of reading data from a file or writing data to it. In IBM BASIC, data is organized in a file in either a sequential or a random manner. The mode in which a file's data is organized determines how that data will be accessed.

### Sequential and Random Files

Two types of IBM BASIC data files are used, sequential data files and random access data files. Cassette BASIC allows only sequential files, while the Disk and Advanced versions allow either.

Each record of a sequential disk file is assigned exactly as much storage space as it requires. There are no blank spaces between records in a sequential file.

In random data files, a constant space is assigned to every record in the file. If the record does not occupy the entire space assigned to it, the remaining space is left blank.

The concepts of sequential and random files are pictured in Illustration 7-1. Notice that the length of each record in the random file is constant at 400 bytes.

Files & File Handling with IBM BASIC  129

The record length of a sequential file is variable. The record length is the sum of the total space used by all the fields in each individual record.

The important difference between random and sequential files lies in how each file is accessed. **Direct Access** of any record in a random file is possible regardless of where that record is located on the file.

**Illustration 7-1. Random and Sequental Data Files**

### Random File

| SECTOR 1 | SECTOR 2 | SECTOR 3 |

Record 1 — 400 Bytes
Record 2 — 400 Bytes
Record 3 — 400 Bytes

### Sequential File

| SECTOR 1 | SECTOR 2 | SECTOR 3 |

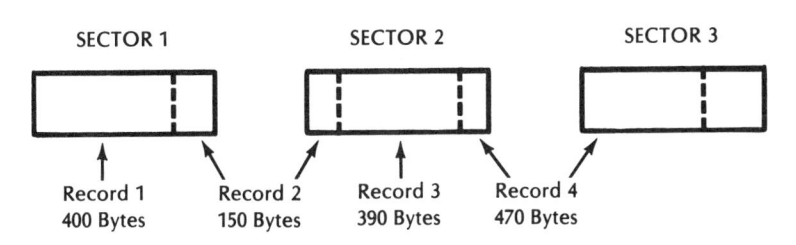

Record 1 — 400 Bytes
Record 2 — 150 Bytes
Record 3 — 390 Bytes
Record 4 — 470 Bytes

***Example assumes 512 bytes per sector***

By direct access, we mean that any record in the file may be retrieved regardless of its position, without having to search through the entire file to find it.

Records in a sequential file can only be retrieved by **sequential access.** In sequential access, the record search begins with the first record in the file and must continue until the desired record is found.

In other words, in a sequential file, to find record 17, IBM BASIC would first have to read the first 16 records, one by one. Since IBM BASIC does not know the record length of sequential files, it has no way of determining the location of record 17, other than by reading the first 16 records.

With random files, IBM BASIC knows the length of each record and can easily calculate the location of any record in the file.

Both random and sequential files have advantages and disadvantages other than file access. Sequential files use less disk space than random files. Since each record in a sequential file is assigned only the disk space it needs, no diskette space is wasted by sequential files. Random files require every record to be assigned the same amount of disk space required by the longest record in that file. This generally results in wasted space.

Random files have an advantage over sequential files in that a record from a random file may be read into memory, changed, and then written back to the disk. A record from a sequential file cannot be read, modified, and then rewritten, as any change that might affect a single record's length could adversely affect the entire file.

**Opening a Sequential File**

Before a file can be read from or written to in IBM BASIC, it must be opened. When a file is opened in IBM BASIC, first of all, the operating system is called upon to read the disk to find information regarding that file in the disk directory. Once this information has been obtained, IBM BASIC will initialize buffer

Files & File Handling with IBM BASIC 131

areas in memory through which data will pass as it is read from and written onto the disk.

Once a file has been opened, the IBM BASIC program can read data from that file one sector at a time. This data is passed to the memory buffer that had been set up when the file was opened. IBM BASIC may then read this data from the buffer area in the same manner that it would read and use any other data stored in memory.

When IBM BASIC writes data to an open file, the data is first written to that file's memory buffer. Data is not actually written to the diskette or cassette until the memory buffer has become filled. When the buffer is full, the data is written to the diskette or cassette one sector at a time.

Once you have opened a file and have finished reading from it and writing to it, you should be certain that you close the file. This is especially important whenever data is written to a file.

When an IBM BASIC file is closed, first of all, any data left in that file's memory buffer will be written to the diskette. This occurs even if the memory buffer is not full. Next, the operating system adds the necessary directory information for that file.

The BASIC statement OPEN is used to open a file. OPEN can be used with either of the following configurations with sequential files. The first is as follows:

OPEN *"file specification"* FOR *mode* AS [#] *filenumber*

The abbreviations in the preceding format can be interpreted as follows:

*file specification*   is the file specification.

*mode*   can be any of the following:

INPUT -- for sequential input. Data can only be

read from the file. Data cannot be written to it. A "File not found" error will occur if an attempt is made to open a file for input that does not already exist.

OUTPUT -- for sequential output. OUTPUT always causes a new file to be created. If a file already exists with the same filename as that specified in an OPEN statement with the OUTPUT mode indicated, existing data in the file will be erased. Data will be written to that file from its beginning point.

APPEND -- for sequential output mode for diskette files only. APPEND is specified when data is to be added to the end of an existing file. If the file being opened for an APPEND already exists, new data will be written to the end of that file. If that file does not exist, a new output file will be created.

*filenumber*  is a required number which is used to refer to a file while it is open. It is much easier to refer to a file as #1 than by its file specification.

The following are examples of valid OPEN statements:

```
OPEN "A:TRANS.DAT" FOR INPUT AS #1
OPEN "B:TEXT.FLE" FOR APPEND AS #2
```

The first example opens TRANS.DAT on drive A for input as file #1. The second example opens TEXT.FLE on drive B for an append as file #2.

The OPEN statement can also be used with the following alternate format for sequential files:

OPEN *altmode,* [#] *filenumber, filespec*

Files & File Handling with IBM BASIC 133

The abbreviations in the preceding format can be interpreted as follows:

*altmode* is a string whose first character is one of the following:
> O -- indicates sequential output mode.
> I -- indicates sequential input mode.
> (APPEND is not available in this configuration)

*filenumber* and *filespec* retain the same meanings as in the first format.

The following are examples of the use of the alternate format of the OPEN statement.

> OPEN "O",#1,"B:FILE.DAT"
> OPEN "I",#2,"A:VENDOR.DAT"
> OPEN "O",#1,"CAS1:CHECKS"

The first example opens FILE.DAT as #1 for output on drive B. The second example opens VENDOR.DAT as #2 for input on drive A. The third example opens CHECKS as #1 for output on the cassette device.

IBM BASIC places a limit on the number of files that may be open at any one time. In Cassette BASIC, only one file may be open at a time. In Diskette and Advanced BASIC, the maximum number of open diskette files is specified in the BASIC command entry (as explained in Chapter 1). From 1 to 15 files may be specified as that maximum.

If no entry is made in the BASIC command, a maximum of three (3) diskette files can be open at any one time. Notice that the use of a filenumber other than 1, 2, or 3 in these cases causes the "Bad file number" error to occur.

One rule to keep in mind when working with files is that the same sequential file may not be open for both input and output at the same time. The following statements would cause an error:

```
100 OPEN "A:ACCOUNT.DAT" FOR OUTPUT AS #2
200 OPEN "A:ACCOUNT.DAT" FOR INPUT AS #1
```

To change ACCOUNT.DAT from input to output, the file must first be closed. This could be accomplished by inserting the following statement:

```
150 CLOSE #1
```

Once ACCOUNT.DAT has been closed as an output file, it may be reopened as an input file.

It is good programming practice to close a file, once the program has finished accessing it. More than one file can be closed with a single CLOSE statement as illustrated below:

```
900 CLOSE #2,#3
```

If the CLOSE statement was executed without an argument as shown below,

```
950 CLOSE
```

all open files would be closed.


**Writing to a Sequential File**

Once a sequential file has been opened, any one of the following statements can be used to output data to it.

```
PRINT#
PRINT# USING
WRITE#
```

PRINT# and PRINT# USING function almost exactly as do PRINT and PRINT USING. The difference lies in the fact that PRINT# and PRINT# USING require that a file number be specified. Data is written to that file rather than to the display. An example of

PRINT# and PRINT# USING is given below.

```
10 OPEN "FILE.DAT" FOR OUTPUT AS #1
20 A = 27.932:B$ = "DON"
30 C = 5.72:D = 9.84
40 PRINT#1,A;B$
50 PRINT#1,USING "**$##.## ";C,D
```

The following will be saved by the PRINT# and PRINT# USING statements in lines 40 and 50.

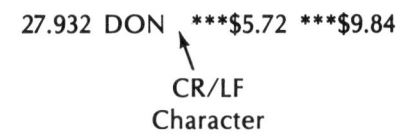

```
27.932 DON  ***$5.72 ***$9.84
            ↑
            CR/LF
            Character
```

We can actually check this output by substituting "SCRN:" for "FILE.DAT" in line 10. This causes our output to appear on the screen.

When WRITE# is used to output data to a sequential file, individual data items are separated with commas, and strings are surrounded by quotation marks.

```
10 OPEN "SCRN:" FOR OUTPUT AS #1
20 A = 27.932:B$ = "DON"
30 C = 5.72:D = 9.84
40 WRITE#1,A,B$,C,D
50 END
RUN
27.932,"DON",5.72,9.84
Ok
```

One advantage of the WRITE# statement is that it outputs data in the same format as that in which it is read by the INPUT# statement.

**Reading from a Sequential File**

The following commands are used in IBM BASIC to input data

from a sequential file:

> INPUT#
> LINE INPUT#
> INPUT$

INPUT# and LINE INPUT# function with sequential files much like INPUT and LINE INPUT do with the keyboard. INPUT# will read the data at the current position in the sequential file and assign that data to the next variable indicated as its argument. The data and variable must be of the same type. If they are not, an incorrect data value may be assigned to a variable.

When INPUT# is reading numeric data, any leading blanks and CR/LF characters will be ignored. INPUT# will begin assigning data beginning with the first numeric character.

When INPUT# is reading string data, any leading blanks and CR/LF characters will again be ignored. If the first character read by INPUT# is a double quotation mark, every subsequent character will be assigned to the string variable until the next double quotation mark is encountered. If the first character read is not a double quotation mark, every subsequent character will be assigned to the string variable until a comma, carriage return, or line feed character is encountered. A maximum of 255 characters can be assigned to a string variable.

```
10 A$ = "Jerry Smith":B$ = "Williams, Dave"
20 OPEN "TEXT.DAT" FOR OUTPUT AS #2
30 PRINT#2,A$;B$
40 CLOSE #2
50 OPEN "TEXT.DAT" FOR INPUT AS #2
60 INPUT#2,A$,B$
70 PRINT A$
80 PRINT B$
90 END
RUN
Jerry SmithWilliams
Dave
Ok
```

In our preceding example, A$ and B$ were output as follows:

Jerry SmithWilliams,Dave*

When INPUT# causes these to be read and assigned to variables, "Jerry Smith Wiliams" was assigned to A$ and "Dave" was assigned to B$. Note that the data was input into A$ until the comma was encountered.

By using quotation marks to delimit the strings when they are output in line 30, we can re-input the string properly. We must use the CHR$ function with the ASCII code for the quotation mark (34) to represent this character. If line 30 of our preceding example was edited as follows:

30 PRINT#2,CHR$(34);A$;CHR$(34);CHR$(34);B$;CHR$(34)

and the program was executed, the following data would be displayed:

Jerry Smith
Williams, Dave

LINE INPUT# is used with the following configuration:

LINE INPUT # *filenumber, variable*

All characters will be assigned to the specified variable until a CR/LF character is encountered.

Note our revised version of the program described on the previous page using LINE INPUT#. LINE INPUT# accepted every character including the double quotations that served as delimiters in INPUT#.

---

* The PRINT# statement does not output the quotation marks specified in the assignment statement in line 10.

```
10 A$ = "Jerry Smith":B$ = "Williams, Dave"
20 OPEN "TEXT.DAT" FOR OUTPUT AS #2
30 PRINT#2,CHR$(34);A$;CHR$(34);CHR$(34);B$;CHR$(34)
40 CLOSE #2
50 OPEN "TEXT.DAT" FOR INPUT AS #2
60 LINE INPUT#2,A$
70 PRINT A$
80 PRINT B$
90 END
RUN
"Jerry Smith""Williams,Dave"
Williams, Dave
Ok
```

INPUT$ is used to retrieve a specific number of characters from a file. INPUT$ is used with the following configuration:

$$z\$ = INPUT\$(x[,\#y])$$

If *x* and *y* are both specified, the next *x* characters from the file indicated by *y* will be read into z$. If a file is not specified, the designated number of characters will be read from the keyboard.

The use of INPUT$ is shown in the following example.

```
10 A$ = "Jerry Smith":B$ = "Williams, Dave"
20 OPEN "TEXT.DAT" FOR OUTPUT AS #2
30 PRINT#2,CHR$(34);A$;CHR$(34);CHR$(34);B$;CHR$(34)
40 CLOSE #2
50 OPEN "TEXT.DAT" FOR INPUT AS #2
60 A$ = INPUT$(13,#2)
70 PRINT A$
90 END
RUN
"Jerry Smith"
Ok
```

## EOF, LOC, & LOF With Sequential Files

The EOF function can be used with sequential files to determine if the end of the file has been reached. The configuration for EOF is given below:

$$A = EOF(filenumber)$$

*filenumber* indicates the file for which the end-of-file condition is to be checked. This function returns a value of true (-1) if the end-of-file has been reached, and a value of false (0) if it has not.

EOF is often used to test for end-of-file while inputting data to avoid an input attempt when the end-of-file has been reached. The following program illustrates this use of EOF.

```
10 OPEN "I",1,"TEXT.DAT"
20 X = 0
30 IF EOF(1) THEN 99
40 INPUT#1,A$(X)
50 PRINT A$(X)
60 X = X + 1:GOTO 30
99 END
RUN
Jerry Smith
Williams,Dave
Ok
```

If we deleted line 30 and edited line 60 as shown below, the following error would occur:

```
10 OPEN "I",1,"TEXT.DAT"
20 X = 0
40 INPUT#1,A$(X)
50 PRINT A$(X)
60 X = X + 1:GOTO 40
99 END
RUN
Jerry Smith
Williams,Dave
Input past end in 40
Ok
```

The LOF function is used with the following configuration:

$$A = \text{LOF}(filenumber)$$

LOF returns the length of the specified file in bytes. The value returned by LOF is always a multiple of 128. That is, if the actual file length is between 1 and 128 bytes, LOF will return a value of 128. If the value is between 129 and 256, LOF will return a value of 256, etc.

LOC returns the location within the file of the last record read or written. LOC is used with the following configuration:

$$A = \text{LOC}(filenumber)$$

Like LOF, LOC is calculated in terms of 128 byte blocks. In other words, LOC will return the number of records (assuming each record consists of 128 bytes) that have been input or output to the file since it was opened. For instance, if 256 records of 16 bytes each (4096 bytes) were written to a sequential file, LOC would return a value of 32.

```
 5 A$ = "ZZZZZZZZZZZZZZZZ"
10 OPEN "TEXTA.DAT" FOR OUTPUT AS 1
20 FOR X = 1 TO 256
30 PRINT#1,A$
40 NEXT X
50 PRINT LOC(1)
60 END
RUN
 36
Ok
```

**RANDOM FILE ACCESS**

Before a random file can be used, the programmer must determine the length of each of its records. The length of each record in the random file must be the same, and can be calculated by adding the length of each of the individual fields in that record.

When a random file is opened, a random file buffer is set up in memory. Data to be written to the random file is first placed in that file's buffer. When all the data for a record has been written to the buffer, that record will be transferred from the buffer to disk.

When data is to be read from a random file, a record is first read from disk into the random file buffer. The individual fields within that record can then be read by instructing the program to access the buffer.

Once you have finished using a random file, you should close it. When a random file is closed, any existing data in the random file buffer will be written to the random file on disk, and the memory space reserved for the buffer will be freed.

**Opening and Closing a Random File**

The following configurations can be used to open a file.

OPEN *filespec* AS [#] *filenumber* [LEN = *rcdlen*]

OPEN "R", [#] *filenumber, filespec* [,*rcdlen*]

*filespec* refers to the file specification. *filenumber* refers to the number that will be assigned to the random file. *rcdlen* specifies the length of each record in the random file in bytes. If this parameter is omitted, a record length of 128 bytes will be assumed. The maximum record length is 32,767 bytes.

The random file's record length may not be greater than that indicated by the /S: option when BASIC was started up. If /S: was not specified in the BASIC command line, a record of up to 128 bytes will be allowed.

CLOSE works with random files exactly as it does with sequential files.

## Field Variables

As we discussed earlier, random file records are read into a random buffer. Each field in the record will correspond to a certain area in the buffer. In order to access a particular field in the random file record, we must actually access the corresponding field in the buffer. In order to do so, we must identify these buffer fields with a **buffer variable** or **field variable.**

A field variable must always be a string variable. You may recall from our discussion of the variable table and string storage, that a string variable via its descriptor can refer to a string value in the string storage space, in the BASIC program itself, or in fact anywhere in the BASIC working area. A string variable can use its descriptor to reference a string constant in the file buffer.

A numeric variable could not be used for a field variable because the value in the field buffer would also have to be stored in the variable table.

The FIELD statement is used to define field variables. FIELD is used with the following configuration:

>   FIELD # *filenumber, size,* AS *fieldvariable,...*

*size* indicates the length of the field in bytes, and *fieldvariable* indicates the string variable used to reference that field.

A FIELD statement cannot be executed until a file has been opened. The sum of the lengths of the field variables specified by FIELD cannot exceed the record length indicated in the OPEN statement. If the combined length of the field variables exceeds that of the record length, the following error message will appear:

>   Field overflow

More than one FIELD statement can be executed concurrently for the same random file. This allows the programmer to create several different types of records within the same random file depending upon how the field variables are defined.

An example of a FIELD statement is given below.

> FIELD 1, 10 AS A$, 15 AS B$, 30 AS C$

In the preceding example, the FIELD statement allocates the first 10 positions in the random file buffer for the string variable A$. The next 15 positions are reserved for B$, and the following 30 positions are reserved for C$.

**Writing Data to a Random File Buffer**

The LSET and RSET statements should be used to assign values to field variables. In effect, LSET and RSET cause data to be placed in the designated field in the buffer. LSET and RSET are used with the following configurations:

> LSET *fieldvariable* = *x$*
> RSET *fieldvariable* = *x$*

*fieldvariable* refers to a string variable referenced in a FIELD statement. *x$* can refer to either a string constant or a string variable.

If *x$* contains fewer bytes than those allowed for in *fieldvariable*, LSET will cause *x$* to be left-justified in the field buffer. In other words, the first character in *x$* will be placed in the leftmost byte in the field buffer. If *x$* does not occupy the entire field buffer, blank spaces will be added to the right of *x$*'s last character.

RSET causes *x$* to be right-justified in the field buffer. If necessary, blank spaces will be added to the left of *x$*'s first character.

If the string to be placed in the field buffer is larger than that allowed for, extra characters will be truncated from the right of the string. This is true regardless of whether RSET or LSET is being executed.

You may already have wondered how we can store numeric values in a random file when only string variables can be used to define field buffers. To store numeric values in a random file, it is necessary to convert the numeric data to a string.

We have already discussed how STR$ can be used to convert a numeric value to a string. The difficulty with using STR$ with random files is that the string values produced by STR$ require more memory storage than a numeric value would. IBM BASIC includes three functions, MKI$, MKS$, and MKD$ which allow a string to be converted to a numeric value that can be stored in memory using the same amount of memory as any other numeric value. These functions are used as follows:

A$ = MKI$(*integer*)
A$ = MKS$(*single precision*)
A$ = MKD$(*double precision*)

*integer, single precision,* and *double precision* refer to integer, single precision, and double precision constants or variables respectively.

MKI$ converts an integer value into a 2-byte string. MKS$ converts a single precision value into a 4-byte string, and MKD$ converts a double precision value into an 8-byte string. MKI$, MKS$, and MKD$ are only meant to be used to convert data for storage in a random file.

If you intend to store numeric data in a random file, you should be certain that your field variables have a sufficient number of bytes reserved in the FIELD statement. For example, the field variables defined by the following FIELD statement could allow for the storage of 4 numbers in a record. Two of these numbers could be integers, one could be single precision, and one could be double precision.

1000 FIELD #2, 2 AS A$, 2 AS B$, 4 AS C$, 8 AS D$

## Writing a Record from the
## Random File Buffer to the File

Once the field buffers have been assigned values via LSET and RSET, the PUT statement can be used to write the random buffer to the random file as a record. PUT is used with the following configuration:

>PUT # *filenumber* [,*rcdnumber*]

*filenumber* refers to the number assigned to the random file when it was opened. If the optional *rcdnumber* parameter is omitted, the contents of the file buffer will be written in the next available position in the random file. If *rcdnumber* is specified, the file buffer's contents will be written at the indicated record number. The record number can range from 1 to 32,767.

In the following example, PUT will cause the contents of the file buffer to be written at the fifth record location in the random file opened as #3.

>100 PUT #3,5

## Reading a Record from the
## Random File into the Buffer

The GET statement is used to read a record from the random file into the buffer. The configuration for GET is very similar to that for PUT.

>GET # *filenumber* [,*rcdnumber*]

If *rcdnumber* is not specified, the record following the last one read will be retrieved.

The following GET statement would cause the tenth record of the random file opened as number 5 to be read into the buffer.

>100 GET #5,10

### Reading Data From the Random File Buffer

Once data has been read into the random file buffer, that data can be read from the buffer by using that buffer's field variables in an assignment statement or by inputting characters with INPUT# or LINE INPUT#.

If a string value in the buffer represents a numeric value, you will want to convert that string to its numeric equivalent. IBM BASIC's CVI, CVS, and CVD functions allow string data to be converted back into numeric data. These are the exact opposites of MKI$, MKS$, and MKD$, respectively. CVI converts a 2-byte string to an integer, CVS converts a 4-byte string to a single precision numeric value, and CVD converts an 8-byte string to a double precision numeric value.

The examples in illustrations 7-2 and 7-3 demonstrate the use of STR$, MKI$, MKS$, MKD$, CVI, CVS, CVD, GET, PUT, OPEN, and LSET in the context of random file processing.

### LOC & LOF With Random Files

LOC and LOF can be used with random files (as they were with sequential files) to determine the location of the last record accessed and the file length respectively. EOF cannot be used with random files.

## Illustration 7-2. Random File Access Using STR$

```
 10 INPUT "ENTER PAYROLL NUMBER ";Z
 20 Z$ = STR$(Z)
 30 Y$ = "PAY" + Z$ + ".DAT"
 40 OPEN Y$ AS #2 LEN = 53
 50 FIELD#2,2 AS RCD.NO$,4 AS EMPL.NO$,15 AS LAST.NAME$,
    15 AS FIRST.NAME$,5 AS NO.HOUR$,5 AS RATE$,7 AS PAY$
 60 X% = 1
 70 A$ = " ":B$ = " ":C$ = " ":D = 0:E = 0
100 INPUT "ENTER EMPLOYEE'S PERSONNEL NO. ";A$
110 INPUT "ENTER EMPLOYEE'S LAST NAME ";B$
120 INPUT "ENTER EMPLOYEE'S FIRST NAME ";C$
130 INPUT "ENTER NUMBER OF HOURS WORKED ";D
140 INPUT "ENTER PAY RATE ";E
145 LSET RCD.NO$ = STR$(X%)
150 LSET EMPL.NO$ = A$
160 LSET LAST.NAME$ = B$
170 LSET FIRST.NAME$ = C$
180 LSET NO.HOUR$ = STR$(D)
190 LSET RATE$ = STR$(E)
200 LSET PAY$ = STR$(D*E)
210 PUT#2,X%
220 INPUT "DO YOU HAVE ADD'L ENTRIES (Y = YES:N = NO) ";FLAG$
230 IF FLAG$ = "Y" THEN X% = X% + 1:GOTO 70
240 IF FLAG$ = "N" GOTO 300 ELSE 160
300 INPUT "DO YOU WISH TO DISPLAY A RECORD (Y = YES:N =
    NO) ";BFLAG$
310 IF BFLAG$ = "N" THEN 999
320 IF BFLAG$ = "Y" THEN 330 ELSE 300
330 INPUT "WHICH RECORD WOULD YOU LIKE TO DISPLAY (0 =
    END) ";Y%
340 IF Y% = 0 THEN 999
350 IF Y% < = X% THEN GET #2,Y% ELSE GOTO 330
360 PRINT RCD.NO$;EMPL.NO$;LAST.NAME$;FIRST.NAME$;
    NO.HOUR$;RATE$;PAY$
365 GOTO 330
370 CLOSE 2
999 END
```

## Illustration 7-3. Random File Access Using MKI$, MKS$, & MKD$

```
 10 INPUT "ENTER PAYROLL NUMBER ";Z
 20 Z$ = STR$(Z)
 30 Y$ = "PAY" + Z$ + ".DAT"
 40 OPEN Y$ AS #2 LEN = 50
 50 FIELD#2,2 AS REC.NO$,4 AS EMPL.NO$,15 AS LAST.NAME$,15 AS
    FIRST.NAME$,4 AS NO.HOUR$,4 AS RATE$,4 AS PAY$
 60 X% = 1
 70 A$ = " ":B$ = " ":C$ = " ":D = 0:E = 0
100 INPUT "ENTER EMPLOYEE'S PERSONNEL NO. ";A$
110 INPUT "ENTER EMPLOYEE'S LAST NAME ";B$
120 INPUT "ENTER EMPLOYEE'S FIRST NAME ";C$
130 INPUT "ENTER NUMBER OF HOURS WORKED ";D!
140 INPUT "ENTER PAY RATE ";E
142 F = D*E
145 LSET REC.NO$ = MKI$(X%)
150 LSET EMPL.NO$ = A$
160 LSET LAST.NAME$ = B$
170 LSET FIRST.NAME$ = C$
180 LSET NO.HOUR$ = MKS$(D!)
190 LSET RATE$ = MKS$(E)
200 LSET PAY$ = MKS$(F)
210 PUT#2,X%
220 INPUT "DO YOU HAVE ADD'L ENTRIES(Y = YES:N = NO) ";FLAG$
230 IF FLAG$ = "Y" THEN X% = X% + 1:GOTO 70
240 IF FLAG$ = "N" GOTO 300 ELSE 160
300 INPUT "DO YOU WISH TO DISPLAY A RECORD(Y = YES:N =
    NO) ";BFLAG$
310 IF BFLAG$ = "N" THEN 999
320 IF BFLAG$ = "Y" THEN 330 ELSE 300
330 INPUT "WHICH RECORD WOULD YOU LIKE TO DISPLAY (0 =
    END ";Y%
340 IF Y% = 0 THEN 999
350 IF Y% < = X% THEN GET #2,Y% ELSE GOTO 330
355 A% = CVI(REC.NO$):B! = CVS(NO.HOUR$):C! = CVS(RATE$):
    D! = CVS(PAY$)
360 PRINT A%;EMPL.NO$;LAST.NAME$;FIRST.NAME$;B!;C!;D!
365 GOTO 330
370 CLOSE 2
999 END
```

# FILE COMMANDS

IBM BASIC includes eight commands designed to allow the user to perform file handling operations while the BASIC interpreter is active. These include SAVE, LOAD, RUN, KILL, NAME, MERGE, FILES, and CHAIN.

## SAVE

SAVE generally is used to store a program on a cassette or a disk file. SAVE is used with the following configuration:

$$\text{SAVE "filespecification"} \begin{bmatrix} ,P \\ ,A \end{bmatrix}$$

*filespecification* indicates the device where the program in RAM is to be saved as well as the filename to be assigned to that file. Note that *filespecification* must be enclosed within double quotation marks.

The optional parameter A indicates that the file is to be saved in ASCII format. Only files saved in this format can be loaded with the MERGE command.

The optional parameter P causes the program file to be saved in encoded binary format. In effect, P results in the program file being protected. If an attempt is made to LIST or EDIT a protected program file, the following error will result.

Illegal function call

When SAVE is used to save a file on disk and no filename extension is indicated in *filespecification,* an extension of .BAS will automatically be assigned. If Cassette BASIC is active, the default device will be CAS1:. If Disk or Advanced BASIC is active, the default device will be A:.

## LOAD

The LOAD command is generally used to load a program file into memory from cassette or diskette. LOAD is used with the following configuration.

LOAD "filespecification" [,R]

LOAD erases any program lines and variables in memory before the specified program is loaded. When LOAD is used without the optional R parameter, any open files will be closed.

When LOAD is executed with R, the program will be automatically run after it has been loaded. Also, if R is specified, all data files will remain open. LOAD is generally executed with the R option in order to chain two or more programs together. Since existing data files remain open, this information can be shared by the programs being chained.

If *filespecification* does not include a filename extension, the .BAS extension will be automatically provided.

When LOAD is used with the cassette device (CAS1:), the filenames present in the cassette will be displayed one by one on the screen. Each filename will be followed by a period and a letter which specifies the file type. These letters are listed with the types of files they reference in Table 7-1.

If the filename displayed matches that indicated by *filespecification*, that file will be loaded into memory and the following message will be displayed.

Found

If these do not match, the message "Skipped" will be displayed, and the next filename on the cassette will be displayed.

The search for the indicated *filespecification* on the cassette tape can be ended at any time by pressing Ctrl-Break.

If *filespecification* is not indicated when LOAD is executed for the cassette unit, the next program file on the cassette will be loaded.

## Table 7-1. File Type Abbreviations During a Cassette LOAD

| File Type Abbrev. | Reference |
|---|---|
| .B | BASIC programs stored in internal format (with SAVE). |
| .A | BASIC programs stored in ASCII format (with SAVE,A). |
| .P | Protected BASIC programs stored in encoded binary format (with SAVE,P). |
| .D | Data files created by OPEN. |
| .M | Memory image files created by BSAVE. |

**RUN**

The RUN command is used to begin execution of a program. RUN is used with the following configuration.

    RUN ["*filespecification*"][,R]

If RUN is executed with *filespecification*, the indicated file will be loaded into memory and executed. If RUN is executed without the *filespecification* parameter, the program currently stored in RAM will be executed. If *filespecification* is indicated, it must be enclosed within double quotation marks.

If the optional parameter R is specified, any open files will remain open. Otherwise, they will be closed.

**KILL**

KILL is used with the following configuration to delete the indicated diskette file. If the filename includes the .BAS extension, that extension must be included in *filespecification*.

    KILL "*filespecification*"

## NAME

NAME is used with the following configuration to change a filename.

>　　NAME *"filespecification"* AS *"newfilename"*

The filename included in *filespecification* will be changed to that specified in *newfilename*. If the filename includes the .BAS extension, that extension must be included in the command line.

## MERGE

The MERGE command loads the specified program file into memory and combines it with existing program lines in memory.

>　　MERGE *"filespecification"*

If the file being loaded contains a program line with the same line number as one of the program lines already present in memory, the program line being loaded will replace that line.

For a program to be loaded with MERGE, it must have been saved in ASCII format using the A option with the SAVE command.

## CHAIN

The CHAIN statement allows one BASIC program to load and run another BASIC program. A COMMON statement can be included in the program containing the CHAIN statement which allows that program to pass the values of some or all of its variables to the program being chained. CHAIN and COMMON are explained in detail in Chapter 9.

## FILES

The FILES command can be used to display the filename of one, several, or all of the files on the indicated drive.

FILES ["*filespecification*"]

If FILES is executed without the optional parameter, all diskette files on the current drive will be displayed. If *filespecification* is included in the command, any files found on that diskette matching that file will be displayed. If filename match characters are used in *filespecification,* several files may be displayed. For example, the following command:

FILES "TEXT?.DAT"

would cause the following filenames to be displayed:

TEXTA.DAT
TEXT7.DAT
TEXTZ.DAT

**File Devices**

Several devices other than the cassette unit (CAS1:) and the disk drives (A:, B:, C:, D:) can accept files. These include the keyboard (KYBD:), screen (SCRN:), printers (LPT1:-LPT3:), and communications devices (COM1:, COM2:).

We have already learned that a disk file can be used either to input or to output data, and that a disk device (ex. A:, B:) can hold a number of different files at once. Some of the other devices can only be used for input or output. For example, SCRN: can only be used as an output file, and KYBD: can only be used as an input file. Moreover, since these devices can only have a single filename, they can only reference one file at a time.

The various devices that can be used as filenames are summarized in Table 7-2.

## Table 7-2. Filename Devices

| Device Name | Reference | Input | Output |
|---|---|---|---|
| CAS1: | Cassette Recorder | x | x |
| A: | Diskette Drive A | x | x |
| B: | Diskette Drive B | x | x |
| C: | First Fixed Disk | x | x |
| D: | Second Fixed Disk | x | x |
| COM1: | First Async. Comm. Adapter | x | x |
| COM2: | Second Async. Comm. Adapter | x | x |
| LPT1: | Line Printer #1 |  | x |
| LPT2: | Line Printer #2 |  | x |
| LPT3: | Line Printer #3 |  | x |
| KYBD: | Keyboard | x |  |
| SCRN: | Screen |  | x |

# CHAPTER 8.
# IBM BASIC GRAPHICS

## INTRODUCTION

Two devices are available with the IBM PC for generating output on the display; the Monochrome Display/Printer Adapter and the Color/Graphics Monitor Adapter. The Monochrome Display/Printer Adapter is generally used with the IBM Monochrome Display, and the Color/Graphics Printer Adapter is used with a color monitor or television set.

The Monochrome Display/Printer Adapter can only display text in black and white. The ASCII graphics characters (see codes 176-223 in Appendix D) can be used to a limited extent in the text mode to output graphics. However, full graphics capability is only available with the Color/Graphics Monitor Adapter.

The Color/Graphics Monitor Adapter includes a text mode and two graphics modes. The text mode generated by the Color/Graphics Monitor Adapter functions much like that of the Monochrome Display Adapter except that 16 colors are available. Therefore, programs written for the Monochrome Display and Printer Adapter can also generally be run on the Color/Graphics Monitor Adapter.

The two graphics modes which are available with the Color/Graphics Monitor Adapter are medium resolution and high resolution.

Both medium and high resolution graphics will be discussed in detail in this chapter.

### Pixels

In medium resolution graphics, the display is divided into a grid consisting of 200 rows of 320 columns each. In high resolution graphics, the display is divided into 200 rows of 640 columns each. Each of the positions on the display can be assigned a coordinate by referencing its column position followed by its row position. This is shown in Illustrations 8-1 and 8-2.

Notice that screen coordinates are enclosed within parentheses and that the row and column values are separated with a comma. Both row and column numbering begin with zero. Each specific screen coordinate is known as a **pixel.**

A pointer known as the LPR (last point referenced) denotes the pixel position last referenced by a BASIC statement in the graphics mode. In the text mode, the location of the cursor is stored with a different pointer.

**Illustration 8-1. Medium Resolution Graphics Coordinates**

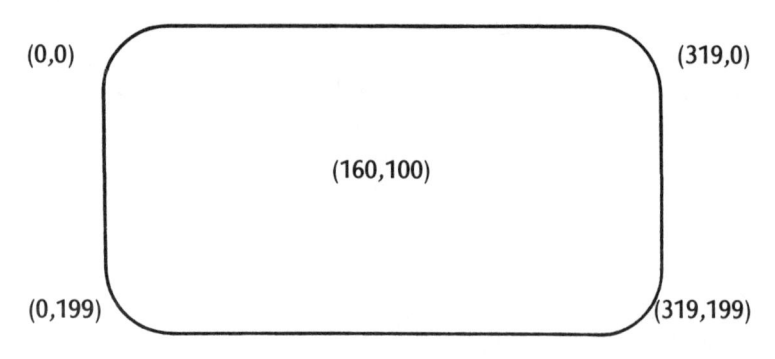

```
(0,0)                                          (319,0)
            ┌─────────────────────────┐
            │                         │
            │                         │
            │       (160,100)         │
            │                         │
            │                         │
            └─────────────────────────┘
(0,199)                                       (319,199)
```

**Illustration 8-2. High Resolution Graphics Coordinates**

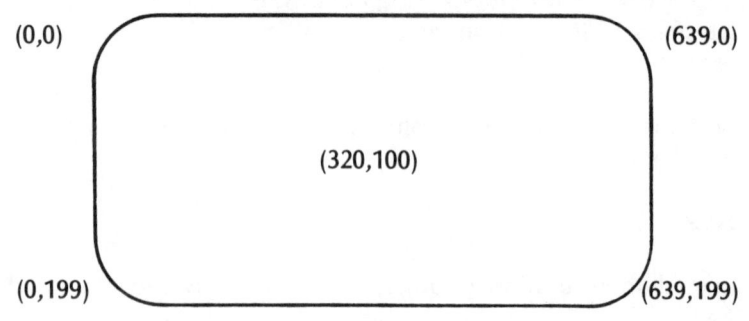

```
(0,0)                                          (639,0)
            ┌─────────────────────────┐
            │                         │
            │                         │
            │       (320,100)         │
            │                         │
            │                         │
            └─────────────────────────┘
(0,199)                                       (639,199)
```

## SCREEN STATEMENT

As we mentioned earlier, three display modes are available with the Color/Graphics Monitor Adapter. These are the text mode, medium resolution graphics mode, and high resolution graphics mode.

The SCREEN statement allows the programmer to select the Color/Graphics Monitor Adapter's display mode. SCREEN uses the following configuration.

SCREEN [mode][,[burst][,[activepg][,visualpg]]]

mode indicates the display mode. SCREEN 0 sets the adapter to the text mode. SCREEN 1 sets the adapter to the medium resolution graphics mode, and SCREEN 2 sets the adapter to the high resolution graphics mode. 1 and 2 are only available with the Color/Graphics Monitor Adapter.

SCREEN can also include an optional second parameter which enables or disables the **color burst signal.** A TV signal contains a component known as the color burst. If the color burst is present, a color picture will be displayed. If it is absent, a black and white picture will be displayed.

In the text mode, if burst evaluates to 0 (false), the color burst will be disabled. A value of 1 (true) in the text mode enables the color burst.

In the medium resolution graphics mode, a true value for burst will disable color, while a false value will enable color. burst has no effect in high resolution as the only colors allowed are black and white.

The Color/Graphics Display Adapter contains more memory than is needed to hold a single screen or **page** of text. This allows more than one page of memory to be stored by the Color/Graphics Display Adapter when SCREEN has set it to the text mode.

If the line width is 80 columns, four pages of text can be stored. These are numbered from 0 to 3, inclusive. If the line width is 80 columns, eight pages of text can be stored. These are numbered from 0 to 7, inclusive.

The final two optional parameters for SCREEN, *activepg* and *visualpg*, allow the programmer to select the page to which output is to be sent (*activepg*), as well as the page which will be displayed on the screen (*visualpg*). This allows the user to write to one page while another is being displayed. *activepg* and *visualpg* can ony be specified in the text mode.

When SCREEN is executed, the display is cleared. With SCREEN 1 and SCREEN 2, the LPR (last point referenced) is set to the center position of the screen.

When one of the first three optional parameters for SCREEN is omitted and another parameter follows this omitted parameter, the position of the omitted parameter must be denoted with a comma.

For example, if the display was initially set to the medium resolution graphics mode with color burst:

SCREEN 1,0

the display could be reset without color burst with the following:

SCREEN ,1

Note that the comma preceding the value for burst indicates that the mode parameter was omitted.

The preceding can be illustrated by executing the following example program.

```
10 SCREEN 1,0:COLOR 2
20 PRINT "222222"
30 FOR X = 1 TO 500
40 NEXT X
60 SCREEN ,1
70 PRINT "222222"
80 END
RUN
222222  ←——— Color will change after
Ok              a few seconds as color
                burst is disabled in line 60.
```

## TEXT MODE

The Color/Graphics Display Adapter's text mode functions much like the Monochrome Display Adapter's text mode. The display consists of 25 rows of 40 or 80 columns each. The number of columns can be controlled via the WIDTH statement.

If the color burst feature was enabled in the SCREEN statement, the Color/Graphics Display Adapter can display foreground text (i.e. characters) in 16 different colors. Any of eight different colors can be selected for the background. Also, the border can be set to any one of 16 different colors in the text mode.

The available colors are as follows:

| 0 | Black   | 8  | Gray                |
|---|---------|----|---------------------|
| 1 | Blue    | 9  | Light Blue          |
| 2 | Green   | 10 | Light Green         |
| 3 | Cyan    | 11 | Light Cyan          |
| 4 | Red     | 12 | Light Red           |
| 5 | Magenta | 13 | Light Magenta       |
| 6 | Brown   | 14 | Yellow              |
| 7 | White   | 15 | High Intensity White|

Notice that each color has a number associated with it. This number, rather than the name of the color, is specified in IBM BASIC's COLOR statement.

The COLOR statement is used to set the colors for the foreground, background, and border screen. The use of the COLOR statement differs depending on whether the text mode or graphics mode is being used. We will discuss the use of COLOR in the text mode in this section.

The configuration for COLOR in the text mode is as follows:

COLOR [foreground][,[background]][,border]

*foreground* is the color of the character and must be a number or numeric expression with a value between 0 and 31. *background* is the color of the background and must be a number or numeric expression with a value between 0 and 7. Only colors 0 to 7 can be used as background colors. *border* is the color for the border screen and must be a number or numeric expression with a value between 0 and 15.

By selecting the *foreground* equal to 16 plus the color desired, the character will blink. In other words, a value of 22 will result in brown blinking.

If you are using the IBM Monochrome Display/Printer Adapter, the following can be used for *foreground*.

- 0 Black
- 1 Underline character with white foreground
- 7 White
- 15 High Intensity White

Again, by adding 16 to the desired value, the character will blink. For example, 16 will result in black blinking.

With the IBM Monochrome Display/Printer Adapter, either of the following may be used for *background*.

- 0 Black
- 7 White

In the following examples, the first COLOR statement sets the foreground to white, the background to blue, and the border to black. The second COLOR statement sets the the border to red. The third COLOR statement sets the foreground to red and the background to white.

*COLOR 7,1,0
COLOR ,,4
COLOR 4,7

* These examples were executed in the 40 column mode.

## MEDIUM RESOLUTION GRAPHICS MODE

The medium resolution graphics screen contains 64,000 pixels arranged in 200 rows with 320 columns each. The rows are numbered from 0 to 199 with row 0 at the top of the display and 199 at the bottom. Column 0 designates the lefthand side of the display, and column 1 designates the righthand side.

Screen positions are referenced using their column position followed by their row position as shown in the following example.

(319,0)

This value references the upper righthand corner of the screen.

A screen position specified in the format given above is known as a screen coordinate. When the screen coordinate references the actual screen position, the coordinate is specified in **absolute form.**

Coordinates can also be specified as an offset from the last coordinate accessed. Coordinates which specify an offset are specified in **relative form.** When a screen coordinate is given in relative form the first coordinate value (known as the x offset) will be added to the column position of the last coordinate referenced. The second coordinate value (known as the y offset) will be added to the row position of the last coordinate referenced. As you may recall from our discussion on page 156, the last coordinate referenced is stored by the LPR pointer in IBM BASIC.

Relative coordinates are generally used with the reserved word STEP in graphics commands. The configuration for STEP is given below.

STEP (*xoffset, yoffset*)

If the last point referenced was (90,150) and STEP(10,-20) was executed, the current coordinates would be (100,130).

COLOR is used in the medium resolution graphics mode with the following configuration.

COLOR [*background*][,[*palette*]]

*background* refers to the background color and must be a number or numeric expression from 0 to 15. The colors used for *background* are listed on page 159. *palette* is the selection of a palette of available colors and must be either 0 or 1, or an expression evaluating to those values. Color 3 from the palette is used for the foreground color by default. The palette selections are listed in Table 8-1.

If palette 0 is chosen, color number 1 will be green, color 2 will be red, and color 3 will be brown. If palette 1 is chosen, color 1 will be cyan, color 2 will be magenta, and color 3 will be white. Color 0 defaults to the background color.

**Table 8-1. Palette Color Selections**

| Color # | Palette 0 | Palette 1 |
|---------|-----------|-----------|
| 0 | Background | Background |
| 1 | Green | Cyan |
| 2 | Red | Magenta |
| 3 | Brown | White |

The COLOR statement cannot be used in the high resolution

graphics mode. Any attempt to do so will result in the "Illegal function call" error.

In the following example, the background is set to green and palette 0 is selected. Notice that the text is displayed in brown.

```
10 SCREEN 1,0
20 COLOR 2,0
30 PRINT "ABC"
RUN
ABC
Ok
```

Text characters can be displayed in medium resolution graphics. In this mode, 40 text characters are displayed per output line. Color 3 of the current palette is used for the foreground of the text character.

You can change only the palette in medium resolution graphics by leaving the background color out of the statement, inserting a comma, and specifying the new palette. This is shown in the following example.

```
10 SCREEN 1
20 COLOR 2,0
30 PRINT "ABC"
40 FOR X = 1 TO 1000
50 NEXT X
60 COLOR ,1
70 END
RUN
ABC
Ok
```

Color will change from brown to white

Notice that when the palette is changed, the color of foreground text and graphics on the display will be changed.

## HIGH RESOLUTION GRAPHICS MODE

In high resolution graphics, the screen is divided into 200 rows of 640 columns each for a total of 128,000 pixels. Only two colors can be used in high resolution graphics -- black and white. Text characters can be output in high resolution graphics and are displayed at 80 characters per line.

## IBM BASIC GRAPHICS STATEMENTS

A number of different statements are available for creating graphics displays in IBM BASIC. These include:

    PSET      DRAW
    PRESET   PAINT
    LINE      GET
    CIRCLE   PUT

Each of these will be discussed in the following sections.

### PSET and PRESET

PSET and PRESET are only used in the graphics mode. These statements are used to draw a point at a given screen location. The configurations for PSET and PRESET are as follows.

    PSET (a,b) [,*color*]
    PRESET (a,b) [,*color*]

*a,b* are the screen coordinates of the point to be set. These may be specified in either absolute or relative form.

*color* is the color to be used (0 to 3). If the optional *color* is not included in the PSET statement, the foreground color will be used (3 in medium resolution; 1 in high resolution). If *color* is not specified in PRESET, the background color (0) will be used.

If *color* is specified, PSET and PRESET work in an identical fashion. If *color* is not specified, PSET and PRESET work in an opposite fashion. This is because the default *color* value for PSET is color 3 in medium resolution graphics. The default for PRESET is color 0 (the background color). This is illustrated in the following example.

```
 10 SCREEN 1:COLOR 4,1
 20 CLS
 30 FOR X = 1 TO 100
 40 PSET(100,X)
 50 PSET(101,X)
 60 NEXT X
 70 FOR Y = 1 TO 2000
 80 NEXT Y
 90 FOR Z = 1 TO 100
100 PRESET(100,Z)
110 PRESET(101,Z)
120 NEXT Z
```

PRESET and PSET also function in high resolution graphics. This can be demonstrated by editing line 10 as follows:

```
10 SCREEN 2
```

**LINE**

In the preceding section, we drew a line using a FOR, NEXT loop. IBM BASIC includes a statement, LINE, which can be used in the graphics mode to draw either lines or boxes. The configuration fo LINE is given below.

LINE [(*a1,b1*)] - (*a2,b2*) [,[*color*][,B[F]][*style*]]

(*a1,b1*),(*a2,b2*) represent the beginning and ending coordinates of the line, respectively. Notice that only the ending coordinate is required.

*color* is the color number which can range from 0 to 3. In medium resolution, *color* chooses the color from the current palette set by the COLOR statement. If *color* is not specified, it will default to 3. In high resolution, a *color* of 0 designates black, while a color of 1 indicates white.

B indicates box. This parameter is used to draw a rectangle. BF indicates filled box. This parameter is used to draw a box filled with color.

*style* is a 16 bit integer mask used to place points in the screen (BASIC 2.0 only). *style* can be used with boxes and lines but not with filled boxes (BF).

The following program illustrates how LINE can be used to draw a horizontal line on the display.

```
10 SCREEN 1
20 COLOR 4,1
30 CLS
40 LINE (20,50)-(200,50)
```

Color 3 from palette 1 will be used by default to draw the line in the preceding example.

The LINE statement can also be used to draw a line where no beginning coordinates are given. In such a case, the line will be drawn from the last point referenced (LPR) to the point specified in the LINE statement.

```
10 SCREEN 1
20 COLOR 4,1
30 CLS
40 LINE (20,50)-(200,50)
50 LINE -(20,10)
60 END
```

The optional parameter B (for box) instructs BASIC to draw a rectangle with the points specified in (*a1,b1*),(*a2,b2*) as the opposite corners. When F (for filled box) is included with B, the interior points of the rectangle will be filled with the color indicated.

The following program illustrates the use of the B and BF options.

```
10 SCREEN 1
20 CLS
30 COLOR 0,1
40 LINE (100,10)-(200,100),,B
50 FOR X = 1 TO 2000
60 NEXT X
70 LINE (100,10)-(200,100),,BF
80 END
```

Notice the inclusion of the commas to denote the position for the optional *color* parameter in lines 40 and 70.

The last optional argument in LINE, *style,* specifies a 16 bit integer mask. Each bit in *style* indicates to LINE whether or not a point is to be plotted. A bit value of 0 causes the point not to be plotted. Any existing data is not erased, but rather is skipped over. A bit value of 1 causes the point to be plotted.

Each group of 4 bits in *style* should be specified with a hexadecimal value.

```
10 SCREEN 1
20 CLS
30 LINE (0,0)-(100,100),2,,&HAAAA
40 END
```

In the preceding example, a line is drawn using coordinates (0,0) and (100,100) as its corners. The line is drawn with dots. The 16 bit integer mask defined by &HAAAA is converted to the following binary value.

1010101010101010

This value causes a point to be plotted at every other bit position resulting in a dotted line being output.

Advanced BASIC should be active if the *style* option is indicated.

## CIRCLE

The CIRCLE statement allows the user to draw a circle, ellipse, or arc on the screen. CIRCLE is only available in Advanced BASIC.

CIRCLE is used with the following configuration.

   CIRCLE(xcenter, ycenter), radius [,color[,start,end[,aspect]]]

*(xcenter,ycenter)* indicates the center of the circle. *radius* gives the radius of the circle.

*color* refers to the color number to be used to draw the circle. The default value for *color* is 3 in medium resolution and 1 in high resolution.

*start,end* are used in drawing arcs. *start,end* refer to the points where the drawing of the circle will begin and end. These are given in radians and may range from −2*PI to 2*PI where PI = 3.141593. If the *start* or *end* angle is negative, the ellipse will be connected to its center point with a line. The angles will be regarded as being positive.

*aspect* denotes the ratio of the x radius to the y radius. The default for *aspect* is 5:6 in medium resolution and 5:12 in high resolution. This ratio will generate a circle in either mode if the standard screen monitor ratio (4:3) is in effect.

A single example of the use of the CIRCLE statement to draw a circle is given in the following program.

```
10  SCREEN 1
20  CLS
30  CIRCLE (160,100),50,2
```

The circle is drawn with its center at coordinate (160,100). The circle's radius is 50 pixels. *(xcenter,ycenter)* will be saved as the LPR once the CIRCLE statement has been executed.

The CIRCLE statement can be used to draw an arc (a portion of a circle). *start* and *end* specify the arc's beginning and ending points respectively. *start* and *end* are specified in radians. The section of a circle indicated by various radian values are specified in Illustration 8-3.

**Illustration 8-3. Degree/Radian Values**

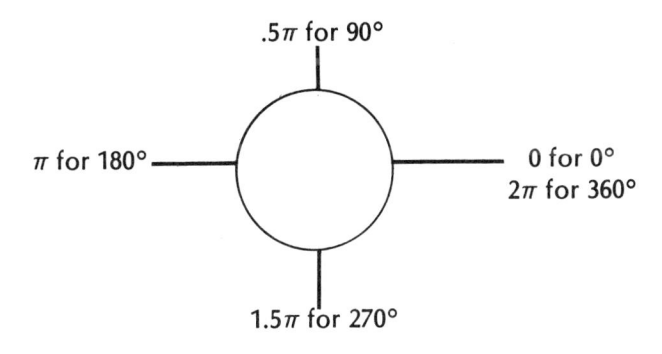

```
              .5π for 90°
                  |
                  |
  π for 180° ───( )─── 0 for 0°
                          2π for 360°
                  |
                  |
              1.5π for 270°
```

The following example causes a semicircle to be drawn. Note that the *color* was omitted. The default (yellow-brown) will be used.

```
10 PI = 3.14159
20 SCREEN 1
30 COLOR 1,0
40 CLS
50 CIRCLE (160,100),50,,0,PI
60 END
```

By specifying *start* and *end* as negative values, a line will be drawn from the center point of the arc to its beginning and ending points. You can demonstrate this by editing line 50 as follows:

```
50 CIRCLE (160,100),50,,-PI*2,-PI*
```

---

\* -0 cannot be specified.

CIRCLE's optional *aspect* parameter can be used to draw an ellipse. An ellipse is an oval shaped circle. The shape of an ellipse is defined by its aspect ratio, which is the ratio of the shape's height to its width.

The aspect ratio defaults to 5:6 in medium resolution and 5:12 in high resolution. CIRCLE uses these default aspect ratios unless *aspect* is specified in the command.

In other words, if *aspect* was omitted, and a radius of 12 pixels was specified in the medium resolution mode, the actual radius would be 12 pixels on the horizontal axis and 10 pixels on the vertical axis. If this ellipse was drawn in the high resolution mode, the horizontal axis would be 12 pixels and the vertical axis would be 5 pixels.

```
10 SCREEN 1
20 COLOR 0,1
30 CLS
40 CIRCLE (160,100),12
50 FOR X = 1 TO 1000
60 NEXT X
70 SCREEN 2
75 CLS
80 CIRCLE (320,100),12
```

The preceding example draws a ellipse in medium and high resolution graphics with a standard aspect ratio.

If an aspect ratio greater than the default is specified, the ellipse will be stretched along the vertical axis. This can be demonstrated by editing lines 40 and 80 in the preceding program as follows:

```
40 CIRCLE (160,100),12,,,,2
80 CIRCLE (320,100),12,,,,2
```

If an aspect ratio less than the default is specified, the ellipse will be stretched along the horizontal axis. This can be demonstrated by editing lines 40 and 80 as follows:

```
40  CIRCLE (160,100),12,,,,1/3
80  CIRCLE (320,100),12,,,,1/3
```

## PAINT

The PAINT statement is used in the graphics mode of Advanced BASIC to place color in a specified area of the screen. PAINT is used with the following configuration:

PAINT (a,b) [[,color][,boundary][,background]

*(a,b)* are the coordinates of a point within the area to be colored in. These coordinates may be specified in absolute or relative form.

*color* is the color to be used (0 to 3). In medium resolution, zero is the background color. Color 3 is the default which is the foreground color. In high resolution, zero indicates black and 1 indicates white. If *color* is a string expression, tiling (described later) is performed.

*boundary* specifies the edges of the shape to be filled in by PAINT. The figure will be PAINT'ed until the *boundary* is encountered. *boundary* can range from 0 to 3.

*background* is a one byte string expression used in tiling (BASIC 2.0 only).

The use of the PAINT statement is illustrated in the following program.

```
10  SCREEN 1:COLOR 2,1
20  LINE (0,0)-(100,150),2,B
30  PAINT (50,50),3,2
```

The (a,b) coordinates for PAINT must be inside the form to be PAINT'ed.

If a complex form is to be PAINT'ed, a large amount of stack space may be required by the PAINT statement. It may be a good idea in such applications to execute a CLEAR command at the beginning of the program to increase the amount of available stack space.

To use PAINT's tiling feature, the *color* parameter must use the following format:

$$CHR\$(\&Hnn) + CHR\$(\&Hnn) + CHR\$(\&Hnn)$$

The tile mask is 8 bits wide. The two hex numbers in the CHR$ function (denoted by nn) indicate these 8 bits.

The string expression used for *color* may consist of as many as 64 bytes, and assumes the following pattern:

```
              X increases

   X,Y  |  8 7 6 5 4 3 2 1
   0,0  |  x x x x x x x x    Tile byte 0
   0,1  |  x x x x x x x x    Tile byte 1
   0,2  |  x x x x x x x x    Tile byte 2
         .
         .
         .
   0,63 |  x x x x x x x x    Tile byte 63 (maximum)
```

Each tile byte masks 8 bits along the screen's x-axis. The tile pattern is repeated across the screen.

The following formula:

$$\text{tile byte mask} = y \bmod \text{tile-length}$$

# IBM BASIC Graphics 173

is used to calculate the starting byte where tiling begins. For example, in the following PAINT statement in the high resolution mode:

PAINT (320,100), CHR$(&H80) + CHR$(&H80) + CHR$(&H80) + CHR$(&H80) + CHR$(&H80) + CHR$(&H80) + CHR$(&H80) + CHR$(&H80)

the beginning byte is calculated as:

tile byte mask = 100 MOD 8

      from PAINT      number of CHR$
      y-coordinate     expressions

which is equal to 4. Plotting will therefore begin with byte 4.

In high resolution, since there is one bit per pixel, a point is plotted at each bit mask position with a value of 1. Our preceding PAINT example causes a series of vertical lines to be plotted on the screen. This is shown in the following program.

```
 5 SCREEN 2
10 CIRCLE (320,100),50
20 TILE$ = CHR$(&H80) + CHR$(&H80) + CHR$(&H80) +
   CHR$(&H80) + CHR$(&H80) + CHR$(&H80) +
   CHR$(&H80) + CHR$(&H80)
30 PAINT (320,100),TILE$
```

Tiling is somewhat different in medium resolution than in high resolution graphics. In medium resolution, each pixel is assigned 2 bits. Therefore, each tile byte in medium resolution identifies just 4 pixels.

Each successive pair of bits in the medium resolution tile byte identifies one of four colors to be used for each of the four pixels which are to be plotted. The following chart summarizes the binary values associated with the available colors.

| Palette 0 | Palette 1 | Number (Binary) | Bit Pattern to Draw Solid Line | Corres. Hex Value |
|---|---|---|---|---|
| Background | Background | 00 | 00000000 | &H00 |
| Green | Cyan | 01 | 01010101 | &H55 |
| Red | Magenta | 10 | 10101010 | &HAA |
| Brown | White | 11 | 11111111 | &HFF |

The following PAINT statement could be used to draw a square with a border of green in palette 0 and cyan in palette 1.

```
PAINT (320,100), CHR$(&H55) + CHR(&H41) +
CHR$(&H41) + CHR$(&H41) + CHR$(&H41) +
CHR$(&H41) + CHR$(&H41) + CHR$(&H55)
```

|  | 76 54 32 10 |  |
|---|---|---|
| Tile byte 0 | 01 01 01 01 | CHR$(&H55) |
| Tile byte 1 | 01 00 00 01 | CHR$(&H41) |
| Tile byte 2 | 01 00 00 01 | CHR$(&H41) |
| Tile byte 3 | 01 00 00 01 | CHR$(&H41) |
| Tile byte 4 | 01 00 00 01 | CHR$(&H41) |
| Tile byte 5 | 01 00 00 01 | CHR$(&H41) |
| Tile byte 6 | 01 00 00 01 | CHR$(&H41) |
| Tile byte 7 | 01 01 01 01 | CHR$(&H55) |

This is shown in the following example.

```
10 SCREEN 1
30 CLS
40 TILE$ = CHR$(&H55) + CHR$(&H41) + CHR$(&H41)
   CHR$(&H41) + CHR$(&H41) + CHR$(&H41) + CHR$(&H41) +
   CHR$(&H55)
45 CIRCLE(160,100),50
50 PAINT(160,100),TILE$
```

## DRAW

The DRAW statement is used to draw an object specified by a string containing drawing commands. These commands are collectively known as a graphics definition language (GDL). The configuration for DRAW is given below:

DRAW *string*

*string* is a string expression containing GDL commands. When DRAW is executed, each GDL command in the string will be interpreted and executed one by one.

**DRAW -- Movement Commands**

The GDL commands can be categorized as movement commands, set angle commands, set color commands, set scale factor commands, and execute substring commands. We will discuss the movement commands first. These commands are described as follows:

| | |
|---|---|
| U$n$ | Move up |
| D$n$ | Move down |
| L$n$ | Move left |
| R$n$ | Move right |
| E$n$ | Move diagonally up and right |
| F$n$ | Move diagonally down and right |
| G$n$ | Move diagonally down and left |
| H$n$ | Move diagonally up and left |

Each of the movement commands is executed in a similar manner. Each indicates a direction in which the plotting will take place. A numeric argument ($n$) follows the command which indicates the distance to be moved.

$n$ does not specify the actual number of points to be moved. This can be calculated by multiplying $n$ times the scaling factor. The scaling factor is set with the scale command using the following configuration:

S$n$

$n$ may range from 1 to 255. The scaling factor can be calculated by dividing $n$ by 4.

The following program illustrates the use of the movement commands and the scale factor.

```
10 SCREEN 1
20 COLOR 1,1
30 CLS
40 A$ = "U30 R40 D30 L40"
50 DRAW A$
60 FOR X = 1 TO 2000
70 NEXT X
80 CLS
90 B$ = "S1 U30 R40 D30 L40"
100 DRAW B$
105 FOR X = 1 TO 2000:NEXT X
110 CLS
120 C$ = "S4 U30 R40 D30 L40"
130 DRAW C$
140 END
```

The first DRAW statement in line 40 draws a square using the default scale (4). The scale is then set to 1 in line 90. DRAW plots the same figure with this new scale in line 100. The scale is then reset to 4 in line 120, and the figure is again plotted in line 130.

Notice that although 40 points were plotted along the x-axis and only 30 points were plotted along the y-axis, that our figure was drawn as a square. This is due to the fact that the screen's aspect ratio in medium resolution graphics is 4:3, which means that four horizontal points occupy the same amount of space as do 3 vertical points.

In high resolution, the aspect ratio is 16:7. This is illustrated in the following example.

```
10 SCREEN 2
30 CLS
40 A$ = "U70 R160 D70 L160"
50 DRAW A$
60 FOR X = 1 TO 2000
```
*program continued on next page*

```
 70 NEXT X
 80 CLS
 90 B$ = "S1 U70 R160 D70 L160"
100 DRAW B$
105 FOR X = 1 TO 2000:NEXT X
110 CLS
120 C$ = "S4 U70 R160 D70 L160"
130 DRAW C$
140 END
```

Aspect ratio will not affect the diagonal move commands. This is shown in the following example program.

```
10 SCREEN 1
30 CLS
40 A$ = "E40 F40 G40 H40"
50 DRAW A$
60 END
```

**DRAW-M Command**

Although the U, D, L, R, E, F, G, and H commands are useful for drawing a figure, they are less useful in situations where a line is to be drawn from the LPR to a specific screen location. The M (movement) command is provided for this purpose. M is used with the following configuration:

$$Mx,y$$

x,y specify the coordinates to which a line is to be drawn from the LPR. If a plus (+) or minus (-) sign prefix x and y, the move will be relative. Otherwise, the move will be absolute. This is illustrated in the following example.

```
10 SCREEN 1
20 CLS
30 A$="U30 R40 D30 L40"
40 DRAW A$
```

*program continued on next page*

```
50 M$="M +20,+30"
55 DRAW M$
70 N$="M 200,100"
80 DRAW N$
```

## DRAW-B Command

If the B command is placed in front of any GDL movement command, the move will be executed, but no points will be plotted. By editing line 70 of the previous program as follows:

```
70 N$="BM 200,100"
```

the effect of B will be illustrated.

## DRAW-N Command

If GDL's N command is placed in front of a movement command, the line will be drawn but the LPR will remain unchanged. The effect of N can be shown by editing line 30 as follows:

```
30 A$="U30 R40 D30 NL40"
```

## DRAW-C Command

The C command can be used to set the color for the shape being drawn. C is used with the following configuration:

*Cn*

*n* specifies the color number. This may range from 0 to 3 in medium resolution and may be specified as either 0 or 1 in high resolution.

The following program illustrates the use of the C command.

```
10 SCREEN 1
15 CLS
20 COLOR 7,0
30 A$="C0 U30 R40 C2 D30 L40"
40 DRAW A$
50 END
```

In the preceding program, a background color of white and palette 1 were specified in line 20. In line 30, the C command specified color 0 from palette 1 (background color) for the U and R commands. Therefore, when the figure is drawn, the U and R commands will be drawn in the background color and will not be visible.

Color 2 from palette 1 (magenta) is specified by the second C command in line 30. This causes the D and L commands to be drawn in that color.

**DRAW-A Command**

The A command is used to set a rotational angle for any subsequent GDL commands. The format for A is as follows:

A*n*

*n* can be any value from 0 to 3, where 0 indicates 0 degrees, 1 indicates 90 degrees, 2 indicates 180 degrees, and 3 indicates 270 degrees.

The following program illustrates the use of A.

```
10 SCREEN 1
20 CLS
30 A$="E50 D50 L50"
40 B$="A1 E50 D50 L50"
50 C$="A2 E50 D50 L50"
60 D$="A3 E50 D50 L50"
70 DRAW A$:GOSUB 110
```

*program continued on next page*

```
80 DRAW B$:GOSUB 110
90 DRAW C$:GOSUB 110
100 DRAW D$:GOSUB 110
105 GOTO 999
110 FOR X=1 TO 2000: NEXT X
120 RETURN
999 END
```

**DRAW-TA Command**

The TA command can be used to turn the figure at the angle indicated by n. n can range from +360 to -360. If n is negative, the angle turns clockwise. This command is only available in BASIC 2.0.

The use of TA is illustrated in the following program.

```
5 CLS
10 FOR X=0 to 360 STEP 45
20 DRAW "TA=X;U30"
30 FOR Y=1 TO 1000:NEXT Y
40 NEXT X
```

**DRAW-S Command**

The S command allows the programmer to set the scale factor. S is used with the following configuration:

$$Sn$$

n can range from 1 to 255. The scale factor is calculated by dividing n by 4. Therefore, the effective range for the scale factor is .25 to 63.75.

By altering our program on page 179 as follows, the shapes will be drawn at 150% of their preceding size.

IBM BASIC Graphics 181

```
10  SCREEN 1
20  CLS
30  A$="S6 E50 D50 L50"
40  B$="S6 A1 E50 D50 L50"
50  C$="S6 A2 E50 D50 L50"
60  D$="S6 A3 E50 D50 L50"
70  DRAW A$:GOSUB 110
80  DRAW B$:GOSUB 110
90  DRAW C$:GOSUB 110
100 DRAW D$:GOSUB 110
105 GOTO 999
110 FOR X=1 TO 2000: NEXT X
120 RETURN
999 END
```

**DRAW-P Command**

The P command specifies the color of the figure being plotted with DRAW as well as the border color. P is only available in BASIC 2.0. Unlike the PAINT statement, the P command does not support tiling. P is used with the following configuration:

P *paint, boundary*

*paint* can range from 0-3 and specifes the color of the figure. *boundary* indicates the border color of the figure to be filled in. *boundary* can also range from 0-3. Both parameters must be specified.

The use of the P command is illustrated in the following program.

```
10 SCREEN 1:COLOR 3,0
20 CLS
30 A$="U30 R40 D30 L40"
35 B$="BE10"
40 C$="P1,3"
50 DRAW A$+B$+C$
```

## DRAW-X Command

The X command allows a DRAW statement to execute a substring from within another command string. The substring is generally specified with a variable name. It must be preceded by X and followed by a semicolon.

The X command allows the user to define a part of a drawing as a separate part from the definition of the entire object.

The use of X is shown in the following program.

```
10 SCREEN 1
20 CLS
30 A$="E50 D50 L50"
40 B$="A1 E50 D50 L50"
50 C$="A2 E50 D50 L50"
60 D$="A3 E50 D50 L50"
70 DRAW "XA$; XB$; XC$; XD$;"
999 END
```

With all of the preceding commands, the argument *n* can either be a constant or it can be a variable. If *n* is a variable, it must be preceded by an equal sign (=). Also, a semicolon must be used to delimit commands where a variable is used for *n*.

The various GDL commands are summarized in Table 8-2.

**Table 8-2. DRAW's GDL Commands**

| Command Format | Reference |
|---|---|
| U*n* | Move up. |
| D*n* | Move down. |
| L*n* | Move left. |

## Table 8-2 (cont). DRAW's GDL Commands

| | |
|---|---|
| R*n* | Move right. |
| E*n* | Move diagonally up and right. |
| F*n* | Move diagonally down and right. |
| G*n* | Move diagonally down and left. |
| H*n* | Move diagonally up and left. |
| M*xy* | Move absolute or relative. If x is preceded by a plus (+) or minus (-) sign it is relative. If not, it is absolute. |
| B | Moves as indicated without the plotting of any points. |
| N | Moves per the command but returns to the original position when the movement has been completed. |
| A*n* | Sets an angle at the value indicated by *n*. *n* can be any value from 0 to 3, where, 0 indicates 0 degrees, 1 indicates 90 degrees, 2 indicates 180 degrees, and 3 indicates 270 degrees. |
| C*n* | Sets the color to the value indicated by *n*. *n* can range from 0 to 3 in medium resolution or from 0 to 1 in high resolution. |
| P *paint, boundary* | Sets the color of the figure to the color specified by *paint* (0-3). *boundary* indicates the border color of the figure to be filled. |
| S*n* | Sets the scale factor. *n* can range from 1 to 255. To calculate the scale factor, divide *n* by 4. |

### Table 8-2 (cont). DRAW's GDL Commands

| | |
|---|---|
| TA*n* | Turns at the angle indicated by *n*. *n* can range from +360 to -360. In *n* is positive, the angle turns counterclockwise. If *n* is negative, the angle turns clockwise. This command is only available in BASIC 2.0. |
| X*string* | Executes the substring. This allows the user to execute a second string from within the original string. |

## GET and PUT -- Graphics Mode

In Chapter 7, we saw how GET and PUT could be used in file handling. GET and PUT can also be used in a separate context in Adanced BASIC for outputting graphics displays.

GET and PUT are particularly useful in defining a graphics shape so that it can be moved across the screen. We have already seen how various graphic statements such as PSET, PRESET, LINE, and DRAW can be used to output stationary figures. In theory, those statements could be used to output a graphics figure, erase that figure, and then redisplay it at a different location. In practice, animated images of greater quality can be generated by GET and PUT. Moreover, it is much easier to program animation using GET and PUT.

Instead of generating graphics directly on the screen, GET and PUT access the Color/Graphics Display Adapter's RAM in order to generate a graphics figure. The GET statement reads a specified rectangular area of the screen and stores the graphics information relating to that image in that area in a numeric array in RAM. PUT accesses this array and places the graphics figure back on the screen.

GET is used with the following configuration:

GET (a1,b1)-(a2,b2), arrayname

a1,b1 & a2,b2 are used to specify the rectangle within which GET will read the colors of the points. This rectangle will have point (a1,b1) as its upper left column and row. (a2,b2) specify the lower right column and row.

arrayname is the name of an array which is used to hold the image. This array must be numeric, and it can be any precision. Generally, the specified array is an integer array.

The required array size in bytes can be calculated with the following formula,

$$4+INT(a*c+7)/8)*b$$

a is the number of screen columns in the rectangle, b is the number of rows. c is 2 in medium resolution and 1 in high resolution.

If we applied this formula to a situation where the GET statement was to be used with a 12 by 12 image in medium resolution, the number of bytes required would be,

$$4+INT((12*2+7)/8)*12$$

or, 40 bytes.

The numer of bytes for each array element is as follows:

- integer → 2 bytes per element
- single precision → 4 bytes per element
- double precision → 8 bytes per element

It is necessary to divide the number of bytes returned by the formula to calculate the array size by the number of bytes required per element. In our preceding example, an integer array of 20 elements (40/2) would be required to store the data in the 12 by 12 image.

As mentioned previously, once GET has stored an image in memory, that image can be written to a specified area of the screen using PUT. The configuration for PUT is as follows.

PUT (a1,b1) array [,operation]

a1,b1 are the coordinates of the top left hand corner of the area to be transferred.

*array* indicates a numeric array which contains the data to be transferred.

*operation* stands for one of the following:

    PSET
    PRESET
    XOR (The default value)
    OR
    AND

We will discuss each of these optional *operations* in the next section.

The following program illustrates the use of GET and PUT.

```
10   SCREEN 1:COLOR 15,0
20   CLS
30   DIM A%(20)
40   FOR Y=0 TO 11
50   FOR X=0 TO 11
60   READ PIX.VALUE
70   PSET(X,Y),PIX. VALUE
80   NEXT X
90   NEXT Y
100  GET (0,0)-(11,11),A%
110  CLS
```

*program continued on next page*

```
120  FOR Y=0 TO 175
130  FOR X=0 TO 300
140  PUT(X,Y),A%
145  FOR Z=1 TO 20:NEXT Z
147  PUT(X,Y),A%
150  NEXT X
160  NEXT Y
200  DATA 0,0,0,2,2,2,2,2,2,0,0,0
210  DATA 0,0,0,2,2,2,2,2,2,0,0,0
220  DATA 0,0,2,2,2,2,2,2,2,2,0,0
230  DATA 0,0,2,2,1,1,1,1,2,2,0,0
240  DATA 0,2,2,1,1,1,1,1,1,2,2,0
250  DATA 2,2,2,1,1,1,1,1,1,2,2,2
260  DATA 2,2,2,1,1,1,1,1,1,2,2,2
270  DATA 2,2,2,1,1,1,1,1,1,2,2,2
280  DATA 0,0,2,2,1,1,1,1,2,2,0,0
290  DATA 0,0,0,2,2,2,2,2,2,0,0,0
300  DATA 0,0,0,0,2,2,2,2,0,0,0,0
310  DATA 0,0,0,0,0,2,2,0,0,0,0,0
```

In the preceding program, and integer array of 20 elements was dimensioned in line 30 as A%. A% will be accessed later by GET in order to store graphics data and by PUT in order to display that data.

Lines 40 through 90 set up a loop in which the graphics data is output into a 12 pixel by 12 pixel rectangle in the upper lefthand corner of the screen. The data to be stored in this rectangle is contained in the 12 DATA statements in lines 200-310. Each number in the DATA statements references a color number in palette 0 (reference the COLOR statement in line 10).

Line 100 contains a GET statement which stores the graphics data in the 12 by 12 rectangle in the integer array A%.

Lines 120 through 160 set up a loop which in effect "moves" the graphics figure across the screen. Notice that the character is placed on the screen in line 140. A delay loop in line 145 displays the character for a fraction of a second at a fixed location. The character is then erased in line 147, after which the loop repeats.

You can end this program by pressing CTRL-BREAK.

**PUT Statement Operators**

As we mentioned in the previous section, the PUT statement includes a number of optional operators. These include:

>XOR (default)
>OR
>AND
>PSET
>PRESET

These operators allow a graphics image to be placed on the screen in a number of different forms.

**XOR, OR, and AND**

When XOR is indicated as the operator in a PUT statement, the color value of each pixel in the * PUT image will be ** XOR'ed with the corresponding pixel in the *** screen image. The resultant color will be a function of these two color values. The effects of color combinations from using PUT with the XOR operator is shown in Table 8-3.

XOR can be very useful for animation. As was evidenced in our previous program, when PUT is executed with XOR (which is the default) twice, the original image will be drawn with the first PUT statement and erased with the second.

---

 *We define PUT image as the figure being transferred to the screen via the PUT statement.
 **The color values are converted to binary for the XOR.
 ***We defined screen image as the graphics data existing on the screen before the PUT image is transferred.

OR and AND can also be used as an operator with PUT. AND will only transfer the points specified by the PUT image if the screen image points underneath that image are plotted in the foreground color (3). The effects of using AND as an operator are shown in Table 8-3.

OR will display an image regardless of the screen image. As can be seen from Table 8-3, some interesting color transformations can occur by using the OR operator.

### Table 8-3. AND, XOR, OR Effects On Color

Image Color Value

| AND | 0 | 1 | 2 | 3 |
|---|---|---|---|---|
| 0 | 0 | 0 | 0 | 0 |
| 1 | 0 | 1 | 0 | 1 |
| 2 | 0 | 0 | 2 | 2 |
| 3 | 0 | 1 | 2 | 3 |

Screen Color Value

Image Color Value

| OR | 0 | 1 | 2 | 3 |
|---|---|---|---|---|
| 0 | 0 | 1 | 2 | 3 |
| 1 | 1 | 1 | 3 | 3 |
| 2 | 2 | 3 | 2 | 3 |
| 3 | 3 | 3 | 3 | 3 |

Screen Color Value

Image Color Value

| XOR | 0 | 1 | 2 | 3 |
|---|---|---|---|---|
| 0 | 0 | 1 | 2 | 3 |
| 1 | 1 | 0 | 3 | 2 |
| 2 | 2 | 3 | 0 | 1 |
| 3 | 3 | 2 | 1 | 0 |

Screen Color Value

## PSET and PRESET

PSET and PRESET can also be used as operators with PUT. PRESET causes the PUT image to be transfered to the screen with its colors inverted, as shown in Table 8-4.

When PUT is used with PSET, the screen image will be transferred exactly as it is stored in the array. Any existing screen graphics will be erased. PSET can be used much like XOR to produce animation. Also, since only one PUT statement is required using PSET as the operator, that animation can be speeded up.

The usage of PSET and PRESET as operators is illustrated in the following program.

**Table 8-4. PUT with PRESET Operator Color Value Inversion**

| PUT Image Color Value | Screen Image If PRESET Used as Operator |
|---|---|
| 0 | 3 |
| 1 | 2 |
| 2 | 1 |
| 3 | 0 |

```
10   SCREEN 1:COLOR 2,1
20   CLS
30   DIM A%(20)
40   FOR Y=0 TO 11
50   FOR X=0 TO 11
60   READ PIX.VALUE
70   PSET(X,Y),PIX.VALUE
80   NEXT X
90   NEXT Y
100  GET (0,0)-(11,11),A%
110  CLS
140  FOR Y=0 TO 175
```

```
145    FOR X=0 TO 300
150    PUT (X,Y),A%,PSET
170    NEXT X
180    NEXT Y
200    DATA 0,0,0,2,2,2,2,2,2,0,0,0
210    DATA 0,0,0,2,2,2,2,2,2,0,0,0
220    DATA 0,0,2,2,2,2,2,2,2,2,0,0
230    DATA 0,0,2,2,2,2,2,2,2,2,0,0
240    DATA 0,2,2,2,2,2,2,2,2,2,2,0
250    DATA 2,2,2,2,2,2,2,2,2,2,2,2
260    DATA 2,2,2,2,2,2,2,2,2,2,2,2
270    DATA 2,2,2,2,2,2,2,2,2,2,2,2
280    DATA 0,0,2,2,2,2,2,2,2,2,0,0
290    DATA 0,0,0,2,2,2,2,2,2,0,0,0
300    DATA 0,0,0,0,2,2,2,2,0,0,0,0
310    DATA 0,0,0,0,0,2,2,0,0,0,0,0
```

In the preceding program, an integer array of 20 elements was dimensioned in line 30 as A%. A% will be accessed later by GET in order to store graphics data and by PUT in order to display that data.

Lines 40 through 90 set up a loop in which the graphics data is output into a 12 pixel by 12 pixel rectangle in the upper lefthand corner of the screen. The data to be stored in this rectangle is contained in the 12 DATA statements in lines 200-310. Each number in the DATA statements references a color number in palette 0 (reference the COLOR statement in line 10).

Line 100 contains a GET statement which stores the graphics data in the 12 by 12 rectangle in the integer array A%.

Lines 140 through 180 set up a loop which plots the graphics image on the screen. Notice that a trail is left behind the image as it "moves" across the screen. PSET only erases that portion of the screen to which it plots. Since the x position was incremented, only the new portion of the image will be erased.

# CHAPTER 9.
# BASIC REFERENCE GUIDE

## INTRODUCTION

In this chapter, we will provide descriptions of the various commands, statements, and functions used in IBM BASIC.

The following rules and abbreviations will be followed in this chapter in our configuration descriptions of the various BASIC commands, statements, and functions.

1. Any capitalized words are keywords. These may be input in either uppercase, lowercase, or both. BASIC automatically converts keywords to uppercase.

2. Any words, phrases, or letters shown in lowercase italics identify an entry that must be made by the operator.

3. Any items enclosed in brackets [ ] are optional.

4. An ellipsis (...) shows that an item may be repeated as often as desired.

5. Any punctuation marks, except the square brackets, (ex. ; , =) must be included where they are shown.

6. The following abbreviations may be used in this chapter:

    *numexp*  any numeric expression
    *intexp*  any integer expression
    *$$$exp*  any string expression

## ABS

- Cassette
- Disk
- Advanced

The ABS function will return the absolute value of its argument.

### Configuration

a = ABS(*b*)

### Example

```
Ok
PRINT ABS(-11)
 11
Ok
```

## ASC

- Cassette
- Disk
- Advanced

The ASC function returns the ASCII code for the first character of its string argument.

### Configuration

a = ASC(*$$$exp*)

### Example

```
Ok
100  X$ = "ABC"
200  PRINT ASC(X$)
RUN
 65
Ok
```

## ATN

- Cassette
- Disk
- Advanced

The ATN function returns the arctangent of its argument.

### Configuration

a = ATN(*b*)

### Example

```
Ok
100 X = 5
200 PRINT ATN(X)
RUN
 1.373401
Ok
```

## AUTO

- Cassette
- Disk
- Advanced

The AUTO command results in a new line number being generated every time the user presses the Enter key.

### Configuration

AUTO [*number*][,][*increment*]

*number* is the beginning line number. *increment* is the amount to be added to the previous line number to generate the next, new line number.

The AUTO command is generally used when entering programs. This saves the user the task of typing every line number.

If no parameters are included in the AUTO command, the beginning line number will be 10 and each new line number generated will be incremented by 10.

If an increment is specified with a comma preceding it, but no beginning line number is specified, the beginning line number will be 0.

If a period (.) is substituted for the beginning line number, the current line will be used as the beginning line number.

The AUTO command might generate a line number that already exists in the program. If this occurs, an asterisk (*) will be printed immediately following the line number. This is meant as a warning to the user. If any data is input into that line, the existing program line will be replaced by it. If the user presses the Enter key immediately after the asterisk without entering any new data, a new line number will be generated, and the existing line will not be replaced.

The AUTO command is ended by pressing the Ctrl-Break key combination. The current line being entered when Ctrl-Break is pressed will be erased. After Ctrl-Break has been pressed, BASIC will return to the command level.

### Examples

AUTO
AUTO 100,20
AUTO 1000
AUTO, 100

## BEEP

- Cassette
- Disk
- Advanced

The BEEP statement is used to cause the speaker to beep.

### Configuration

BEEP

### Example

100 IF X = Y THEN BEEP

## BLOAD

- Cassette
- Disk
- Advanced

BLOAD can be used to load any segment defined as the source file by the DEF SEG statement. The BLOAD command is generally used for loading machine language programs.

### Configuration

BLOAD *filespec* [,*offset*]

*filespec* refers to the file specification for the file being loaded. *offset* refers to the address at which loading is to start. This address is designated as an offset into the segment specified in the last DEF SEG statement.

### BLOAD With Cassette BASIC

Unless a device name is specified, the device CAS1: will be assumed. When BLOAD is executed in the direct mode, the filenames for the files on the cassette tape will be listed one by one on the screen. These filenames will be followed by a period and one of the following letters (which indicates the file type).

- **.B** indicates a BASIC program stored in internal format and created by the SAVE command.
- **.P** indicates a protected BASIC program in internal format and created with the SAVE.P command.
- **.A** indicates a BASIC program in ASCII format and created via the SAVE,A command.
- **.M** indicates a memory image file created with the BSAVE command.
- **.D** indicates a data file created by the OPEN statement.

As the files are displayed on the screen, they will be followed by one of the following messages:

> Skipped
> Found

"Skipped" indicates the file displayed does not match the file named in BLOAD. "Found" indicates that the file displayed was named in BLOAD.

If BLOAD is executed in a BASIC program, the filenames will not be displayed on the screen.

### BLOAD With Disk or Advanced BASIC

If the device name is not included, the current disk drive is assumed to be the device.

## BSAVE

■ Cassette
■ Disk
■ Advanced

The BSAVE command makes it possible to save a part of memory on a device. Generally, BSAVE is used for saving machine language programs.

### Configuration

BSAVE *filespec, offset, length*

*filespec* is the file specification for the file to be saved. *offset* is the offset in the segment last designated by the previous DEF SEG statement. This is where saving will begin. *length* is the length of the memory image to be saved.

If you are using Cassette BASIC, the device CAS1: will be assumed, and a memory image file will be written on the magnetic tape.

If you are using Disk or Advanced BASIC, the designated device name will receive the file. If no device name is given, the current drive will receive the file.

## CALL

- Cassette
- Disk
- Advanced

The CALL statement is used to call a machine language subroutine.

### Configuration

CALL *numericvar* [(*variable* [,*variable*]...)]

*numericvar* designates the name of a numeric variable, the value of which gives the starting address in memory of the subroutine being CALL'ed. This address is given as an offset into the current segment of memory (i.e. the one given in the last DEF SEG statement).

*variable* refers to the name of a variable which is to be given as an argument to the machine language subroutine.

### Example

1200 CALL A(X,Y$,Z)

## CDBL

- Cassette
- Disk
- Advanced

The CDBL function is used to convert its argument to a double precision number.

### Configuration

a = CDBL(*b*)

### Example

```
Ok
100 A = 367.55
200 PRINT A;CDBL(A)
RUN
 367.55        367.549877929688
Ok
```

## CHAIN

- ☐ Cassette
- Disk
- Advanced

The CHAIN statement is used to transfer program control to another program.

### Configuration

CHAIN [MERGE] *filespec* [,[*line*][,[ALL][,DELETE *range*]]]

*filespec* refers to the name of the program that is to be CHAIN'ed. *line* refers to a line number within the program being CHAIN'ed. That is the point within the program where execution is to begin.

If the MERGE option is included, a section of the code may be brought into the BASIC program as an overlay. In other words, a

MERGE operation will be performed with the current program and the program being CHAIN'ed. The program being CHAIN'ed must be an ASCII file if it is to be MERGE'd (see explanation of MERGE command).

An example of the use of the MERGE command in a CHAIN statement is given below.

CHAIN MERGE "A:NTW",1000

In this example, the program NTW on drive A will be brought into the program as an overlay with a starting point for execution in line 1000.

Once an overlay has been used, it is generally deleted so that a new overlay can be instituted. This is accomplished with the DELETE option. The DELETE option, when used in the CHAIN statement, functions much like the DELETE command.

In the following example,

CHAIN MERGE "A:NTW",1000,DELETE 1000-3000

lines 1000 through 3000 in the current program will be deleted before the loading of the overlay.

The ALL option passes every variable in the current program to the program being CHAIN'ed. In cases where the ALL option is not included in the CHAIN statement, the current program must contain a COMMON statement which lists all variables that are to be passed to the programs being CHAIN'ed

☐ Cassette
■ Disk
## CHDIR
■ Advanced

CHDIR is used in BASIC 2.0 to change the current directory.

### Configuration

CHDIR *path*

*path* is a string expression of 63 characters or less which identifies the new current directory.

### Example

CHDIR " \ "
CHDIR "ACCT\CHECKS\INV"

In the first example, the root directory becomes the current directory. In the second example, INV becomes the current directory.

## CHR$

- Cassette
- Disk
- Advanced

The CHR$ function is used to convert an ASCII code to its corresponding character.

### Configuration

a$ = CHR$(*b*)

where *b* is a number or numeric expression from 0 to 255.

CHR$ is often used to send a special character to either the screen or the printer.

### Example

```
Ok
100 PRINT CHR$(33)
RUN
 !
Ok
```

In the preceding example, the exclamation point is sent to the screen.

## CINT

■ Cassette
■ Disk
■ Advanced

The CINT function is used to convert its argument to an integer.

### Configuration

a = CINT(*b*)

The fractional portion of the argument will be rounded to determine the integer result.

### Example

```
Ok
PRINT CINT(15.46)
 15
Ok
```

## CIRCLE

□ Cassette
□ Disk
■ Advanced

The CIRCLE statement is used in the graphics mode to draw an ellipse on the screen.

### Configuration

CIRCLE (*xcenter,ycenter*), *radius* [,*color* [,*start,end* [,*aspect*]]]

*xcenter,ycenter* gives the center of the ellipse. *radius* gives the radius of the ellipse.

*color* refers to the color of the figure being drawn. The default value for color is 3 in medium resolution and 1 in high resolution.

*start,end* refers to the points where the drawing of the ellipse will begin and end. These are given in radians and may range from −2*PI to 2*PI where PI = 3.141593. If the *start* or *end* angle is negative, the ellipse will be connected to its center point with a line.

*aspect* affects the ratio of the x-radius to the y-radius. The default value for *aspect* is 5/6 in medium resolution and 5/12 in high resolution.

If the *aspect* given is less than 1, the radius given is the x-radius. In other words, the radius is measured in points in the horizontal direction. If the *aspect* given is greater than one, the y-radius will be given.

## CLEAR

- Cassette
- Disk
- Advanced

The CLEAR command is used to set all numeric variables to zero and to set all string variables to null. CLEAR can also optionally be used to set the end of memory and the amount of stack space.

### Configuration

CLEAR [,[exp1][,exp2]]

*exp1* is a byte count which sets the maximum number of bytes available for BASIC to store programs and data files.

*exp2* reserves stack space for BASIC. The default value is either 512 bytes or one eighth of available memory -- whichever is smaller.

## CLOSE

■ Cassette
■ Disk
■ Advanced

The CLOSE statement is used to end input and/or output to the specified device or file.

### Configuration

CLOSE [[#]*filenum*[,[#]*filenum*]...]

*filenum* refers to the number of the file which was used in the OPEN statement.

If the CLOSE statement is used without an optional file number, all devices and files which were open will be closed.

## CLS

■ Cassette
■ Disk
■ Advanced

The CLS statement is used to clear the screen.

### Configuration

CLS

The CLS statement also causes the cursor to return to the home position. In the text mode, this is the upper left hand corner of the screen. In the graphics mode, this is the point in the center of the screen (160,100 -- medium resolution; 320,100 -- high resolution).

Also, if the screen is in the text mode, the active page will be cleared to the background color. If the screen is in the graphics mode, the screen buffer will be cleared to the background color.

## COLOR

- Cassette
- Disk
- Advanced

The COLOR statement is used to set the colors for the foreground, background, and border screen. The use of the COLOR statement differs depending on whether the text mode or graphics mode is being used. This is set by the SCREEN statement.

The text mode allows the user to set the following:

| | |
|---|---|
| Foreground | 1 of 16 colors |
| Background | 1 of 8 colors |
| Border | 1 of 16 colors |

The border is an area on the TV set or monitor which is outside the area used for characters. The color for the border can be set with the COLOR statement.

Every character on the screen consists of two portions; the foreground and the background. The foreground is the actual character, while the background is a box that outlines the character.

In the graphics mode, the user can set the following:

| | |
|---|---|
| Background | 1 of 16 colors |
| Palette | 1 of 2 palettes of 3 colors each |

In the graphics mode, the border is the same color as the background.

### Configuration (Text Mode)

COLOR [foreground][,[background][,border]]

*foreground* is the color of the character and must be a number or numeric expression from 0 to 31.

*background* is the color of the background and must be a number or numeric expression from 0 to 7.

*border* is the color for the border screen and must be a number from 0 to 15.

The following colors are available for *foreground* if the color/graphics monitor adapter is being used.

| | | | |
|---|---|---|---|
| 0 | Black | 8 | Gray |
| 1 | Blue | 9 | Light Blue |
| 2 | Green | 10 | Light Green |
| 3 | Cyan | 11 | Light Cyan |
| 4 | Red | 12 | Light Red |
| 5 | Magenta | 13 | Light Magenta |
| 6 | Brown | 14 | Yellow |
| 7 | White | 15 | High Intensity White |

By selecting the *foreground* equal to 16 plus the color desired, the character will blink. In other words, a value of 22 will result in brown blinking.

Colors 0 through 7 can be selected for *background*.

If you are using the IBM Monochrome Display and Printer Adapter, the following can be used for *foreground*.

- 0 Black
- 1 Underline character with white foreground
- 7 White
- 15 High Intensity White

Again, by adding 16 to the desired value, the character will blink. For example, 16 will result in black blinking.

With the IBM Monochrome Display and Printer Adapter, either of the following may be used for *foreground*.

- 0 Black
- 7 White

**Example**

100 COLOR 0,7

In the preceding example, the *foreground* is set to black. The *background* is set to white, assuming the Monochrome Display/Printer Adapter is used.

**Configuration (Graphics Mode)**

COLOR [*background*][,[*palette*]]

*background* is the background color and must be a number or numeric expression from 0 to 15.

*palette* is the selection of a palette of available colors and must be either 0 or 1 or an expression evaluating to those values.

The COLOR statement will set the colors used by the PSET, PRESET, LINE, CIRCLE, PAINT, and DRAW statements.

The *background* colors allowed are 0 through 15 in the list given previously. The palette selections available are given in Table 9-1.

If palette 0 is chosen, color number 1 will be green, color 2 will be red, and color 3 will be brown. If palette 1 is chosen, color 1 will be cyan, color 2 will be magenta, and color 3 will be white.

**Table 9-1. Palette Color Selection**

| Color # | Palette 0 | Palette 1 |
|---|---|---|
| 1 | Green | Cyan |
| 2 | Red | Magenta |
| 3 | Brown | White |

The COLOR statement can only be used in medium resolution. Attempting to use the COLOR statement in the high resolution mode will result in an "Illegal function call" error.

### Example

100 SCREEN 1
200 COLOR 8,0

In the preceding example, the background is set to gray and palette 0 is selected.

## COM

☐ Cassette
☐ Disk
■ Advanced

The COM statement is used to allow or disallow the trapping of communications on the Communications Adapter.

### Configuration

COM(n) ON
COM(n) OFF
COM(n) STOP

*n* is the number of the communications adapter (1 or 2).

Before trapping is allowed by the ON COM statement, a COM ON statement must have been executed. Once a COM ON statement has been executed, if a line number was specified in the ON COM statement, then BASIC will check every statement to see if characters have arrived from the communications line.

If the COM OFF statement was last executed, then communications trapping will not take place.

If the COM STOP statement has been executed, then no communications trapping can occur. However, any occurrences of communications activity will be retained. This will result in an immediate trap upon execution of COM ON.

## COMMON

☐ Cassette
■ Disk
■ Advanced

The COMMON statement passes the variables listed as its arguments to all CHAIN'ed programs.

### Configuration

COMMON *variable* [,*variable*]

It is recommended that the COMMON statement appear at the beginning of a program. Any array variable included in a COMMON statement must be followed with parentheses ( ). If all variables are to be passed to the programs being CHAIN'ed, this can be accomplished by using the ALL option with CHAIN.

### Example

100 COMMON A,B,C,D ( )


## CONT

■ Cassette
■ Disk
■ Advanced

The CONT command is used to restart program execution after it had been stopped.

### Configuration

CONT

Program execution may be stopped if the Ctrl-Break keys were pressed, if a STOP or END statement was executed, or if an error occurred. The CONT command will resume execution at the point where the program break occurred.

## COS

- Cassette
- Disk
- Advanced

The COS function returns the cosine of its argument.

### Configuration

$a = \text{COS}(b)$

### Example

```
Ok
100  A = 4*COS(.6)
200  PRINT A
RUN
 3.301342
Ok
```

## CSNG

- Cassette
- Disk
- Advanced

The CSNG function converts its argument to a single precision number.

### Configuration

$a = \text{CSNG}(b)$

### Example

```
Ok
100  X# = 963.3721422#
200  PRINT X#,CSNG(X#)
RUN
 963.3721422#     963.3721
Ok
```

## CSRLIN

- ■ Cassette
- ■ Disk
- ■ Advanced

The CSRLIN variable returns the cursor's vertical coordinate.

### Configuration

a = CSRLIN

The CSRLIN variable returns the current row position of the cursor on the active page (as explained in the SCREEN statement). The value returned will be between 1 and 25.

## CVI, CVS, CVD

- □ Cassette
- ■ Disk
- ■ Advanced

The CVI, CVS, and CVD functions are used to convert string variable types to numeric variable types.

### Configuration

a = CVI(*2-byte string*)
a = CVS(*4-byte string*)
a = CVD(*8-byte string*)

CVI converts a 2-byte string to an integer. CVS converts a 4-byte string to a single precision number, and CVD converts an 8-byte string to a double precision number.

## DATA

- ■ Cassette
- ■ Disk
- ■ Advanced

DATA statements contain the numeric and string constants which later are accessed by READ statements.

### Configuration

DATA *constant [,constant]*

*constant* may be any numeric or string constant. Expressions are not allowed in a DATA statement.

Numeric constants may be in integer, fixed point, floating point, hex, or octal format. String constants in DATA statements need not be enclosed in quotation marks unless the string contains commas, colons, trailing blanks, or leading blanks.

An unlimited number of DATA statements may be included in a program. As many constants as can be contained on a line can be included with a DATA statement.

The constants included in the DATA statements can be envisioned as one long list of items. The READ statements access the constants in the DATA statements sequentially. The variable type in the READ statement must correspond with the constant being read from the DATA statement. Otherwise, a "Syntax error" will occur.

## DATE$

☐ Cassette
■ Disk
■ Advanced

DATE$ is used to set or retrieve the date. It can be used as a variable or as a statement.

### Configuration

a$ = DATE$ → variable
DATE$ = b$ → statement

When used as a variable in the following format:

a$ = DATE$

the current date is returned as a 10 character string in the form mm-dd-yyyy. The "mm" gives the month. The "dd" gives the day in the month, and the "yyyy" gives the year.

When used as a statement in the following format:

DATE$ = b$

the current date will be set to that given in *b$*. *b$* can take any of the following forms.

mm-dd-yy
mm/dd/yy
mm-dd-yyyy
mm/dd/yyyy

The year must be between 1980 and 2099. If the month or days is entered as a single digit, a zero will be assumed to precede it. If only 2 digits are given for the year, these digits will be assumed to be preceded by 19.

### Example

```
Ok
100  DATE$ = "7/15/82"
200  PRINT DATE$
RUN
 07-15-1982
Ok
```

## DEF FN

■ Cassette
■ Disk
■ Advanced

The DEF FN statement is used to define a function written by the user.

### Configuration

DEF FN*name* [(*argument*[,*argument*]...)] = *function definition* *name* is a variable name, which when preceded by FN becomes the name of the function.

*argument* is an argument of the function being defined. The argument is a variable name in the function definition. When the function is called, the argument will be replaced with a value.

*function definition* are the statements which perform the function's operations.

Any *arguments* appearing in the *function definition* are used only to define the function. If a variable with the same name as an *argument* appears in the program, these variables will not be affected.

The function may return either a string or a numeric value depending upon the function type. The function type is given in *name* in the same way as variable types are defined. If the *function definition* does not return the type of data specified in the *name*, a "Type mismatch" error will occur.

The DEF FN statement must appear in a program prior to the point where it is called. If a function is called before it is defined, the following error will appear:

Undefined user function

### Example

```
Ok
100 DEF FNTT(X) = SQR(X) + 1
200 X = 49
300 Y = FNTT(X)
400 PRINT Y
RUN
 8
Ok
```

## DEFDBL, DEFSTR
## DEFINT, DEFSNG

- Cassette
- Disk
- Advanced

These statements are used to declare variable types as integer, single-precision, double-precision, or string.

### Configuration

DEF { INT / SNG / DBL / STR } alpha[-alpha] [,alpha[-alpha]]...

alpha is a letter of the alphabet

The letter specified in the DEF statement will be the type of variable defined. However, if the variable appears with a type declaration character (%, !, #, or $), that will supercede the DEF statement.

If DEF statements are to be used, they must be executed before any variables being defined are encountered in the program.

### Example

```
100  DEFINT A-D
200  DEFSTR E
300  DEFDBL F-M, Z
```

In line 100, the variables A through D are declared as integer variables. In line 200, the variable E is defined as a string variable. In line 300, the variables F through M and Z are defined as double precision variables. All other variables will be assumed to be single-precision.

## DEF SEG

■ Cassette
■ Disk
■ Advanced

DEF SEG is used to define the current segment used for storage. A succeeding BLOAD, BSAVE, CALL, PEEK, POKE, VARPTR, or USR definition will define an actual physical address in memory as an offset into this segment.

### Configuration

DEF SEG [= address]

address is a number or numeric expression from 0 to 65535.

If the optional address is not included, the segment will be set to BASIC's Data Segment (DS), which is the beginning of the user work area in memory.

If an address is specified, that value should be predicated upon a 16 byte boundary. The value given in address is moved left 4 bits (times 16) to create the segment address to be used for any ensuing operation.

### Example

100 DEF SEG = &HB800

## DEF USR

■ Cassette
■ Disk
■ Advanced

DEF USR is used to give the starting address of a machine language subroutine which is to be called later by the USR function.

### Configuration

DEF USR [digit] = offset

digit can be any digit from 0 to 9. offset is an integer or integer expression from 0 to 65535.

*Digit* refers to the number of the USR routine for which an address is being specified. *Digit's* default value is 0.

The value given in *offset* is added to the current segment value to give the USR routine's starting address.

### Example
```
100  DEF SEG = 0
200  DEF USR0 = 25000
```

## DELETE

■ Cassette
■ Disk
■ Advanced

The DELETE command is used to delete program lines.

### Configuration

DELETE [*line*] [-*line*]
DELETE [*line*-]

In the first configuration, the *line* or range of lines specified will be erased. A period may be used in place of *line* to denote the current line. If a specified *line* does not exist, an "Illegal function call" error will result.

In the second configuration, all lines from the *line* indicated to the end of the program will be deleted (BASIC 2.0).

### Example

DELETE 100 ⟶ line 100 is erased
DELETE 60-70 ⟶ lines 60 to 70 are erased
DELETE -20 ⟶ all lines up to and including 20 are erased.

## DIM

■ Cassette
■ Disk
■ Advanced

DIM is used to initialize and reserve space in memory for arrays.

### Configuration

DIM variable(subscript) [,variable(subscript)]

The DIM statement assigns a value of zero to all of the elements of numeric arrays and the null value to the elements of string arrays.

If an array variable name that was not defined with a DIM statement is used in a program, that array will be allowed a maximum subscript value of 10.

### Example

DIM A(15), B(7)

## DRAW

☐ Cassette
☐ Disk
■ Advanced

The DRAW statement is used to draw an object specified by a string containing drawing commands. The DRAW statement is only used in the graphics mode.

### Configuration

DRAW string

*string* is a string expression containing drawing commands.

We will discuss the movement commands first. These commands are described as follows:

| | |
|---|---|
| U*n* | Move up. |
| D*n* | Move down. |
| L*n* | Move left. |
| R*n* | Move right. |
| E*n* | Move diagonally up and right. |
| F*n* | Move diagonally down and right. |
| G*n* | Move diagonally down and left. |
| H*n* | Move diagonally up and left. |

*n* gives the distance to be moved. The number of points to be moved is calculated by multiplying *n* times the scaling factor, which is set by the S command.

| | |
|---|---|
| M x,y | Move absolute or relative. If x is preceded by a plus (+) or minus (−) sign it is relative. If not, it is absolute. |

The spacing of the horizontal, vertical, and diagonal points is determined by the aspect ratio of your screen. The standard aspect ratio is 4/3. This means that four horizontal points are the same length as three vertical points.

The movement commands can be preceded by the prefix commands, B and N. These are described below:

- B Moves as indicated without the plotting of any points.
- N Moves per the command but returns to the original position when the movement has been completed.

The following commands can also be used with DRAW:

| | |
|---|---|
| A*n* | This command sets an angle at the value indicated by *n*. *n* can be any value from 0 to 3, where 0 indicates 0 degrees, 1 indicates 90 degrees, 2 indicates 180 degrees, and 3 indicates 270 degrees. |

Cn	This command sets the color to the value indicated by *n*. *n* can range from 0 to 3 in medium resolution or from 0 to 1 in high resolution. In medium resolution, the color specified (*n*) is from the current palette as defined in color. 0 is the background color. The default (3) is the foreground color. In high resolution, *n*=0 results in black while *n*=1 (default) indicates white.

P *paint, boundary*	This command sets the color of the figure to the color specified by *paint* (0-3). The border color of the figure to be filled is indicated by *boundary* (0-3). This feature is only available in BASIC 2.0.

S*n*	This command is used to set the scale factor. *n* can range from 1 to 255. To calculate the scale factor, divide *n* by 4. The scale factor is multiplied by the distances given with the movement commands to determine the actual distance to be moved.

TA*n*	This command can be used to turn the angle previously set with A. *n* can range from +360 to -360. If *n* is positive, the angle turns counterclockwise. If *n* is negative, the angle turns clockwise. This command is only available in BASIC 2.0.

X *string*	This command executes the substring. This allows the user to execute a second string from within the original string. The X command allows the user to define a part of a drawing as a separate part from the definition of the entire object.

With all of the commands, the argument *n* can either be a constant or it can be a variable. If *n* is a variable, it must be preceded by an equal sign (=). Also, a semicolon must be used to delimit commands where a variable is used for *n*.

**Example**

```
100 SCREEN 1
200 X = 30
300 DRAW "U=X; R=X;"
```

**EDIT**
■ Cassette
■ Disk
■ Advanced

The EDIT command is used to display a line for editing purposes.

**Configuration**

EDIT *line*

*line* is the line number of a line in a program. If the *line* specified does not exist, the following error message will appear:

Undefined line number

A period can be used for *line* if the user wishes to specify the current line. The EDIT statement displays the specified line. The cursor is positioned at the beginning of the line number. The line may then be edited as described in Chapter 1.

**END**
■ Cassette
■ Disk
■ Advanced

The END statement is used to end program execution. The END statement closes any open files and returns control to the command level.

## Configuration

END

The END statement can be placed anywhere in the program.

### Example

1000 IF X = Y THEN END ELSE GOTO 100

## EOF

- Cassette
- Disk
- Advanced

The EOF function is used to test for the end of file condition.

### Configuration

a = EOF(*filenumber*)

*filenumber* is the number of the file as specified in the OPEN statement.

If the end of file has been reached, the EOF file will return a value of −1 (true). If the end of file has not been reached, the EOF file will return a value of 0.

EOF(0) when executed in BASIC 2.0 will return the end of file condition on standard input devices used with I/O redirection.

### Example

100 OPEN "TEXT.DAT" FOR INPUT AS #5
200 IF EOF(5) THEN 999

## ERASE

- Cassette
- Disk
- Advanced

The ERASE statement is used to erase arrays from a program.

### Configuration

ERASE *arrayname* [,*arrayname*]...

*arrayname* refers to the name of the array.

ERASE is often used when an array is to be redimensioned in a program. If the user attempts to redimension an array without it previously having been ERASE'd, the following error message will be displayed:

Duplicate Definition

The ERASE statement is also often used in situations where a program is running short of storage space. Once the arrays have been ERASE'd, the memory space previously allocated for arrays will be freed for use by the program.

### Example

```
100 DIM A(10,10),B(5),C(7,5)
150 PRINT FRE(1)
200 ERASE A
250 PRINT FRE(1)
300 DIM A(5,5)
350 PRINT FRE(1)
```

## ERR, ERL

- Cassette
- Disk
- Advanced

The ERR and ERL variables can be used to return the error code and the line number associated with that error.

### Configuration

$a$ = ERR
$b$ = ERL

The ERR variable returns the error code for the last error. The ERL variable returns the line number of the line in the program where that error was discovered.

The ERL and ERR variables are often used in conjunction with an IF...THEN statement to test for an error condition as shown in the following example.

### Example

```
100  ON ERROR GOTO 900
150  A% = 9
170  PRINNT A%
350  GOTO 1100
900  CLS
950  IF ERR= 2 THEN LOCATE 1,1:
     PRINT "CHECK FOR SYNTAX ERRORS"
1000 RESUME NEXT
1100 END
```

## ERROR

- Cassette
- Disk
- Advanced

The ERROR statement allows the user to duplicate a BASIC error. The ERROR statement can also be used to allow a user to define his own error codes.

### Configuration

ERROR *n*

*n* is an integer or integer expression from 0 to 255.

If the argument *n* specified with ERROR is the same as an error code used in BASIC, then the ERROR statement will duplicate that error's occurrence when it is executed. If an error routine had previously been defined with an ON ERROR statement, then the error routine will be executed after that ERROR statement has been executed. If an error routine had not been previously defined, then the appropriate error message will be printed and program execution will stop.

If a value is used for *n* that is different than any of the error codes used by BASIC, then the user will have the opportunity to define his own error code. The newly-defined error code should have an error handling routine. If it does not, the following message will be printed:

Unprintable error

and program execution will stop.

An example of ERROR is given in the program on page 225.

**EXP**
- Cassette
- Disk
- Advanced

The EXP function is used to calculate the exponential function.

### Configuration

*a* = EXP(*b*)

The value returned by the EXP function is the mathematical function e raised to the power specified by the argument *b*. The argument *b* must be less than or equal to 88.02969. Otherwise, the Overflow message will be displayed, infinity will be given as the value *a*, and program execution will continue.

**Example**

```
Ok
100 B = 4
200 PRINT EXP(B)
RUN
54.59815
Ok
```

## FIELD

□ Cassette
■ Disk
■ Advanced

The FIELD statement is used to reserve space for variables in a random file buffer.

**Configuration**

FIELD[#] *filenumber, width* AS *string variable*
[*,width* AS *stringvariable*]...

*filenumber* is the number of the file. This was specified in the OPEN statement.

*width* is a number or numeric expression which indicates the number of character positions which are to be allocated to *stringvariable*. *stringvariable* is a string which is used for random file access.

FIELD statements are used to enter data into a random buffer for a PUT statement or to extract random data from a buffer after a GET statement has been executed. The FIELD statement does not actually place data into the random file buffer. This is performed by the LSET and RSET statements.

In the following example, the FIELD statement allocates the first 10 positions in the random file buffer for the string variable A$. The next 15 positions are reserved for B$, and the following 30 positions are reserved for C$.

**Example**

FIELD 1, 10 AS A$, 15 AS B$, 30 AS C$

## FILES

☐ Cassette
■ Disk
■ Advanced

The FILES command is used to display the filenames of the files contained on a diskette.

**Configuration**

FILES [*filespec*]

*filespec* is a filespecification.

If the optional file specification is not included with the FILES command, then all of the files on the current drive will be listed.

The filename match characters (? and *) may be used in the filename portion of the file specification. All files on the current drive that match the filename portion of the file specification will be listed.

**Examples**

FILES

FILES "*.DAT"

FILES "B:*.*"

In the first example, all of the files in the current drive will be listed. In the second example, all files on the current drive with an extension of .DAT will be listed. In the final example, all files on drive B will be listed.

Files can also be used to display the files in a sub-directory. When FILES is used without an argument, the current sub-directory will be listed. When used with an argument, FILES will list the sub-directory specified. A backslash must be used following the directory name as shown in the following example.

FILES "ARINV \ "

## FIX

- Cassette
- Disk
- Advanced

The FIX function truncates its argument to an integer.

### Configuration

a = FIX(b)

The FIX function deletes the decimal portion of its argument and returns only the integer portion. The FIX function differs from the INT function in that FIX does not return the next lower number when its argument is negative.

### Example

```
Ok
PRINT FIX(67.345)
 67
Ok
PRINT FIX(-63.99)
 -63
Ok
```

## FOR...NEXT

■ Cassette
■ Disk
■ Advanced

The FOR...NEXT statements are used to execute a sequence of statements a set number of times.

### Configuration

FOR *variable* = *a* TO *b* STEP *c*
.
NEXT [*variable*][,*variable*]

*variable* is set to a single precision variable or an integer (*a*,*b*,*c*), and is used as a counter. *a* is the initial value of the counter, and *b* is the final value. The counter is incremented by the amount named after STEP(*c*). If a value is not given after STEP, it is assumed to be 1.

The program lines following the FOR statement are executed until the NEXT statement is encountered. At this point, the counter is incremented by the value specified after STEP. If no such value is specified, the counter will be increased by 1.

The value for the counter is then compared with its maximum value (*b*). As long as the counter's value is less than the final value, program control will branch back to the statement following the FOR statement. This entire process will then be repeated.

When the counter's value is greater than the specified maximum value (*b*), program execution will continue with the statement immediately following the NEXT statement. This will exit the FOR...NEXT loop.

One FOR...NEXT statement may be placed within another FOR...NEXT statement. This is known as **nesting.** When FOR...NEXT loops are nested, each FOR...NEXT loop must use a different variable name for the counter. Also, the NEXT statement for the inside loop must appear before the NEXT statement for the outside loop. However, if both loops end at the same point, a single NEXT statement may be used to end these. Be certain that the *variable* for the inside loop appears before that of the outside loop. A NEXT statement like the following,

NEXT A,B

would be interpreted as follows:

NEXT A
NEXT B

A NEXT statement can be used without a variable. In such a situation, the NEXT statement will be applied to the last FOR statement.

**Example**

```
Ok
100 B = 5
200 FOR A = 1 TO B
300 PRINT A;
400 NEXT
RUN
 1 2 3 4 5
Ok
```

■ Cassette
■ Disk
**FRE** ■ Advanced

The FRE function returns the number of "free" bytes in memory (i.e. those not being used).

**Configuration**

$a = \text{FRE}(b)$
$a = \text{FRE}(b\$)$

The arguments used with FRE are dummy arguments. When FRE is used with a string argument, a **housekeeping** will be performed before the function returns the number of free bytes. A housekeeping is where BASIC gathers all useful data and frees any areas of memory which were once used for strings, but are currently unused.

Areas assigned to strings can become unused because strings in BASIC can have variable lengths. Every time a different value is assigned to a string variable, its length may change. This may cause the space assigned to a string to become partially unused. A housekeeping eliminates this unused space.

Whenever BASIC determines that the available work area in memory is being depleted, a housekeeping will be automatically undertaken.

**Example**

Ok
PRINT FRE(1)
 17397
Ok

## GET

☐ Cassette
■ Disk
■ Advanced

The GET statement is used to read a record from a random file into a random buffer.

**Configuration**

GET [#] *filenumber* [,*number*]

*filenumber* is the number assigned to the file when it was opened. *number* is the number of the record which is to be read.

If the optional parameter *number* is omitted, the next record following the last GET statement will be read into the buffer.

The GET statement can also be used with communications files. In these instances, the optional parameter *number* specifies the number of bytes to be read from the communications buffer.

An example of the use of the GET statement is given in line 350 in the program on page 148.

## GET (Graphics)

☐ Cassette
☐ Disk
■ Advanced

The GET statement is used in the graphics mode to read points from an area of the video screen.

### Configuration

GET (a1,b1)-(a2,b2), arrayname

*a1,b1* and *a2,b2* are used to specify a rectangle within which GET will read the colors of the points. This rectangle will have points (*a1,b1*) and (*a2,b2*) as opposite corners.

*arrayname* is the name of an array which is used to hold the image. This array must be numeric, but it can be any precision. The required array size in bytes can be calculated with the following formula,

$$4 + INT((a * c + 7)/8) * b$$

where *a* is the length of the horizontal side of the rectangle, *b* is the length of the vertical side, and *c* is 2 in medium resolution and 1 in high resolution.

If we applied this formula to a situation where the GET statement is to be used with a 12 by 12 image in medium resolution, the number of bytes required would be,

$$4 + INT((12*2+7)/8)*12$$

or, 40 bytes.

The number of bytes for each array element is as follows:

- integer          2 bytes per element
- single precision   4 bytes per element
- double precision   8 bytes per element

In this situation, an integer array with at least 20 elements could be used.

## GOSUB, RETURN

■ Cassette
■ Disk
■ Advanced

The GOSUB, RETURN statements are used to branch to a subroutine and then return from it.

### Configuration

GOSUB *line*

RETURN

A subroutine is called by the GOSUB statement. When the RETURN statement is encountered within that subroutine, program control will branch back to the statement following the GOSUB statement just executed.

Subroutines may appear at any point within the program. However, it is good programming practice to group all subroutines near the beginning of the program.

### Example

```
10 FOR J = 0 TO 2
20 GOSUB 100
30 NEXT J
40 J = 5
50 GOSUB 100
60 END
100 PRINT J;
110 RETURN
RUN
 0 1 2 5
```

## GOTO

■ Cassette
■ Disk
■ Advanced

The GOTO statement is used to branch program control to another program line.

### Configuration

GOTO *line*

The ON...GOTO statement allows the program to branch to a number of different lines depending upon the answer to the conditional expression.

### Example

```
100 ON X GOTO 500,600,700,999
  .
  .
999 END
```

## HEX$

- Cassette
- Disk
- Advanced

The HEX$ function returns a string which contains the hexadecimal equivalent of the function's argument (assumed to be decimal).

### Configuration

a$ = HEX$(*b*)

The decimal argument (*b*) is rounded to an integer before the function is executed.

### Example

```
Ok
100 INPUT A
200 A$ = HEX$(A)
300 PRINT "DECIMAL VALUE IS";A
400 PRINT "HEXADECIMAL VALUE IS ";A$
RUN
 ?50
 DECIMAL VALUE IS 50
 HEXADECIMAL VALUE IS 32
```

## IF

- Cassette
- Disk
- Advanced

The IF statement sets a condition which will influence the program flow.

### Configuration

IF *expression* [,] THEN *clause* [[,] ELSE *clause*]
IF *expression* GOTO *line* [[,] ELSE *clause*]

*clause* can be either a BASIC statement, a series of statements, or a line number.

In the first configuration, if the *expression* following the IF statement evaluates as true (not zero), the *clause* following the THEN statement will be executed. If the *expression* following the IF statement evaluates as false (zero), the *clause* following THEN will be disregarded, and the *clause* following the optional ELSE statement will be executed (if present). If an ELSE statement is not present, the program will proceed to the next line.

In the second configuration, if the *expression* following the IF statement evaluates as true, program control will branch to the *line* specified. If the *expression* evaluates as false, the statement will be ignored and the program will proceed to the next line.

**Example**

```
100 IF X = 1 THEN Y = 1 ELSE Y = 2
200 IF Y = 1 GOTO 999
    .
    .
999 END
```

## INKEY$

■ Cassette
■ Disk
■ Advanced

INKEY$ is used to read a character from the keyboard.

**Configuration**

a$ = INKEY$

The value returned by INKEY$ is a string consisting of either zero, one, or two characters. If no characters are waiting at the keyboard, then the null string will be returned. If a one character string is returned, that string will contain the character read from the keyboard. If a two character string is returned, an extended character code is being returned. The first character is hex 00, followed by the extended character code. The extended character codes are listed in Appendix E.

While the INKEY$ variable is being executed, characters will not be displayed on the screen. However, all characters will be transmitted to the program except for the following:

Ctrl-Break → used to stop the program.
Ctrl-Number → used to send the system into a writing state.
Alt-Ctrl-Del → used to perform a system reset.
Prtsc → used to print the screen.

One character returned by INKEY$ can be assigned to a string variable and used in conjunction with another BASIC statement to check for an operator entry.

**Example**

```
100 PRINT "PRESS X TO CONTINUE";X$
150 X$ = INKEY$
200 IF X$ = "X" GOTO 300 ELSE 150
300 PRINT "CONTINUED"
400 END
```

- Cassette
- Disk
- Advanced

## INP

INP returns the byte read from the port specified by its argument.

**Configuration**

$a = INP(b)$

**Example**

```
100 X = INP(255)
```

## INPUT

■ Cassette
■ Disk
■ Advanced

The INPUT statement permits data entry while the program is being executed.

### Configuration

INPUT ["*prompt*";] *variable* [,*variable*]

*prompt* is a string which is to be displayed on the console before data is accepted from the keyboard. *prompt* is optional, and need not be included in the INPUT statement.

When an INPUT statement is executed, program execution will stop temporarily. A question mark will be displayed on the screen. If *prompt* was included in the INPUT statement, the prompt will be displayed in front of the question mark.

If you do not want the question mark prompt printed, you can eliminate this by using a comma rather than a semicolon after INPUT.

After the INPUT statement has been executed, the user may enter the desired data at the keyboard. That data is assigned to the *variable(s)* listed in the INPUT statement. The number of data items input must equal the number of *variables* listed. Also, the type of data entered must agree with the type specified in *variable*. The data items must be delimited by commas when input.

If the operator enters the wrong number of data items, or the wrong type of data, the following error message will be displayed:

Redo from start

If data is to be entered for just one variable and you wish to enter a null value for a string variable or 0 for a numeric variable, you may do so by pressing Enter.

### Example

```
Ok
100 INPUT "ENTER A NUMBER";A
200 PRINT "THE NUMBER ENTERED IS" A
300 END
RUN
 ENTER A NUMBER? 7.93
 THE NUMBER ENTERED IS 7.93
Ok
```

## INPUT#

- Cassette
- Disk
- Advanced

The INPUT# statement is used to read data items from a sequential file or device and to assign those items to program variables.

### Configuration

INPUT# *filenumber, variable* [*,variable*]...

*filenumber* is the number assigned to the file when it was OPEN'ed. *variable* is the name of the variable that will be assigned a data item from the file.

The data items being read and assigned to the *variable(s)* may either be from a sequential file on diskette or cassette, from a communications adapter, or from the keyboard.

With the INPUT# statement, a prompt (?) is not displayed as with INPUT.

Like the INPUT statement, the type of data being read from the file must agree with the *variable* type.

The data items should appear in the data file just as they would if they were being keyed in as a response to an INPUT prompt.

When numeric items are being read, any leading blank spaces, carriage returns, and line feeds will be disregarded. When a character is encountered that is neither of the above, this character will be regarded as the start of a number. When a blank space, a comma, line feed, or carriage return is encountered, the number will be assumed to have ended.

When string items are being read, again leading blank spaces, carriage returns, and line feeds will be disregarded. When a character is encountered that is neither of the above, this character will be regarded as the start of the string. If the first character is a quotation mark, the string will include all of the characters between that first quotation mark and the next. Note that a quotation mark should not appear within the string itself, as BASIC will interpret this as the end of the string.

If the first character of the string is not a quotation mark, the end of the string will be interpreted as the first comma, carriage return, or line feed encountered.

If the end of file is encountered when either a numeric or sting item is being input, the entry of that item will be ended.

## INPUT$

- Cassette
- Disk
- Advanced

The INPUT$ function returns a string with a length specified in the function which is read from either the keyboard or from a file number specified in the function.

## Configuration

$$a\$ = \text{INPUT}\$(b[,[\#]c])$$

a$ is the string returned by the function. b is the number of characters to be returned. c is the optional file number.

If the keyboard is used for input, characters will not be displayed on the screen. Also, all control characters except Ctrl-Break will be passed through. Ctrl-Break is used to interrupt program execution. The user need not press the Enter key to end his response to INPUT$ when the entry is from the keyboard.

The INPUT$ function is preferred over INPUT# and LINE INPUT# for use with communications files. The INPUT# is the least desirable method of data input from a communications file, as input stops when either a carriage return or comma is encountered. The INPUT$ function allows every character read to be included in the string. Because all ASCII characters may be significant in communications, INPUT# is the preferred method when communications files are being used.

### Example

```
100  PRINT "ENTER END TO EXIT"
200  A$ = INPUT$(3)
300  IF A$ = "END" GOTO 999 ELSE 100
999  END
```

■ Cassette
■ Disk
■ Advanced

## INSTR

The INSTR function searches for the initial appearance of one string within another string. The position where the match occurs is returned by the function.

## Configuration

$a = \text{INSTR}([b,]c\$,d\$)$

*a* is the value returned by the function. *b* is an optional number or numeric expression from 1 to 255. *b* specifies the position within *d$* where the search is to begin.

*c$* is the string to be searched. *c$* may be a string variable, string expression, or string constant. *d$* is the string which is to be searched for. *d$* may be a string variable, string expression, or string constant.

### Example

```
Ok
100 C$ = "ABCDEFG"
200 D$ = "C"
300 PRINT INSTR(C$,D$)
RUN
 3
Ok
```

## INT

- Cassette
- Disk
- Advanced

The INT function returns the integer value of its argument regardless of whether the argument is positive or negative. INT will return the largest integer which is less than or equal to the argument.

### Configuration

$a = \text{INT}(b)$

### Example

Ok
PRINT INT(49.99)
 49
Ok
PRINT INT(-40.01)
 -41
Ok

## KEY

■ Cassette
■ Disk
■ Advanced

The KEY statement is used to either set or display the soft keys.

The soft keys are initialized with the following values:

| | |
|---|---|
| F1 = LIST | F6 = ,"LPT1:" < Enter > |
| F2 = RUN < Enter > | F7 = TRON < Enter > |
| F3 = LOAD" | F8 = TROFF < Enter > |
| F4 = SAVE" | F9 = KEY |
| F5 = CONT < Enter > | F10 = SCREEN 0,0,0 < Enter > |

The KEY ON statement lists the soft key assignments on the 25th line of the screen. If the screen width is 40, 5 of the 10 soft keys will be displayed. If the screen width is 80, all 10 of the soft keys will be displayed. In either the 40 or 80 column widths, the first six characters will be displayed.

The KEY OFF statement erases the display of the soft key assignments on the 25th line of the video display. The KEY OFF statement does not turn off the soft keys.

KEY LIST displays all 15 characters of all 10 soft keys on the screen.

The first configuration,

> KEY *keynum, b$*

is used to assign the string *b$* to the key specified in *keynum*. *b$* may range from 1 to 15 characters. If *b$* is longer than 15 characters, only the first 15 will be recognized.

If a null string is assigned to a soft key, that key will be disabled.

When a soft key is pressed, one character is returned via the INKEY$ function every time the soft key is pressed. When a soft key is pressed that has previously been disabled, INKEY$ will return a two character string with the first character being binary zero and the second the key scan code. The key scan codes are given in Appendix E.

After a soft key has been reassigned, or after the last character has been received via INKEY$ from a soft key string, the following DEF SEG statement should be executed.

DEF SEG:POKE 106,0

This will help avoid problems with the input buffer.

### Examples

```
100 KEY ON
200 KEY OFF
300 KEY 1,"LPRINT"
400 KEY 1," "
```

In the preceding example, program line 100 displays the soft keys in line 25 of the video screen. Line 200 turns off the display. In line 300, "LPRINT" is assigned to soft key 1. In line 400, function key 1 is disabled as a soft key.

In BASIC 2.0, *keynum* can range from 1 to 20, and there are 6 additional definable key traps. These allow the user to trap any Control, Shift, or Super/Shift key. The configuration for these additional key traps is:

KEY *n*, CHR$(*shift*) + CHR$(*scan code*)

*n* is a numeric expression from 15 to 20. *shift* is a numeric value which corresponds to the trapped key. These are as follows:

| | |
|---|---|
| Caps Lock | &H40 |
| Num Lock | &H20 |
| *Shift | &H01, &H02, &H03 |
| Alt | &H08 |
| Ctrl | &H04 |

Multiple shift states can be trapped. The *shift* value must be in hexadecimal notation.

*scan code* is a number from 1 to 83 that identifies the key to be trapped. Appendix F contains a listing of the key scan codes and their associated key postions.

**KEY(a)**

☐ Cassette
☐ Disk
■ Advanced

The KEY(a) statement is used to specify a key which is to be trapped in a BASIC program.

### Configuration

KEY(a) ON
KEY(a) OFF
KEY(a) STOP

*a* is a number or numeric expression from 1 to 14. This number indicates the key which is to be trapped. The following numbers correspond with the keys to be trapped.

---

\* Key trapping assumes the left and right shift keys to be the same. Therefore, &H01, &H02, or &H03 (combination of 01H and 02H) can be used to indicate shift.

1-10   F1 to F10 function keys
11   Cursor Up
12   Cursor Left
13   Cursor Right
14   Cursor Down
15-20   Trapped only in BASIC 2.0. Defined by KEY*n*, CHR$(*shift*) + CHR$(*scan code*)

The KEY(a) ON statement causes the function or cursor control key specified to be trapped. Once a key has been specified with the KEY(a) ON statement, BASIC will check to see if that key was pressed every time a statement is executed. If a line number is specified in an ON KEY(a) statement, BASIC will perform a GOSUB to the line number indicated if it senses that the key specified in KEY(a) ON was pressed.

The KEY(a) OFF statement deactivates the KEY(a) ON statement.

In the KEY(a) STOP statement, no trapping of the specified key actually occurs. However, if the specified key is pressed, that event will be stored in memory. If a KEY(a) ON statement is executed for that key, a trap will occur immediately.

**KILL**

☐ Cassette
■ Disk
■ Advanced

The KILL command is used to delete the file specified from a diskette.

**Configuration**

KILL *filespec*

*filespec* is a file specification. If the file includes a filename extension, that must be included in the *filespec* used with the KILL command. In BASIC 2.0, *filespec* can also be a path.

If the device or drive specifier is not included in *filespec*, then the current disk drive will be assumed.

A file that is open cannot be KILL'ed. If a KILL command is executed for an open file, the following error will occur:

File already open

KILL can only remove a file. RMDIR must be used to remove a directory.

### Example

100 KILL "A:TEXT.DAT"

## LEFT$

- Cassette
- Disk
- Advanced

The LEFT$ function returns the number of characters specified in the second expression of the argument to the leftmost of the string specified in the first part of the argument.

### Configuration

a$ = LEFT(*b$,x*)

a$ is the string returned by the function. *b$* is the string searched by the function. *x* is the number of characters to be returned.

## LEN

- Cassette
- Disk
- Advanced

The LEN function returns the length of the string specified in the expression.

## Configuration

$l$ = LEN(a$)

$l$ is the length of the string. a$ is the string.

## LET

■ Cassette
■ Disk
■ Advanced

The LET statement is an optional keyword often found in an assignment statement. An assignment statement is one that determines the value of an expression and then assigns that result to the variable named in the assignment statement.

### Configuration

LET *variable* = *expression*

The *variable* must be of the same data type as the expression. For example, if *variable* is a string, *expression* must also be a string. If *variable* is an integer or real number, then *expression* must also be numeric.

### Example

```
100 LET A$ = "JOHN"
200 Z = Z + Y
```

## LINE

■ Cassette
■ Disk
■ Advanced

The LINE statement is used only in the graphics mode to draw a line or box on the screen.

## Configuration

LINE [(a1,b1)]-(a2,b2) [,[color][,B[F]][style]

(a1,b1),(a2,b2) are the coordinates.

*color* is the color number from 0 to 3. In medium resolution, *color* chooses the color from the current palette set by the COLOR statement. Color 0 will be used for the background color, and color 3 for the foreground. In high resolution, a *color* of 0 designates black, while a color of 1 indicates white.

B indicates box. BF indicates filled box.

*style* is a 16 bit integer mask used to place points in the screen (BASIC 2.0 only). *style* can be used with boxes and lines but not with filled boxes (BF).

The LINE statement can be used as follows to draw a line:

LINE(0,50)-(319,50)

The first set of coordinates specify the starting and ending coordinates. The foreground color will be used for the line as no value is given for *color*.

The LINE statement can also be used to draw a line where no beginning coordinates are given:

LINE -(319,150)

In such a case, the last point referenced will be used as the starting point.

The color can be specified in the LINE statement as per the following, in which color 1 is specified.

LINE (0,0)-(50,100),1

The optional parameter B (for box) instructs BASIC to draw a rectangle with the points specified in (a1,b1),(a2,b2) as the opposite corners. When F (for filled box) is included with B, the interior points of the rectangle will be filled with the color indicated.

In the preceding example, the LINE statement was used in absolute form. The LINE statement can also be used in relative form. In relative form, the coordinates are given as follows:

LINE (150,150)-STEP(-50,-50)

Here, a line will be drawn from (150,150) to (100,100).

The current bit in *style* is used by LINE to plot points on the screen. If the bit is 1, the point is plotted. If the bit is 0, the point is not plotted, but is skipped over. After each bit causes a point to be plotted or skipped, the next bit is evaluated. When the last bit in *style* is evaluated, LINE will begin again with the first bit.

■ Cassette
■ Disk
## LINE INPUT ■ Advanced

The LINE INPUT statement is a variation of the INPUT statement. The LINE INPUT statement allows an entire line (maximum of 254 characters) to be input to a string variable.

### Configuration

LINE INPUT[;]["*prompt*"] *variable$*

*prompt* is a prompt message that will be displayed on the screen before data can be input.

*variable$* is the string variable that will accept the data being input.

Unlike the INPUT statement, a question mark will not be printed by the LINE INPUT statement.

## LINE INPUT#

- Cassette
- Disk
- Advanced

The LINE INPUT# statement is a variation of the INPUT statement. The LINE INPUT# statement allows an entire line (maximum of 254 characters) to be input from a sequential file to a string variable.

### Configuration

LINE INPUT# *filenumber, variable$*

*filenumber* is the number assigned to a file when it was opened. *variable$* is the string variable that will accept the data being input.

The LINE INPUT# statement is often used in instances where each line in a file has been separated into different fields. LINE INPUT# is also used in situations where a BASIC program saved in ASCII code is read as data by another program.

### Example

```
10 A$ = "Jerry Smith":B$ = "Williams, Dave"
20 OPEN "TEXT.DAT" FOR OUTPUT AS #2
30 PRINT#2,CHR$(34);A$;CHR$(34);CHR$(34);B$;CHR$(34)
40 CLOSE#2
50 OPEN "TEXT.DAT" FOR INPUT AS #2
60 LINE INPUT#2,A$
70 PRINT A$
80 PRINT B$
90 END
RUN
 "Jerry Smith""Williams,Dave"
 Williams, Dave
Ok
```

## LIST

- Cassette
- Disk
- Advanced

The LIST command is used to list the program stored in memory on the video display or another device.

### Configuration

LIST [*line*[-[*line*]]] [,*filespec*]

*line* is a line number. *filespec* is the file specification.

If *filespec* is not included in the LIST command, the *line* indicated will be sent to the screen. If the range given by *lines* is omitted, then the entire program will be listed.

When a dash (-) is used with *lines*, the following possibilities will be available.

1. If only the first *line* is specified, only that line number and any higher line numbers will be listed.
2. If only the second *line* is specified, all of the program lines from the beginning of the program through the *line* named are listed.
3. If both *lines* are included, that range will be listed.

A period (.) can be used to indicate the current line.

Listings being sent to the screen by default can be stopped by pressing Ctrl-Break. Listings being sent to a specified device cannot be terminated with Ctrl-Break.

### Examples

```
LIST
LIST 20,"LPT1:"
LIST 100-200
LIST 50-100,"B:SUB1.BAS"
```

In the first example, the whole program is listed to the screen. In the second, line 20 is listed on the printer. In the third example, lines 100 to 200 are listed to the screen. In the final example, lines 50 through 100 are listed to a file named SUB1.BAS in drive B.

## LLIST

- Cassette
- Disk
- Advanced

LLIST is used to list all or part of the program held in memory to the printer (LPT1:).

### Configuration
LLIST [*line*[-[*line*]]]

*line* is a line number. The use of the *line* ranges for LLIST functions exactly like LIST.

To stop LLIST, you must turn the printer off for 10 seconds. Ctrl-Break will not terminate LLIST.

### Examples
LLIST
LLIST 100
LLIST 110-120
LLIST 130-
LLIST -100

In the first example, LLIST will print a listing of the whole program. In the second, line 100 will be listed on the printer. In the third example, lines 110 through 120 will be listed on the printer. In the fourth example, all lines from 130 to the end of the program will be listed on the printer. In the final example, all lines from the beginning of the program through line 100 are listed.

## LOAD

- Cassette
- Disk
- Advanced

The LOAD command is used to load a program from the device specified into memory. When the R option is specified, the program will execute after it has been loaded.

### Configuration

LOAD *filespec* [,R]

*filespec* is the file specification.

If you are using Cassette BASIC, CAS1: is the only device that can be used. If no device is given in *filespec*, CAS1: is the default device.

If you enter the LOAD command in the direct mode, the filenames on the cassette tape will be displayed on the screen followed by a period and a single letter. These letters indicate the type of file and are as follows:

- B   for BASIC programs created with the SAVE command (in internal format).

- P   for BASIC programs which are protected (created with the SAVE,P command).

- A   for BASIC programs in ASCII format (created with the SAVE,A command).

- M   for memory image files created with the BSAVE command.

- D   for data files created by OPEN followed by output statements.

The filenames on the cassette will be displayed one by one. If the file encountered does not match that named in *filespec*, the following message will be displayed:

> Skipped

If the file on the cassette matches that in *filespec*, the following message will be displayed:

> Found

The LOAD command can be aborted by pressing Ctrl-Break. If this occurs, the search will stop for the named file and BASIC will return to the direct mode.

When the LOAD command is executed within a BASIC program, the filenames are not displayed on the video display.

If the LOAD command is executed when using Disk or Advanced BASIC, a filename extension of .BAS is assumed if no device is given in *filespec*.

**Example**

> LOAD "MENU",R

## LOC

☐ Cassette
■ Disk
■ Advanced

The LOC function returns the current position within the file specified. With a random file, LOC returns the record number of the last number read from or written to that file. With a sequential file, LOC returns the number of records read from or written to the file since it was opened.

**Configuration**

> a = LOC(*filenumber*)

*filenumber* is the number assigned to the file when it was opened.

When LOC is used with a communications file, the function returns the number of characters in the input file waiting to be read.

### Example

100 IF LOC(1) > 100 THEN GOTO 999
:
:
999 END

## LOCATE

- Cassette
- Disk
- Advanced

The LOCATE statement is used to position the cursor on the screen.

### Configuration

LOCATE [*row*][,[*column*][,[*cursor*][,[*start*][,*stop*]]]]

*row* is the line number on the screen (1-25). *column* is the column number on the screen (1-40 or 1-80).

*cursor* is a value which indicates whether the cursor is on or off (0 indicates off, 1 indicates on).

*start* is the starting scan line (0-31). *stop* is the ending scan line (0-31).

Once the cursor is positioned with the LOCATE statement, any succeeding input or output statements to the screen will initially send characters to the position specified by LOCATE.

The optional *start* and *stop* parameters allow the user to regulate the size of the cursor. The size is specified via scan lines. The scan line at the top of the character position is 0. The bottom scan line is 7 when the Color/Graphics Monitor Adapter is installed; 13 with the IBM Monochrome Display and Printer Adapter. If the *start* scan line is specified and *stop* is not, the *stop* will take on the value used for *start*. If *start* is greater than *stop*, then a two part cursor will extend from the bottom line back to the top.

Usually, line 24 on the video display is reserved for messages. However, by using the KEY OFF statement, the user can turn off the soft key display. The LOCATE function can then be used as follows to place information in line 25.

LOCATE 25,1:PRINT...

**Example**

100 LOCATE 1,1

## LOF

☐ Cassette
■ Disk
■ Advanced

The LOF function (length of file) returns the number of bytes which were allotted for a file.

### Configuration (Diskette Files)

a = LOF(*filenumber*)

*filenumber* is the number assigned to the file when it was opened.

When LOF is used with diskette files in BASIC 1.0, the value returned by the function will be a multiple of 128. For example, if the actual number of bytes contained in a file were 244, the number returned by LOF would be 256 (128 x 2).

When LOF is used with files created under BASIC 2.0 or outside

BASIC, LOF will return the actual number of bytes allocated to the files.

LOF can also be used in communications to return the amount of free space in the input buffer.

**Example**

A = LOF(1)

## LOG

■ Cassette
■ Disk
■ Advanced

The LOG function returns the natural logarithm of its argument.

**Configuration**

a = LOG(*b*)

**Example**

Ok
PRINT LOG(15)
 2.70805
Ok

## LPOS

■ Cassette
■ Disk
■ Advanced

LPOS returns as its argument, the position of the printhead within the printer buffer. This is not necessarily the physical position of the printhead on the printer.

**Configuration**

a = LPOS(*b*)

In Cassette BASIC, *b* is a dummy argument. In Disk and Advanced BASIC, *b* specifies which printer is to be tested. The following are used:

     0 or 1  LPT1:
      2   LPT2:
      3   LPT3:

### Example
100 IF LPOS(1) > 80 GOTO 900

## LPRINT

- Cassette
- Disk
- Advanced

LPRINT is used to output data to the printer.

### Configuration

LPRINT [*data*][,]...

*data* includes the string or numeric expressions to be printed. These may be separated by either commas or semicolons.

The LPRINT statement functions exactly like PRINT except that it sends data to the printer. LPRINT assumes the printer width to be 80 characters. This value may be changed with a WIDTH "LPT1:" statement.

### Example

```
Ok
100 FOR I = 1 TO 3
200 LPRINT "CUSTOMER";I
300 NEXT I
RUN
 CUSTOMER 1
 CUSTOMER 2
 CUSTOMER 3
```

## LPRINT USING

■ Cassette
■ Disk
■ Advanced

LPRINT USING is used to send data to the printer.

### Configuration

LPRINT USING *format$; data* [,]

*format$* is a string constant or string variable which consists of special formatting characters. These are described in the PRINT USING statement section.

*data* includes the string or numeric expressions to be printed. These may be separated by either commas or semicolons.

The LPRINT USING statement functions exactly like PRINT USING except that it sends data to the printer. LPRINT assumes the printer width to be 80 characters. This value may be changed with a WIDTH "LPT1:" statement.

### Example

```
Ok
LPRINT USING "##.##";.59
 0.59
Ok
```

## LSET, RSET

□ Cassette
■ Disk
■ Advanced

LSET and RSET are used to move data from memory to a random file buffer. LSET and RSET are generally used prior to a PUT statement.

**Configuration**

LSET variable$ = x$
RSET variable$ = x$

variable$ is a string variable to be used for random file access.

In some cases, the string returned by LSET or RSET (x$) will require a fewer number of bytes than the amount reserved by the FIELD statement. In these situations, RSET will right-justify that string and LSET will left-justify it. Blank spaces will be used to fill the excess positions.

If x$ is longer than the space reserved by FIELD, then the extra characters are deleted from the right.

Numeric values must first be converted to strings via the MKI$, MKS$, or MKD$ functions before they can be used with LSET or RSET.

**Example**

100  RSET Z$ = MKS$(TOTAL)

## MERGE

■ Cassette
■ Disk
■ Advanced

The MERGE statement is used to merge program lines from an ASCII program file to the program currently held in memory.

**Configuration**

MERGE filespec

filespec is the file specification.

When the MERGE statement is executed, the device specified will be searched for the file specified. In Cassette BASIC, the default value for device is CAS1: (the only device allowed with the MERGE statement in Cassette BASIC). In Disk and Advanced BASIC, the default for the device name is the current drive.

When the specified file is located, the program lines in that file will be merged with the program in memory. If any of the lines in the file specified in the MERGE statement have the same line number as lines in the program in memory, the lines from the file being merged will replace those in memory.

Once the MERGE statement has finished executing, the resulting file will be held in memory, and program control will return to command level.

The program being merged must have been saved in ASCII format. This is accomplished by using the SAVE command with the A option. If the file being merged was not saved in ASCII format, the following error will occur,

Bad file mode

and the program in memory will not be altered.

**Example**

MERGE "B:PROGRAM2.BAS"

## MID$
■ Cassette
■ Disk
■ Advanced

When used as a function, MID$ returns a part of a string as specified by its arguments. When used as a statement, MID$ will replace a part of one string with another string.

**Configuration (Function)**

a$ = MID$(b$,c[,d])

*a$* is the string returned by the function. *b$* is the string from which *a$* is being returned. *c* is the beginning character in *b$* from which *a$* is to be returned. *d* is the number of characters to be returned in *a$* from *b$*. If *d* is not included, all characters to the right of *c* will be returned.

### Configuration (Statement)

MID$(*b$*,*c*[,*d*]) = *a$*

When used as a statement, MID$ replaces the characters in *b$* with those in *a$*, beginning at position *c*. The optional value *d* gives the number of characters from *a$* which will be used. If *d* is not included, all of *a$* will be used.

When MID$ is used as a statement to replace characters in *b$*, the length of *b$* will not change. For example, if *b$* consists of seven characters and *a$* consists of nine characters, the length of *b$* will remain at seven characters.

### Example (Function)

```
Ok
100  A$ = "ANNETTE"
200  PRINT MID$(A$,3,3)
RUN
NET
Ok
```

### Example (Statement)

```
Ok
100  A$ = "PHILADELPHIA"
200  MID$(A$,6,7) = "NTHROPY"
300  PRINT A$
RUN
PHILANTHROPY
Ok
```

## MKDIR

☐ Cassette
■ Disk
■ Advanced

MKDIR is used only in BASIC 2.0 to create a directory on the indicated diskette.

### Configuration

MKDIR *path*

### Example

MKDIR "ACCT\INV"

In the preceding example, the sub-directory INV is created under the directory ACCT.

## MKI$, MKS$, MKD$

☐ Cassette
■ Disk
■ Advanced

MKI$, MKS$, and MKD$ are used to convert numeric values to string values.

### Configuration

a$ = MKI$(*integer*)
a$ = MKS$(*single precision*)
a$ = MKD$(*double precision*)

a$ is the string value returned by the function. *integer* is an integer or an expression that evaluates to an integer.

*single precision* is a single precision number or an expression that evaluates to a single precision number. *double precision* is a double precision number or one that evaluates to a double precision number.

MKI$ converts an integer to a 2-byte string. MKS$ converts a single precision number to a 4-byte string. MKD$ converts a double precision number to an 8-byte string.

MKI$, MKS$, and MKD$ are often used to convert numeric values to string values before placing them in a random file buffer with LSET or RSET.

Refer to page 148 for an example of the use of MKI$, MKS$, and MKD$.

## MOTOR

■ Cassette
■ Disk
■ Advanced

The MOTOR statement is used to turn on or turn off the cassette player from within a program.

### Configuration

MOTOR [*condition*]

*condition* is a value which determines whether the motor will be on or off. A value of zero for *condition* turns off the motor. A non-zero value turns it on. If no *condition* is given, the motor will be switched to its opposite state. That is, if the motor was on, it will be off, and vice versa.

## NAME

□ Cassette
■ Disk
■ Advanced

The NAME command is used to change a diskette file's name.

### Configuration

NAME *filespec* AS *filename*

*filespec* is the file specification of the file whose name is to be changed. *filename* is the new filename.

In the following example, a file named TEXT.DAT on drive B will be renamed as FILE1.DAT.

**Example**

100 NAME "B:TEXT.DAT" AS "FILE1.DAT"

**NEW**
- Cassette
- Disk
- Advanced

The NEW command erases the program currently stored in memory and clears all variables.

**Configuration**

NEW

The NEW command is usually executed to free memory space before a new program is entered. All files will be closed when the NEW command is executed. After the NEW command has been executed, program control will return to the command level.

**OCT$**
- Cassette
- Disk
- Advanced

OCT$ is a function which returns the octal value of its argument (which is in decimal).

**Configuration**

a$ = OCT$(*b*)

*b* is a decimal argument. *b* is converted to an integer before conversion to octal is effected.

**Example**

Ok
PRINT OCT$(32)
   40
Ok

## ON COM

☐ Cassette
☐ Disk
■ Advanced

The ON COM statement is used to set up a line number which is to be trapped by BASIC when data is transmitted into the communications buffer.

**Configuration**

ON COM(a) GOSUB *line*

*a* is the number identifying the communications adapter (1 or 2). *line* is the line number where a GOSUB will execute to if any characters have come into the communications buffer. If zero is used for *line*, the trapping of communications activity will be discontinued.

Before an ON COM statement can be executed, a COM ON statement must have been previously executed for the same communications adapter (specified in *n*). Once a COM ON statement has been executed and if a non-zero line number was used in ON COM, BASIC will check the communications adapter named before executing every statement to see if any data has been received. If so, a GOSUB will be executed to the *line* given.

If a COM OFF statement had been executed, no trapping will occur for the adapter.

If a COM STOP statement had been executed, no trapping will occur for the adapter. However, unlike the COM OFF statement, if a character is received by the adapter, this event is remembered. When a COM ON statement is executed, an immediate trap will occur.

When a character is received while the COM ON and ON COM statements are executing, and program control branches to a subroutine, a COM STOP statement is executed to prevent additional data being received from causing additional traps.

When a RETURN statement is executed in the subroutine, a COM ON statement will be automatically executed.

It is not a good idea to use the communications trap for single character messages. In these situations with high baud rates, the trapping and reading of every single character may result in an overflow of the interrupt buffer for communications.

Generally, the communications trap routine is used to read an entire message from the communications line.

### Example

```
100  ON COM(1) GOSUB 900
      .
      .
      .
900  REM COMMUNICATIONS ROUTINE
      .
      .
      .
950  RETURN
```

## ON ERROR

- Cassette
- Disk
- Advanced

The ON ERROR statement allows errors to be trapped and transfers program control to an error handling routine.

### Configuration

### ON ERROR GOTO *line*

*line* is a program line number.

Once the ON ERROR statement has been effected, when an error is detected, program control will branch to the specified *line*.

To disable error trapping, use zero (0) for *line*. Any future errors will result in the error code being printed and program execution being stopped.

If an ON ERROR statement with a line of zero (0) is used in the error routine itself, execution will stop and the error message for the error causing the trap will be printed.

It is good programming practice to include the following,

### ON ERROR GOTO 0

in error trapping routines where there is no recovery procedure for that error. As discussed previously, the error message for that error will print.

Error trapping does not occur within the error handling subroutines themselves.

Refer to page 225 for an example of the use of ON ERROR.

## ON...GOSUB, ON...GOTO

- Cassette
- Disk
- Advanced

The ON...GOSUB and ON...GOTO statements are used to branch program control to one of several line numbers depending on the value appearing after ON.

## Configurations

ON a GOTO *line* [,*line*]...
ON a GOSUB *line* [,*line*]...

The value of *a* controls which *line* is to be branched to. For instance, if *a* evaluates to 1, program control will branch to the line number given in the first *line*. If *a* evaluates to 2, program control will branch to the second *line*, etc.

If the ON...GOSUB statement is being used, the line number specified in *line* must be that of a subroutine. In other words, a RETURN statement eventually will have to be executed to return program control to the main routine.

If *a* evaluates to zero or to a number greater than the number of *lines* specified after GOTO or GOSUB, then the program will continue with the next executable statement.

### Example

100 ON X GOSUB 200,300,400

## ON KEY

☐ Cassette
☐ Disk
■ Advanced

The ON KEY statement specifies the line number of a subroutine to be branched to when the specified control or function key is pressed.

### Configuration

ON KEY(a) GOSUB *line*

*a* is a number or numeric expression between 1 and 20 which indicates the key which when pressed will cause the branch in program control. These keys are as follows:

| | |
|---|---|
| 1-10 | Function keys F1 through F10 |
| 11 | Cursor Up |
| 12 | Cursor Left |
| 13 | Cursor Right |
| 14 | Cursor Down |
| 15-20 | (BASIC 2.0) Keys defined by KEY*n*, CHR$ (*shift*) + CHR$(*scan code*) |

A KEY ON statement must have been executed prior to the ON KEY statement. Once KEY ON has been executed, an ON KEY statement can be executed. This will result in BASIC checking to see if the function key specified in ON KEY was pressed before the execution of every statement. If that key was pressed, a GOSUB to the indicated line will be executed.

If a KEY OFF statement was executed, the ON KEY statement will no longer have any effect.

If a KEY STOP statement was executed, the key specified in ON KEY will not cause a branch to the indicated subroutine. However, if that key is pressed, the event will be remembered. If a KEY ON statement is subsequently executed, a branch to the *line* indicated in ON KEY will immediately be executed.

If the key specified in ON KEY is pressed while the KEY ON is on, a KEY STOP will be executed. This will prevent the pressing of the specified key a second time from having any immediate effect. Once the RETURN statement in the subroutine has been executed, the KEY OFF statement will be executed as well.

### Example

100  ON KEY(7) GOSUB 900

## ON PEN

☐ Cassette
☐ Disk
■ Advanced

The ON PEN statement transfers control to a specified subroutine when the light pen is activated.

### Configuration

ON PEN GOSUB *line*

*line* is the line number of the subroutine to be branched to. If a *line* of zero is specified, the ON PEN statement will have no effect.

A PEN ON statement must have been executed for the ON PEN statement to have an effect. If a PEN ON statement has been executed, BASIC will check to see if the light pen was turned on before it executes every statement. If so, the ON PEN statement will execute a GOSUB to the *line* indicated.

If the PEN OFF statement had been executed, then the ON PEN statement will have no effect.

If a PEN STOP statement had been executed, then the occurrence of turning on the light pen will be remembered. When a PEN ON statement is executed, a GOSUB to the *line* specified in the ON PEN statement will be executed.

When the pen is turned on with the PEN ON statement in effect, a PEN STOP statement will be executed immediately. Once a RETURN statement in the subroutine being branched to is executed, a PEN ON will be executed.

### Example

100 ON PEN GOSUB 900

## ON PLAY

☐ Cassette
☐ Disk
■ Advanced

This statement is used in BASIC 2.0 only to play continuous background music during program execution.

### Configuration

ON PLAY(n) GOSUB *line*

*n* is an integer expression from 1 to 32 which indicates the notes to be trapped.

*line* is the beginning line number of PLAY's trap routine. A *line* of 0 stops trapping.

A PLAY ON statement must have been used to begin the ON PLAY routine. Once PLAY ON has been executed, if a non-zero *line* was specified, BASIC will check the music buffer to see if it has gone from *n* to *n* − 1 notes every time a new statement is executed. If this has occurred, a GOSUB will be executed to the indicated lines.

PLAY OFF ends trapping. PLAY STOP halts trapping until PLAY ON is executed.

## ON STRIG

☐ Cassette
☐ Disk
■ Advanced

The ON STRIG statement specifies the line of a subroutine to be branched to if one of the joysticks is pressed.

### Configuration

ON STRIG (a) GOSUB *line*

a is 0 for the first joystick and 2 for the second. *line* is the line number of the subroutine to be branched to. If 0 is specified for *line*, the ON STRIG statement will be disabled.

A STRIG ON statement for the joystick indicated must have been executed for the ON STRIG statement to execute. If so, BASIC will check to see if the specified joystick had been pressed before executing each new statement. If it has, a GOSUB to the *line* indicated will be executed.

If a STRIG OFF statement had been executed, then pressing the joystick will have no effect.

If a STRIG STOP statement had been executed, then pressing the joystick button will not have an immediate effect. However, if the joystick is pressed, that event will be remembered. If a STRIG ON statement is later executed, a branch to the indicated *line* will be effected.

If a joystick is pressed with STRIG ON and ON STRIG executing, a STRIG STOP statement will be immediately executed. This prevents any further pressing of the joystick from having an immediate effect. However, if a RETURN statement is executed in the subroutine, a STRIG ON statement will be executed.

### Example

100 ON STRIG GOSUB 900

## ON TIMER

☐ Cassette
☐ Disk
■ Advanced

This statement transfers control to the specified line number when a specific period of time has elapsed.

### Configuration

ON TIMER (*n*) GOSUB *line*

*n* is a numeric expression in the range 1-86,400. *line* is the initial line number for the ON TIMER statement trap routine. If a *line* of zero is indicated, timer trapping will be ended.

TIMER ON must have been executed prior to the ON TIMER statement to begin trapping. ON TIMER instructs BASIC to count the passing seconds. When *n* seconds have been counted, a GOSUB will be executed to the *line* specified. BASIC then begins counting again from 0.

TIMER OFF ends trapping. TIMER STOP halts trapping until a TIMER ON is executed.

## OPEN

■ Cassette
■ Disk
■ Advanced

The OPEN statement allows input and output to the specified file.

### Configuration 1

OPEN *filespec* [FOR *mode*] AS [#] *filenumber* [LEN = *rcdlength*]

*filespec* is the file specification or path. *mode* can be any one of the following:

    INPUT  for sequential input mode.

    OUTPUT  for sequential output mode.

    APPEND  for sequential output mode where the file is positioned to the end of the data file when that file is opened. If the specified file does not exist, the APPEND causes that file to be created for the sequential output mode and positioned to its beginning. APPEND may only be used with diskette files.

In cases where *mode* is not included, random access will be assumed.

*filenumber* is an integer or integer expression with a value between 1 and the maximum allowable number of files. In Cassette BASIC, this maximum is 4. In Disk and Advanced BASIC, this maximum is 3, however it can be altered with the F: option in the BASIC command. *filenumber* is used in subsequent statements and commands for file identification purposes.

*rcdlength* is an integer or integer expression which initializes the record length for random files. *rcdlength* may range from 1 to 32767. However, *rcdlength* may not be greater than the number specified in the /S: option in the BASIC command. The default value for *rcdlength* is 128 bytes. In BASIC 2.0, *rcdlength* can be used for sequential files, while this is not the case in earlier versions.

### Configuration 2

OPEN *altmode*, [#] *filenumber*, *filespec* [,*rcdlength*]

*altmode* is a string or string expression with one of the following as its first character.

    O   indicates sequential output mode.
    I    indicates sequential input mode.
    R   indicates random input/output mode.

The OPEN statement reserves an input/output buffer for a file or device. The OPEN statement also specifies the mode of access to that buffer.

An OPEN statement must have been executed for a file or device before any input/output statements can be executed for that device. These include the following:

| GET | PRINT# |
| INPUT$ | PRINT USING# |
| INPUT# | PUT |
| LINE INPUT# | WRITE# |

In IBM BASIC, the same file may be open under more than one file number. This allows the same file to be open under differing modes of access.

In Cassette BASIC, the default value for the device is CAS1:. In Disk or Advanced BASIC, the current drive is the default value for the device.

### Example

```
100 OPEN "TEXT.DAT" FOR INPUT AS #1
200 OPEN "O",#1,"FILEA"
```

## OPEN COM

☐ Cassette
■ Disk
■ Advanced

The OPEN COM statement is used to open a communications file.

### Configuration

OPEN "COM*a*: [*speed*][*parity*][,*data*][,*stop*][,RS][,CS[*n*]][,CD[*n*]][,LF][,PE]" AS [#] *filenum* [LEN = *number*]

*a* indicates the number of the communications adapter (1 or 2).

*speed* is an integer constant which indicates the transmit/receive rate in bits per second (bps). *speeds* that can be used include 75, 110, 150, 300, 600, 1200, 1800, 2400, 4800, and 9600. The default value is 300 bps.

*parity* is a one character constant which specifies the parity for transmitting and receiving. These are as follows:

S   for SPACE. The parity bit is transmitted and received as the space (0) bit.

O   for ODD. Odd transmit and odd receive parity checking.

M   for MARK. The parity bit is transmitted and received as a mark (1 bit).
E   for EVEN. Even is used for transmission parity, and even receive parity checking.
N   for NONE. No transmit parity, and no receive parity checking.

The default value is EVEN (E).

*data* is an integer constant which specifies the number of transmit/receive data bits. The following values can be used:

4, 5, 6, 7, and 8

The default value is 7.

*stop* is an integer constant that specifies the number of stop bits. Either 1 or 2 are valid. The default values are as follows:

2   75 and 110 bps
1   for all others

*filenumber* is an integer or integer expression that indicates a valid file number.

*number* is the maximum number of bytes that can be read from the communications buffer when a GET or PUT is executed. The default is 128.

RS suppresses RTS (Request To Send). CS[n] controls CTS (Clear To Send). DS[n] controls DSR (Data Set Ready). CD[n] controls CD (Carrier Detect). LF sends a line feed after each carriage return. PE enables parity checking.

The *n* following CS, DS, and CD indicates the number of milliseconds that the statement will wait for the signal before a "Device timeout" error occurs. *n* can range from 0 to 65535. If *n* is not specified or set equal to zero, the line status is not checked. The defaults are CS1000 and CD0.

Generally, if CS or DS are off, the communications attempt will not be successful.

Generally, CD (Carrier Detect) is disregarded by an OPEN COM statement. By specifying the parameter *n* with CD, the CD option allows the Carrier Detect test to occur.

The LF parameter automatically sends the line feed character (0AH) after each carriage return character (0CH). LF allows communications files to be printed via a serial printer.

The PE parameter enables parity checking. When PE is specified, a "Device I/O" error will occur upon parity errors. If a parity error occurs, the high order bit will be turned on for 7 or fewer data bits.

The OPEN COM statement reserves a buffer for input and output to communications files. The OPEN COM statement allows RS232 asynchronous communication with other computers and peripherals. A communications device may only be open to one file number at any one time.

If 8 bits are indicated, parity N must be specified. If 4 data bits are indicated, a parity other than N must be specified. When numeric data is being transmitted or received, 8 data bits must be specified.

**Example**

100 OPEN "COM1:1200,N,8" AS #2

## OPTION BASE

- Cassette
- Disk
- Advanced

The OPTION BASE statement is used to specify a minimum value for array subscripts.

## Configuration

OPTION BASE a

a is a default base of 1 or 0. The default for OPTION BASE is 0.

### Example

100 OPTION BASE 1

## OUT

- Cassette
- Disk
- Advanced

The OUT statement is used to send a byte to a machine output port.

### Configuration

OUT a, b

a is the port number. b is the data to be transmitted.

The OUT statement is used to adjust the video output of devices connected to the Color/Graphics Adapter board. In the following example, the display will be shifted 5 characters to the right (assuming an 80 column width).

### Example

OUT 980,2:OUT 981,85

## PAINT

- ☐ Cassette
- ☐ Disk
- Advanced

The PAINT statement is used in the graphics mode of Advanced BASIC to place color in a specified area of the screen.

### Configuration

PAINT (a,b)[[,color][,boundary][,background]

(a,b) are the coordinates of a point within the area to be colored in. These coordinates may be specified in absolute or relative form.

*color* is the color to be used (0 to 3). In medium resolution, zero is the background color. Color 3 is the default which is the foreground color. In high resolution, zero indicates black and 1 indicates white. If *color* is a string expression, tiling (see Chapter 8) is performed.

*boundary* is the color of the edges of the form to be colored in (0 to 3).

*background* is a one byte string expression used in tiling (BASIC 2.0 only).

The figure with edges of the boundary color is filled in with the color specified.

The (a,b) coordinates for PAINT must be inside the form to be PAINT'ed. If the optional *color* is not included, the foreground color will be used.

If a complex form is to be PAINT'ed, a large amount of stack space may be required by the PAINT statement. It may be a good idea in such applications to execute a CLEAR command at the beginning of the program to increase the amount of available stack space.

PAINT is discussed in detail in Chapter 8.

## PEEK

■ Cassette
■ Disk
■ Advanced

The PEEK function will return the byte read from the memory location specified as its argument.

### Configuration

a = PEEK(b)

a is the value returned by the function. a must be an integer from 0 to 255.

b is the offset from the current segment as defined in the DEF SEG statement.

### Example

100 IF PEEK(&H50) = THEN GOSUB 900

## PEN

■ Cassette
■ Disk
■ Advanced

The PEN statement and function are used to read the light pen.

### Configurations

PEN ON
PEN OFF
PEN STOP
a = PEN(b)

a is the integer returned by PEN. b is a number or numeric constant which returns an integer from 0 to 9. These are as follows.

0   a flag which specifies whether the pen was down since the last pull (−1 indicates down; 0 indicates not down).
1   gives the x coordinate where the pen was last utilized. X can range from 0 to 319 in medium resolution and from 0 to 639 in high resolution.
2   gives the y coordinate where the pen was last utilized. Y can range from 0 to 199.
3   gives the current pen switch value (−1 indicates down; 0 indicates up).
4   gives the last known valid x coordinate.
5   gives the last known valid y coordinate.
6   gives the character row position where the pen was last utilized (1 to 24).
7   gives the character column position where the pen was last utilized (1 to 40 or 1 to 80).
8   gives the last known valid character row (1 to 24)
9   gives the last known valid character column position (1 to 40 or 1 to 80).

The PEN ON statement must be executed before any of the PEN functions can be used. Initially, the PEN function is off. Therefore, a PEN ON statement must be executed before PEN functions can be executed.

As explained in the ON PEN statement section, the PEN ON statement must be executed for trapping to occur with the ON PEN statement.

The PEN STOP statement is only used in Advanced BASIC. The PEN STOP statement remembers light pen activity so that the event is immediately trapped upon execution of a subsequent PEN ON statement.

### Example

```
100 PEN ON
200 X = PEN(2)
300 PRINT X
400 PEN OFF
500 END
```

## PLAY

■ Cassette
■ Disk
■ Advanced

The PLAY statement is used to play music.

### Configuration

PLAY *music$*

*music$* is a string constant or string expression consisting of music commands. These are as follows.

A-G {#, +, -}  The note given is played. # or + after the note means sharp, while - means flat.

Lx  This is used to set the length of each note. L1 indicates a whole note; L2 a half note; L4 a quarter note; L16 a sixteenth note, etc...*x* may range from 1 to 64.

If you wish to change the length for only one note, you can do so by placing the length directly after the letter for the note (ex. A4 would be a quarter note A).

MF  This causes music to run in the foreground. Each note or sound will not begin to play until the preceding note or sound has finished playing. MF (music foreground) is the default value.

MB  This causes music to play in the background. Each note or sound is placed in a buffer. This allows the BASIC program to continue execution as music plays in the background. As many as 32 notes can be played in the background at any one time.

MN or music normal, results in every note being played at 7/8th of the value given in L (length).

ML or music legato. This causes each note to be played at the entire length specified in L.

MS or music staccato. This causes each note to be played at ¾ of the time specified in L.

N*a* is used to play the note specified in *a*, where *a* can range from 0 to 84. Since there are 7 octaves available, there are 84 notes available. If *a* is 0, a rest is indicated.

O*b* is used to set the current octave. Seven octaves are available. These are numbered from 0 to 6. Each octave extends from C to B. Octave 3 begins with middle C.

P*c* is used to indicate a pause. The length of the pause (as given in *c*), may range from 1 to 64 and is calculated as in L (length).

T*d* is used to indicate the tempo. Tempo is defined by the number of quarter notes per second. *d* may range from 32 to 255. The default value for *d* is 120.

*string* causes execution of the specified *string*.

. A period following a note causes it to be played as a dotted note (the note's length is multiplied by 1.5). More than one period may follow a note. If more than one period does follow a note, it's length will be adjusted as indicated. For instance, "A..." will play 3.37 times as long as "A". Periods may also follow a pause to lengthen it in the same manner.

< X is used to play the note given in X in the next higher octave. Each time the note specified is played, the next higher octave is used, until octave 6 is attained. (BASIC 2.0 only.)

> X functions as does > X. Each note is played in the next lower octave. (BASIC 2.0 only.)

## PLAY Function

☐ Cassette
☐ Disk
■ Advanced

The PLAY function returns the number of notes in the music background buffer (BASIC 2.0 only).

### Configuration

$x = \text{PLAY}(z)$

z is a dummy argument. This function only returns a value when the Music Background (MB) mode is active.

## PMAP

☐ Cassette
☐ Disk
■ Advanced

PMAP is available in BASIC 2.0 graphics mode only and is used to map physical to world coordinates or vice versa.

### Configuration

$A = \text{PMAP}(m, z)$

m is the coordinate to be mapped. z may assume a value of 0 to 3. A value of 0 maps the world coordinate x to the physical coordinate x. A value of 1 maps the world coordinate y to the physical coordinate y. A value of 2 maps the physical coordinate x to the world coordinate x. A value of 3 maps the physical coordinate y to the world coordinate y.

The world system is defined by the WINDOW statement, and the physical coordinate system is defined by the VIEW statement.

PMAP (m,0) and PMAP (m,1) are used to map indices from the world to the physical coordinate system. PMAP (m, 2) and PMAP (m, 3) are used to map indices from the physical to the world coordinate system.

For example, if the following statements were executed:

SCREEN 2: WINDOW (-1, -1) - (1, 1)

PMAP (-1, 0) would return the physical x coordinate value for the world coordinate -1. This would be 0.

PMAP (-1, 1) would return the physical y coordinate value for the world coordinate -1. This would be 199.

PMAP (1, 0) would return the physical x coordinate value for the world coordinate value of 1. This would be 639.

PMAP (1, 1) would return the physical y coordinate value for the world coordinate 1. This would be 0.

Note in the preceding example that SCREEN 2 is specified. This example shows us that the world coordinate (-1, -1) corresponds to the physical coordinate (0,199). This is the screen's lower left-hand corner. The upper right hand corner corresponds to (1, 1) in world coordinates and (639,0) in physical coordinates.

## POINT

- Cassette
- Disk
- Advanced

The POINT function returns the color of the point on the screen indicated as its argument. The POINT function is only used in the graphics mode.

### Configuration

$c = POINT(a,b)$

c is the color value returned by the function. a,b are the coordinates of the point to be used as the argument. If the point specified is out of range, the value returned is −1.

### Example

100 IF POINT(100,100) = 1 THEN GOTO 900

The POINT function can also be used with the following configuration in BASIC 2.0 to return the value of the current x or y graphics coordinate.

### Configuration

c = POINT(z)

z can have a value of 0 to 3. A value of 0 returns the current physical x coordinate. A value of 1 returns the current physical y coordinate. A value of 2 returns the current world x coordinate if WINDOW is active. If not, the physical x coordinate is returned. A value of 3 returns the current world y coordinate if WINDOW is active. If not, the current physical y coordinate is returned.

## POKE

- Cassette
- Disk
- Advanced

The POKE statement is used to write a byte to a specified address in memory.

### Configuration

POKE a,b

a is an address memory in the range of 0 to 65535. a is given as an offset from the current segment as given in the DEF SEG segment. b is the data to be written to the memory location specified in a. b can range from 0 to 255.

### Example

100 POKE 200,13

## POS

■ Cassette
■ Disk
■ Advanced

The POS function returns the present column position of the cursor.

### Configuration

a = POS(*b*)

*a* is the cursor column position. *b* is a dummy argument.

### Example

100 IF POS(0) > 40 THEN PRINT CHR$(13)

## PRINT

■ Cassette
■ Disk
■ Advanced

The PRINT statement is used to display data on the screen.

### Configuration

PRINT [*expressions*][;]
? [*expressions*][;]

If the optional *expressions* is omitted, a blank line will be displayed on the video screen. If *expressions* are included, these will be displayed on the screen. These *expressions* may be either numeric or string.

The position on the screen where each item is displayed is determined by the punctuation mark used to separate the items in *expressions*. Each display line is divided into print zones of 14 spaces each. A comma causes the next item encountered in *expressions* to be printed at the beginning of the next print zone.

A semicolon causes the next item to be printed immediately following the preceding value. If one or more blank spaces is used to separate the items in *expressions,* the effect will be the same as using a semicolon.

If the last item in *expressions* is ended with a semicolon, the next PRINT statement will begin printing on the same line as the last PRINT statement immediately following the last item.

If a comma is used to end the list of items in *expressions,* the next PRINT statement will again print on the same line. However, that item will be printed at the next print zone.

If neither a comma nor a semicolon ends the items in *expressions,* a carriage return will be executed before the next item is printed.

When numbers are PRINT'ed to the screen, they are always followed by a blank space.

**Configuration**

```
Ok
100  A$ = "ABC"
200  B$ = "DEF"
300  C = 5
400  PRINT A$;B$,C,C
500  END
RUN
ABCDEF         5           5
Ok
```

■ Cassette
■ Disk
## PRINT USING
■ Advanced

The PRINT USING statement is used to print string or numeric data in a pre-defined format.

### Configuration

PRINT USING *format$; expressions* [;]

*format$* is a string constant or variable consisting of the formatting characters. These are explained in Chapter 3.

*expressions* consist of the string or numeric items that are to be printed. Each item in *expressions* must be separated with commas or semicolons.

## PRINT#, PRINT# USING

- Cassette
- Disk
- Advanced

The PRINT# and PRINT# USING statements are used to write data to a file sequentially.

### Configuration

PRINT# *filenumber,* [USING *format$;*] *expressions*

*filenumber* is the number assigned to the file when it was opened.

*format$* is a string constant or expression consisting of special formatting characters. These were explained in Chapter 3.

*expressions* is one or more numeric and/or string items that are to be written to the file specified.

The PRINT# statement can also be used with the optional reserved word USING to print data to the file in a format specified by a format string.

## PSET & PRESET

■ Cassette
■ Disk
■ Advanced

PSET and PRESET are only used in the graphics mode. These statements are used to draw a point at a given screen location.

### Configuration

PSET (a,b) [,color]
PRESET (a,b) [,color]

a,b are the screen coordinates of the point to be set. These may be specified in either absolute or relative form.

color is the color to be used (0 to 3). If the optional color is not included in the PSET statement, the foreground color will be used (3 in medium resolution; 1 in high resolution). If color is not specified in PRESET, the background color (0) will be used. If color is specified, PRESET and PSET work in an identical fashion.

### Example

300 PSET(100,100),2

## PUT (Files)

□ Cassette
■ Disk
■ Advanced

The PUT statement is used to write a record from a random buffer to a random file.

### Configuration

PUT [#] *filenumber* [,*rcdnumber*]

*filenumber* is the number assigned to the file when it was opened.

*rcdnumber* is the record number of the record to be written. If *rcdnumber* is not included, the next available record (after the last PUT) will be used. When PUT is used with communications files, *rcdnumber* is used to designate the number of bytes to be written to the communications file.

**Example**

500  PUT#1,X%


## PUT (Graphics)

☐ Cassette
☐ Disk
■ Advanced

The following configuration of the PUT statement is used only in the graphics mode to write colors to a specified area on the screen.

**Configuration**

PUT (*a1,b1*) array [,*operation*]

*a1,b1* are the coordinates of the top left hand corner of the area to be transferred. *array* stands for a numeric array which contains the data to be transferred. *operation* stands for one of the following:

> PSET
> PRESET
> XOR (The default value)
> OR
> AND

The PUT statement when used in the graphics mode takes data out of the specified *array* and places it onto the video screen.

The optional *operation* provides a means whereby the data being transferred can be used in conjunction with existing data to gain some sort of special effect.

If PSET is used as the *operation,* the data from the *array* is stored on the screen. PRESET functions like PSET except that it forms a negative image.

AND is sometimes used as the *operation* in cases where an image is already in place beneath the image to be transferred. AND is used to transfer the image only.

OR is used to overlay the image specified in PUT over an image already in place.

XOR is used for animation purposes. When used with XOR the PUT statement can be used to move an object over a background without erasing it.

Examples of programs utilizing the PUT statement are included in Chapter 8.

## RANDOMIZE

■ Cassette
■ Disk
■ Advanced

The RANDOMIZE statement is used to reset the seed of the random number generator.

### Configuration

RANDOMIZE [a]
RANDOMIZE TIMER

a is the new seed. If a is omitted, the user will be prompted to enter the new seed.

If a seed is not specified, RANDOMIZE will prompt the operator to enter one. In BASIC 2.0, by specifying the TIMER function with RANDOMIZE, a new seed will be generated without the operator prompt.

## READ

- Cassette
- Disk
- Advanced

The READ statement is used to read items from the DATA statement and assign these items to the variables specified in the READ statement.

### Configuration

READ variable [,variable]

variable may be either numeric or string. The variable type must agree with the data type being read.

READ statements are always used in combination with DATA statements. The items in the DATA statement are assigned to the variables given in the READ statement one by one. If the number of variables in the READ statement is greater than the number of items available in the DATA statement, the following error will occur:

### Out of data

If the number of variables given in the READ statement are fewer than the number of data items given in the DATA statement, any future READ statements will begin reading at the first item which had not previously been read. If there are no more READ statements, these extra data items will be ignored.

By executing a RESTORE statement, the data items will be read into the READ variables beginning with the first data item once again.

### Example

```
100 DATA "MIAMI","FLORIDA",33507
200 READ CITY$
300 READ STATE$
400 READ ZIP.CODE
500 PRINT CITY$,STATE$,ZIP.CODE
RUN
  MIAMI         FLORIDA         33507
```

## REM

- Cassette
- Disk
- Advanced

The REM statement is used to include programmer's remarks in the program listing. These remarks are generally used to detail the program's operation.

### Configuration

REM *remark*

*remark* can be any sequence of characters. Remarks may also be included at the end of a line by placing a single quote mark (') in front of the *remark*.

Whenever a *remark* is placed on the same line with other BASIC statements, the *remark* must be the final statement on the line.

REM statements are not executed. However, they are output just as they were entered when the program is listed. REM statements cause execution to be slowed somewhat as they use available memory.

A GOTO or GOSUB statement can branch directly to a REM statement. In these cases, program execution will continue with the next executable statement following the REM statement.

### Example

```
100 REM Calculate Future Value
200 I = 10 ' Set interest rate to 10%
```

## RENUM

- Cassette
- Disk
- Advanced

The RENUM command is used to renumber a program's line numbers.

### Configuration

RENUM [new#][,old#][,value]

new# is the first new line number to be used in the renumbering process. The default value for new# is 10.

old# is the line in the program where renumbering is to begin. The default is the program's first line.

value is the amount to be added or subtracted from the present new line number to generate the next new line number. The default for value is 10.

The RENUM command will also change any references to a line number that has been changed. These references could be present in GOTO, GOSUB, ON...GOTO, ON...GOSUB, ERL, THEN, and ELSE statements.

### Example

RENUM 100,500,50

## RESET

☐ Cassette
■ Disk
■ Advanced

The RESET command is used to close all diskette files and reset the system buffer.

### Configuration

RESET

BASIC Reference Guide  299

## RESTORE

■ Cassette
■ Disk
■ Advanced

The RESTORE statement resets the DATA statement pointer to the line specified.

### Configuration

RESTORE [*line*]

*line* is a line number in the program containing a DATA statement.

If a RESTORE is executed without a *line* being given, the next READ statement executed will read the first data item in the first DATA statement in the program. If a *line* is given with the RESTORE statement, the next READ statement will read the first data item in the DATA statement named in *line*.

### Example

```
Ok
100 DATA 29,39,49,59,69,79
200 READ A,B,C
300 READ D,E
400 RESTORE
500 READ F
600 PRINT A,B,C,D,E,F
RUN
 29    39    49    59    69
 29
Ok
```

## RESUME

■ Cassette
■ Disk
■ Advanced

The RESUME statement is used to continue program execution after an error recovery routine was executed.

### Configuration

RESUME [0]
RESUME NEXT
RESUME *line*

*line* refers to a program line number.

When RESUME [0] is used, program execution will continue at the program statement which caused the error. When RESUME NEXT is used, execution will continue at the statement directly after the statement causing the error. When RESUME *line* is used, execution will continue at the specified line number.

If a RESUME statement is used in an area other than an error trap routine, the following error message will be printed:

RESUME without error

### Example

```
100  ON ERROR GOTO 999
200  OPEN "GIT" FOR OUTPUT AS #1
300  GOTO 1100
999  IF ERR=71 THEN PRINT "INSERT DISKETTE"
1000 RESUME
1100 END
```

■ Cassette
■ Disk
## RETURN ■ Advanced

When the RETURN statement is executed, program execution will resume with the statement following the most recently executed GOSUB statement.

### Configuration

RETURN [*line*]

*line* is a program line number. The use of *line* in a RETURN statement is only allowed in Advanced BASIC. This option allows the user to transfer program control to a specified line number while eliminating the GOSUB entry. This option is generally used in event trapping routines.

### Example

```
100 ON Y GOSUB 300,400,500
    .
    .
    .
300 REM SUBROUTINE #1
    .
    .
    .
399 RETURN
400 REM SUBROUTINE #2
    .
    .
    .
499 RETURN
500 REM SUBROUTINE #3
    .
    .
    .
599 RETURN
```

## RIGHT$

- Cassette
- Disk
- Advanced

The RIGHT$ function returns the rightmost characters of a string specified as its argument. The number of characters returned is also given in the argument.

### Configuration

*a$* = RIGHT$(*b$,c*)

*a$* is the string returned by the function. *b$* is the string from which the characters are to be returned.

c is the number of characters to be returned. If c is zero, the null string is returned. If c is greater than or equal to the length of the string given in b$, then that entire string will be returned.

**Example**

```
Ok
100 B$ = "SAN FRANCISCO, CALIFORNIA"
200 PRINT RIGHT$(B$,10)
RUN
CALIFORNIA
Ok
```

## RMDIR

☐ Cassette
■ Disk
■ Advanced

RMDIR is used only in BASIC 2.0 to remove a directory from the disk indicated.

**Configuration**

RMDIR *path*

*path* is a string expression which specifies the sub-directory to be removed. With the exception of '.' and '..' entries, the directory being removed must be void of all files and sub-directories.

**Example**

RMDIR "ACCT \ INV"

In the preceding example, the sub-directory, INV, is removed.

## RND

■ Cassette
■ Disk
■ Advanced

RND is used to return a random number between 0 and 1.

### Configuration

a = RND[(b)]

a is the random number generated. b is used to reseed the random number generator when b is given as a negative value. If b is positive or is left out, RND(b) will generate the next random number in the sequence. RND(0) repeats the last number generated.

The same series of random numbers will be generated unless a new seed is specified for the random number generator. This can be accomplished via the RANDOMIZE statement or by using a negative value for b, as described earlier.

### Example

```
Ok
100 FOR I = 1 TO 3
200 PRINT RND(I);
300 NEXT
RUN
 .7291626      .1425771      .7301725
Ok
```

## RUN

■ Cassette
■ Disk
■ Advanced

The RUN command is used to begin program execution.

### Configuration

RUN [*line*]
RUN *filespec* [,R]

*line* is a program line number. If *line* is included, execution will begin with that line number. If *line* is not specified, execution will begin with the lowest line number. *filespec* is a file specification.

In the first configuration, the RUN command will execute the program currently held in memory.

In the second configuration, the file given in *filespec* is loaded from a cassette or diskette into memory and run. The current memory contents will be erased before the program to be run is loaded. Also, all open files are closed unless the R option is included. If so, all data files will remain open.

### Example

```
Ok
100 PRINT "This is being run."
RUN
This is being run.
Ok
```

## SAVE

- Cassette
- Disk
- Advanced

The SAVE command is used to save a BASIC program file on diskette or cassette.

### Configuration

SAVE *filespec* [,A]
SAVE *filespec* [,P]

*filespec* is the file specification for the file to be saved.

The program file named in *filespec* is written to the device indicated. For diskette files, if the filename consists of 8 or fewer characters and a filename extension is not given, the filename extension .BAS is automatically added to the filename.

If a file already exists on the diskette with the same filename as that of the program file to be saved, the file to be saved will be written over the existing file.

CAS1: is the default device name in Cassette BASIC. In fact, in Cassette BASIC, CAS1: is the only allowable device. The default device is the current drive for Disk and Advanced BASIC.

If the optional A is included in the SAVE command, the program will be saved in ASCII format. If A is not included, the file will be saved in compressed binary format.

The P (or Protection) option causes the program to be saved in an encoded binary format. A protected program cannot be used with the LIST or EDIT commands.

**Example**

SAVE "A:NEW",A

## SCREEN Function

■ Cassette
■ Disk
■ Advanced

The SCREEN function will return the ASCII code for the character displayed at the screen location given in the function.

**Configuration**

a = SCREEN(*row, column* [,*b*])

*a* is the ASCII code returned by the function. *row* is a number or numeric expression corresponding to the row (1 to 25) on the screen. *column* is a number or numeric expression corresponding to the column (1 to 40 or 1 to 80) on the screen.

*b* is a number or numeric expression which evaluates to a value of true (non-zero) or false (zero). If *b* is included and evaluates to true, the color attribute for the character will be returned instead of its ASCII code. The values returned for the color attribute may range from 0 to 255, and can be interpreted as follows.

(a MOD 16)  will be the foreground color.
(a MOD 128) will return the background color.
a>127 will evaluate as true (-1) if the character is blinking; false (0) if not.

### Example

```
100 A = SCREEN(10,10)
200 B = SCREEN(10,10,1)
300 PRINT A:PRINT B
```

## SCREEN Statement

■ Cassette
■ Disk
■ Advanced

The SCREEN statement is used to set the screen attributes which are to be used by any subsequent statements.

### Configuration

SCREEN [*mode*][,[*colorenable*][,[*activepg*][,*visualpg*]]]

*mode* is a number or numeric expression which will evaluate to an integer value of 0, 1, or 2. 0 indicates the text mode at the current width (40 or 80). 1 indicates the medium resolution graphics mode (320 x 200). 2 indicates the high resolution graphics mode. 1 and 2 are only available with the Color/ Graphics Monitor Adapter.

*colorenable* is a numeric expression which returns a value of true or false. *colorenable* enables the color. In the text mode, a false value for *colorenable* disables color allowing only black and white. A true value enables color. In the medium resolution graphics mode, a true value for *colorenable* will enable color. *colorenable* has no effect in high resolution as the only colors allowed are black and white.

*activepg* or active page, can be a number or numeric expression evaluating to an integer from 0 to 7 for screens with a width of 40, or from 0 to 3 for screens with a width of 80. *activepg* selects the page which is to be written to by output statements to the screen.

*visualpg* or visual page, selects the page to be displayed on the screen. The ranges for *visualpg* are the same as for *activepg*.

Any of these parameters may be omitted from the SCREEN statement. If this is the case, the parameter omitted will keep its old value.

If the new screen mode matches that of the previous mode, the screen won't be changed. However, if the new screen mode differs from the old, the new screen mode will be stored and the old screen mode will be erased.

### Example

100 SCREEN 1

## SGN

- Cassette
- Disk
- Advanced

SGN returns the sign of its argument.

### Configuration

$a = SGN(b)$

If the argument *b* is positive, SGN returns a value of 1. If *b* is zero, SGN returns a value of 0. If *b* is negative, SGN returns a value of −1.

### Example

100 ON SGN(A) + 2 GOTO 100,200,300

## SIN

- Cassette
- Disk
- Advanced

The SIN function is used to calculate the sine of its argument.

### Configuration

$a = SIN(b)$

*b* is an angle in radians.

### Example

```
Ok
PRINT SIN(1.7)
 .9916648
Ok
```

## SOUND

- Cassette
- Disk
- Advanced

The SOUND statement is used to transmit sounds from the PC's speaker.

### Configuration

SOUND *frequency, ticks*

*frequency* is the frequency desired in cycles per second (Hertz). *frequency* may range from 37 to 32707.

*ticks* is the length of the sound in clock ticks. There are 18.2 clock ticks per second. *ticks* may range from 0 to 15535.

When the SOUND statement is used to produce a sound, the program continues execution until another SOUND statement is executed. The current SOUND statement can be turned off by executing another SOUND statement with a *ticks* of zero. If the current SOUND statement is not turned off in this manner, it will continue to execute, and no new SOUND statements will be executed until the first SOUND statement has been completed.

### Example

```
100 REM CREATE SOUNDS
200 SOUND 100,2
300 FOR X = 1 TO 1000
400 NEXT X
500 END
```

## SPACE$

- Cassette
- Disk
- Advanced

The SPACE$ function returns a string consisting of the number of blank spaces given as the function's argument.

#### Configuration

$a\$ = SPACE\$(b)$

#### Example

```
Ok
100 FOR X = 1 TO 3
200 A$ = SPACE$(X)
300 PRINT A$;X
400 NEXT
RUN
 1
  2
   3
Ok
```

## SPC

- Cassette
- Disk
- Advanced

SPC is used to print the number of spaces given as its argument.

#### Configuration

PRINT SPC(a)

a is the number of spaces (0 to 255).

SPC can only be used in conjunction with PRINT, LPRINT, and PRINT# statements.

#### Example

```
Ok
100 PRINT SPC(10) "JOHN" SPC(10) "CLARK"
RUN
          JOHN          CLARK
Ok
```

## SQR

- Cassette
- Disk
- Advanced

SQR returns the square root of its argument.

### Configuration

a = SQR(b)

### Example

```
Ok
100 X = 49
200 PRINT SQR(X)
RUN
 7
Ok
```

## STICK

- Cassette
- Disk
- Advanced

The STICK function returns the X and Y coordinates of the two joysticks.

### Configuration

a = STICK(b)

b may range from 0 to 3 and will return the coordinate listed as follows:

```
0   Returns the X coordinate for joystick A.
1   Returns the Y coordinate for joystick A.
2   Returns the X coordinate for joystick B.
3   Returns the Y coordinate for joystick B.
```

### Example

100  X = STICK(2):Y = STICK(3)

## STOP

■ Cassette
■ Disk
■ Advanced

The STOP statement is used to end program execution and return program control to the command level.

### Configuration

STOP

When a STOP statement is executed, the following message will be displayed:

Break in xxxxx

where xxxxx is the line number where the STOP statement was executed.

The STOP statement differs from the END statement in that it does not close open files.

If a CONT command is executed following a STOP statement, program execution will continue.

### Example

```
100  INPUT X,Y
200  Z = X + Y
300  STOP
400  A = Z * 4
500  PRINT A
RUN
?4,8
```

```
Break in 300
Ok
PRINT Z
 12
Ok
CONT
 48
Ok
```

## STR$

■ Cassette
■ Disk
■ Advanced

STR$ returns the string representation of its argument.

### Configuration

a$ = STR$(a)

In the following example, A$ would consist of the string "40". In this case, "40" is a string -- not a number. In other words, "40" (in its string equivalent) would not be used in calculations.

### Example

100  A$ = STR$(40)

## STRIG

■ Cassette
■ Disk
■ Advanced

STRIG returns the status of the joystick button.

### Configuration

STRIG ON
STRIG OFF
a = STRIG(b)

*a* is the value returned by the function.

*b* is a number or numeric expression between 0 and 3. The values returned for *b* are as follows:

0   A value of −1 is returned if the button for joystick A was pressed since the execution of the last STRIG(0) statement. If not, a value of 0 is returned.

1   A value of −1 is returned if the button for joystick A is currently being pressed, and 0 if not.

2   A value of −1 is returned if the button for joystick B was pressed since the execution of the last STRIG(2) statement, and 0 if not.

3   A value of −1 is returned if the button for joystck B is currently pressed, and 0 if not.

A STRIG ON must have been executed before any form of the STRIG(*b*) function can be executed. Once STRIG ON has been executed, BASIC will check to see if a joystick button has been pressed before beginning a new statement.

☐ Cassette
☐ Disk
■ Advanced

## STRIG( )

STRIG( ) is used to enable or disable trapping of the joystick buttons by ON STRIG.

### Configuration

STRIG(*a*) ON
STRIG(*a*) OFF
STRIG(*a*) STOP

*a* is a number or numeric expression that evaluates to 0 or 2. 0 represents joystick A, and 2 represents joystick B.

STRIG ON must be in effect before the pressing of a joystick button can be trapped by ON STRIG. Once STRIG ON has been executed, a check will be made by BASIC at the beginning of the statement to determine whether or not a joystick button had been pressed.

If STRIG OFF is executed, no trapping of the pressing of a joystick button will take place.

If STRIG STOP is executed, trapping of the pressing of a joystick button does not occur. However, if a button is pressed, that event will be stored in memory. When a STRIG ON is executed, an immediate trap will take place.

## STRING$

- Cassette
- Disk
- Advanced

The STRING$ function prints a string of the length specified in its argument. All of the characters returned by the STRING$ function will either be the character corresponding to the ASCII code specified in its argument, or the first character in the string specified in its argument.

### Configuration

a$ =STRING$(*b,c*)   c is ASCII code
a$ = STRING$(*bc$*)   c$ is string

### Example

```
Ok
100 A$ = STRING$(5,61):PRINT A$
RUN
=====
Ok
100 B$ = "JOHN"
200 C$ = STRING$(5,B$)
300 PRINT C$
RUN
JJJJJ
Ok
```

## SWAP

- ■ Cassette
- ■ Disk
- ■ Advanced

The SWAP statement is used to exchange values between two variables.

### Configuration

SWAP *variable1, variable2*

Be careful that you do not use the SWAP statement with variables storing different data types (ex. A% and A$). If the SWAP statement is used with variables of different types, the following error will occur:

Type Mismatch

### Example

```
Ok
100 A$ = "JOHN":B$ = "JACK"
200 PRINT A$,B$
300 SWAP A$,B$
400 PRINT A$,B$
RUN
 JOHN      JACK
 JACK      JOHN
Ok
```

## SYSTEM

- □ Cassette
- □ Disk
- ■ Advanced

The SYSTEM command is used to return to DOS from BASIC. All files are closed by the SYSTEM command prior to the return to DOS.

## TAB

- Cassette
- Disk
- Advanced

The TAB function is used to move the print position (on screen or line printer) to that indicated in its argument.

### Configuration

PRINT TAB(a)
LPRINT TAB(a)

a is the position to which the print position is to be moved. If the current print position on a line is already beyond a, then TAB will move the print position to that specified by a on the next line.

The first position (to the left) is position 1. The position farthest to the right can be calculated by subtracting 1 from the value specified in WIDTH.

### Example

```
Ok
100 PRINT "FIRST NAME" TAB(25) "LAST NAME"
200 PRINT "JOHN" TAB(25) "JOHNSON"
RUN
   FIRST NAME        LAST NAME
   JOHN              JOHNSON
```

## TAN

- Cassette
- Disk
- Advanced

The TAN function returns the tangent of its argument.

### Configuration

a = TAN(b)

*b* is the angle in radians. Degrees can be converted to radians by multiplying by PI/180 where PI = 3.141593.

### Example

```
Ok
100  A = TAN(35*3.141593/180)
200  PRINT A
RUN
 .7002076
Ok
```

## TIME$

☐ Cassette
■ Disk
■ Advanced

TIME$ can be used as a statement to set the current time. TIME$ can also be used as a variable to obtain the current time.

### Configuration (Statement)

TIME$ = *a$*

### Configuration (Variable)

*a$* = TIME$

*a$* is a string expression or constant containing the current time value.

When TIME$ is used as a statement to set the current time, *a$* may be specified in any of the following three formats:

    *hh*    where *hh* sets the hour (0 to 23). The minutes and seconds will be set at 00 by default.

  *hh:mm*  will set the hours and minutes. The range for minutes is 0 to 59. The seconds will be set to 00 by default.

*hh:mm:ss*   will set the hours, minutes, and seconds. The range for seconds is 0 to 59.

When TIME$ is used to obtain the current time, that time will be returned as an 8 character string in the form *hh:mm:ss* where *hh* specifies hours in the range of 00 to 23, *mm* specifies minutes in the range of 00 to 59, and *ss* specifies seconds in the range of 00 to 59.

### Example

```
Ok
100 A$ = TIME$
200 PRINT A$
RUN
 11:52:57
Ok
```

## TIMER

☐ Cassette
■ Disk
■ Advanced

The TIMER function returns a single precision number which indicates the number of seconds since the last System Reset or since midnight (BASIC 2.0 only).

### Configuration

*x* = TIMER

## TRON & TROFF

■ Cassette
■ Disk
■ Advanced

The TRON and TROFF commands are used to trace the execution of program statements.

### Configuration

TRON
TROFF

The TRON (Trace On) command sets a trace flag which prints the line number of each statement in the program as it is executed. The numbers will be displayed within brackets. The TROFF (Trace Off) command turns off the TRON command.

### Example

```
Ok
100  X = 100
200  FOR I = 1 TO 3
300  X = 2 * X
400  PRINT X
500  NEXT
600  END
TRON
Ok
RUN
[100] [200] [300] [400] 200
[500] [300] [400] 400
[500] [300] [400] 800
[500] [600]
Ok
TROFF
Ok
```

## USR

■ Cassette
■ Disk
■ Advanced

USR is used to call the machine language subroutine with the argument specified (c).

### Configuration

a = USR[b] (c)

*b* is the number of the USR routine as given in the DEF USR statement. If *b* is not included, USR0 will be assumed.

### Example

500  A = USR(X/2)

## VAL

■ Cassette
■ Disk
■ Advanced

The VAL function returns the numeric value of its string argument.

### Configuration

a = VAL(*b$*)

*a* is the numeric value returned by the function. *b$* is the string argument whose numeric value is to be returned.

The VAL function eliminates all leading blanks, tabs, and line feeds from the string argument before determining its numeric equivalent.

### Example

```
Ok
100 DATA "JOHN WILSON","212-759-2050"
200 READ NA$,PHONE$
300 A$ = LEFT$(PHONE$,3)
400 A = VAL(A$)
500 IF A = 212 THEN PRINT NA$ TAB(20) "IS LOCATED IN NY"
600 END
RUN
JOHN WILSON     IS LOCATED IN NY
Ok
```

## VARPTR

■ Cassette
■ Disk
■ Advanced

The VARPTR function will return the memory address of the variable specified or the starting memory address of the file control block for the file specified.

### Configuration

a = VARPTR(*variable*)
b = VARPTR(#*filenumber*)

*a* and *b* is the address returned (0 to 65535). This will be an integer which specifies the offset into the current memory segment. This was defined by the DEF SEG statement.

*variable* may be any type of variable (numeric, array, string). *#filenumber* is the filenumber whose file control block starting address is to be returned.

### Example

200  FCB = VARPTR(#1)

## VIEW

□ Cassette
□ Disk
■ Advanced

VIEW is only available in BASIC 2.0's graphics mode. VIEW allows viewports to be defined on the screen surface. Window contents can then be mapped on these viewports, which are in fact, portions of the screen surface.

### Configuration

VIEW [[SCREEN][(x1,y1)-(x2y2)[,[color][,[boundary]]]]]

(x1, y1) - (x2, y2) represent the upper-left and lower-right viewport coordinates.

*color* can be used optionally to fill the viewport with color. *color* can range from 0 to 3. In medium resolution, *color* = 0 denotes the background color, and *color* = 3 denotes the foreground color. In high resolution, *color* = 0 denotes black, and *color* = 1 denotes white.

*boundary* allows a boundary to be drawn around the viewport. *boundary* can be assigned a value from 0 to 3. The color indicated by that value will be used for the boundary.

If the SCREEN argument is not included, all points are plotted relative to the viewport's x1, y1 coordinate. For example, if the following statement was used to define the viewport:

    100 VIEW (50,50) - (100,100)

the point plotted by:

    150 PSET (5,5), 2

would actually be plotted at the screen coordinate (55,55).

If SCREEN is included, points are plotted in absolute terms, and those points plotted outside the viewport will not be visible. If the SCREEN argument was included in our preceding example, the point plotted would not have been visible as it lay outside the viewport.

When VIEW is used without any arguments, the entire viewing surface is defined as the viewport. In medium resolution, this equates to VIEW(0,0)-(319,199). In high resolution, this equates to VIEW(0,0)-(639,199). Using VIEW without any arguments in fact disabled existing viewports.

Multiple viewports may be defined. However, only one viewport can be active at a given moment. The RUN and SCREEN statements will disable the viewports.

VIEW allows the user to make graphics designs appear either larger (by using a larger viewport) or smaller (by using a smaller viewport).

When VIEW is active, CLS will only clear the active viewport. If you wish to clear the entire screen, the viewports must be disabled, and CLS must then be executed.

## WAIT
- Cassette
- Disk
- Advanced

The WAIT statement is used to halt program execution while examining the status of a machine input port.

### Configuration

WAIT port#, a[,b]

port# is the port number (0 to 65535). b is an integer constant or expression with which the data read at the port specified is to be XOR'ed. a is an integer or integer expression which is AND'd with the value returned by the XOR.

When WAIT is executed, the contents of the port address specified will be returned. The value returned is XOR'ed with the value given in b. If no value is specified for b, the default is 0.

The value obtained from the XOR is AND'd with the value given in a. If this value equals 0, WAIT will remain in a loop, stopping program execution.

When the result of the WAIT, XOR, and AND operations does not equal 0, program execution will continue with the statement following WAIT.

## WHILE, WEND

■ Cassette
■ Disk
■ Advanced

The WHILE, WEND statement is a loop which begins with the WHILE statement and ends with a corresponding WEND statement. The loop will continue to execute as long as the expression named after WHILE evaluates as true (not zero).

**Configuration**

WHILE *expression*
⋮
⟵*loop statements*
⋮
WEND

If the *expression* following WHILE is true (not zero), the *loop statements* will be executed until WEND is reached. Program control will then branch back to WHILE where it will again check the *expression* to determine whether or not it evaluates as true. If it does, the *loop statements* execute again. If not, program control will branch execution to the statement following WEND.

All WHILE statements must have a corresponding WEND statement. If not, the following error will be displayed:

WEND without WHILE

### Example

```
Ok
100  X = 3
200  WHILE X
300  PRINT X
400  X = X - 1
500  WEND
600  END
END
 3
 2
 1
Ok
```

## WIDTH

- Cassette
- Disk
- Advanced

The WIDTH statement is used to set the output line width.

### Configuration

WIDTH *characters*
WIDTH *filenumber, characters*
WIDTH *device, characters*

*characters* indicates the number of characters that WIDTH is to be set to.

*filenumber* is the number assigned to a file when it was opened.

*device* is a string constant or expression which identifies the device.

When WIDTH is used with a filenumber as per the second configuration example, the width of the device given in the file specification for the file with that filenumber will be set as indicated. This allows the device width to be changed while the file is still open.

## Example

100 WIDTH "LPT1:",80*

* This line must precede the OPEN statement for LPT1:.

## WINDOW

☐ Cassette
☐ Disk
■ Advanced

The WINDOW statement is used in BASIC 2.0's graphics mode to redefine the screen coordinates.

### Configuration

WINDOW [[SCREEN] (x1, y1) - (x1, y2)]

x1,y1 and x2,y2 are known as **world coordinates.** These coordinates define the world coordinate space that will be mapped into the physical coordinate space defined by VIEW.

The region defined by the world coordinates is known as a **window.** The window allows the programmer to create graphics figures under the world coordinate system and not be limited by the screen boundaries (physical coordinate system.) BASIC will convert the world coordinates into the corresponding physical coordinates for display within the screen.

Under the physical coordinate system, when the following statements are executed:

NEW:SCREEN 2

the screen will assume the following coordinates.

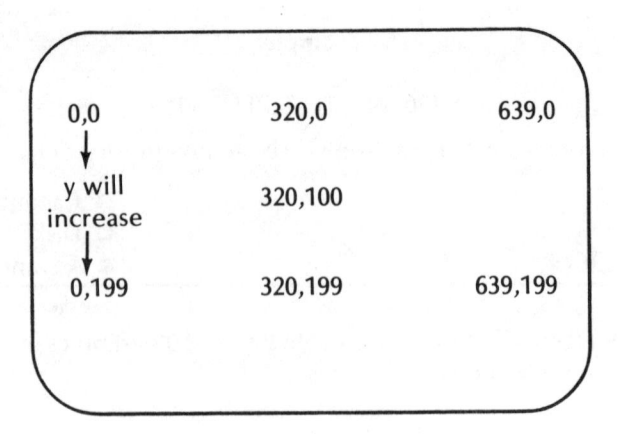

```
┌─────────────────────────────────────────┐
│                                         │
│   0,0              320,0         639,0  │
│    ↓                                    │
│   y will          320,100               │
│   increase                              │
│    ↓                                    │
│   0,199           320,199       639,199 │
│                                         │
└─────────────────────────────────────────┘
```

When WINDOW is executed as follows without the optional parameter SCREEN:

$$\text{WINDOW } (-1, -1) - (1, 1)$$

the following screen is generated:

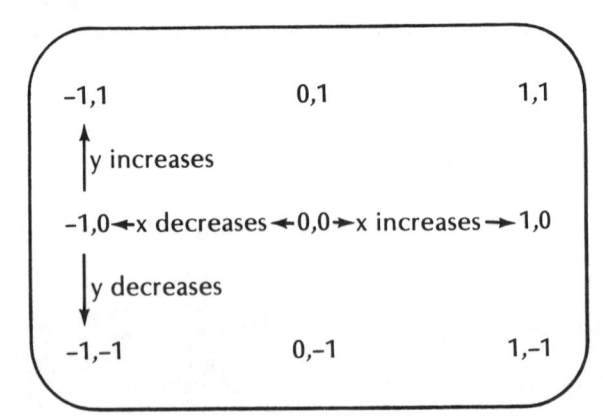

```
┌─────────────────────────────────────────┐
│                                         │
│  -1,1              0,1            1,1   │
│   ↑                                     │
│   │y increases                          │
│                                         │
│  -1,0 ← x decreases ← 0,0 → x increases → 1,0 │
│   │                                     │
│   │y decreases                          │
│   ↓                                     │
│  -1,-1             0,-1           1,-1  │
│                                         │
└─────────────────────────────────────────┘
```

Notice that this screen corresponds to a true cartesian graphics axis. Also, note that the y-coordinate in the WINDOW statement is inverted. This results in (x1, y1) being the lower left-hand coordinate, and (x2, y2) being the upper-right hand coordinate.

When the SCREEN parameter is not included in the WINDOW statement, these coordinates are not inverted. In other words, (x1, y1) defines the upper-left coordinate, and (x2, y2) defines the lower-right coordinate.

For example, the following WINDOW statement:

WINDOW SCREEN (-1, -1) - (1, 1)

defines the screen coordinates as pictured below.

```
(-1,-1)            (0,-1)            (-1,-1)

↑ y decreases

(-1,0)             (0,0)             (1,0)

↓ y increases

(-1,1)             (0,1)             (1,1)
```

WINDOW will rearrange the x and y coordinates so that x1 and y1 are assigned the lowest values. For example, the following statement:

WINDOW (-20, 20) - (20, -20)

would be redefined as:

WINDOW (-20, -20) - (20, 20)

WINDOW allows an image to be displayed as being either smaller or larger. When a larger window is used, the image will appear smaller within the window and will be surrounded with blank spaces.

By using a window with coordinates smaller than the graphics object, only a portion of that object will be displayed, and that portion will appear larger. The areas outside of the window will be **clipped.** Clipping refers to the fact that the points outside of the defined window will not be visible.

## WRITE

■ Cassette
■ Disk
■ Advanced

The WRITE statement is used to send data to the screen.

### Configuration

WRITE [*expressions*]

*expressions* may be string and/or numeric. These may be delimited by either commas or semicolons.

The WRITE statement outputs data much as the PRINT statement does. One difference between the WRITE statement and the PRINT statement, is that when the *expressions* are displayed on the screen with the WRITE statement, they are separated by commas. Also, with the WRITE statement, strings will be delimited by quotation marks. Also, with the WRITE statement, blank spaces are not placed in front of positive numbers.

A carriage return/line feed is output after the last item in *expressions* has been output.

## Example

```
Ok
100 A$ = "JOHN":B$ = "SMITH":C = 2207
200 WRITE A$,B$,C
RUN
"JOHN"   "SMITH", 2207
Ok
```

## WRITE#

- Cassette
- Disk
- Advanced

The WRITE# statement is used to write data to a sequential file.

### Configuration

WRITE# *filenumber, expressions*

*filenumber* is the number assigned to the file when it was opened. *expressions* can either be string or numeric constants or variables. These will be output to the specified file. The items in *expressions* must be separated with commas or semicolons.

WRITE# is much like PRINT# except that it delimits strings with quotation marks and inserts commas between the items in *expressions* as they are written. Therefore, specific delimiters need not be included in the list of items output by WRITE#.

A carriage return/line feed character is inserted after the last item in *expressions* has been output.

Refer to page 135 for an example of the use of WRITE#.

## Appendix A. BASIC Reserved Words

**Reserved words** are words which have a special meaning in BASIC. They include all BASIC commands, statements, function names, and operator names.

Reserved words are not allowed to be used as variable names in BASIC statements. Also, reserved words must be delimited in BASIC statements so that they can be recognized. Generally, words can be delimited through the use of blank spaces or special characters.

### IBM BASIC Reserved Words

| | | | | |
|---|---|---|---|---|
| ABS | DELETE | INT | ON | SIN |
| AND | DIM | INTER$ | OPEN | SOUND |
| ASC | DRAW | IOCTL | OPTION | SPACES |
| ATN | EDIT | IOCTL$ | OR | SPC( |
| AUTO | ELSE | KEY | OUT | SQR |
| BEEP | END | KEY$ | PAINT | STEP |
| BLOAD | ENVIRON | KILL | PEEK | STICK |
| BSAVE | ENVIRON$ | LEFT$ | PEN | STOP |
| CALL | EOF | LEN | PLAY | STR$ |
| CDBL | EQV | LET | PMAP | STRIG |
| CHAIN | ERASE | LINE | POINT | STRING$ |
| CHDIR | ERDEV | LIST | POKE | SWAP |
| CHR$ | ERDEV$ | LLIST | POS | SYSTEM |
| CINT | ERL | LOAD | PSESET | TAB( |
| CIRCLE | ERR | LOC | PRINT | TAN |
| CLEAR | ERROR | LOCATE | PRINT# | THEN |
| CLOSE | EXP | LOF | PSET | TIME$ |
| CLS | FIELD | LOG | PUT | TIMER |
| COLOR | FILES | LPOS | RANDOMIZE | TO |
| COM | FIX | LPRINT | READ | TROFF |
| COMMON | FNxxxxxxxx | LSET | REM | TRON |
| CONT | FOR | MERGE | RENUM | USING |
| COS | FRE | MID$ | RESET | USR |
| CSNG | GET | MKDIR | RESTORE | VAL |
| CSRLIN | GOSUB | MKD$ | RESUME | VARPTR |
| CVD | GOTO | MKI$ | RETURN | VARPTR$ |
| CVI | HEX$ | MKS$ | RIGHT$ | VIEW |
| CVS | IF | MOD | RMDIR | WAIT |
| DATA | IMP | MOTOR | RND | WEND |
| DATE$ | INKEY$ | NAME | RSET | WHILE |
| DEF | INP | NEW | RUN | WIDTH |
| DEFDBL | INPUT | NEXT | SAVE | WINDOW |
| DEFINT | INPUT# | NOT | SCREEN | WRITE |
| DEFSNG | INPUT$ | OCT$ | SGN | WRITE# |
| DEFSTR | INSTR | OFF | SHELL | XOR |

## Appendix B. IBM Personal Computer Device Names

### Device Names

| Device Name | Interpretation |
|---|---|
| KYBD: | **Keyboard**--Used in all versions of BASIC for input. |
| SCRN: | **Screen**--Used in all versions of BASIC for output. |
| LPT1: | **First printer**--Used in all versions of BASIC for output. |
| LPT:2 | **Second printer**--Used only in Disk and Advanced versions of BASIC for output. |
| LPT3: | **Third printer**--Used only in Disk and Advanced versions of BASIC for output. |
| COM1: | **First asynchronous communications adater**-- Used in Disk and Advanced BASIC for input and output. |
| COM2: | **Second asynchronous communications adapter**-- Used only in Disk and Advanced BASIC for input and output. |
| CAS1: | **Cassette tape unit**--Unit in all versions of BASIC for input and output. |
| A: | **First or system disk drive**--Used in Disk and Advanced versions of BASIC for input and output |
| B: | **Second disk drive**--Used in Disk and Advanced versions of BASIC for input and output. |
| C: | **First fixed drive**--Disk and Advanced BASIC |
| D: | **Second fixed drive**--Disk and Advanced BASIC |

## Appendix C. IBM BASIC Error Messages

The following give all of the BASIC error messages along with the related error message number and a description of the error.

1 **NEXT without FOR** The variable that follows NEXT does not match with any preceding FOR statement.

2 **Syntax Error** The program line contains errors in punctuation or spelling (ex. misspelled reserved word, deleted parentheses, etc.).

3 **RETURN without GOSUB** A RETURN statement is found which does not have a corresponding GOSUB.

4 **Out of Data** A READ statement is encountered where no more items are available to be read from DATA statements.

5 **Illegal Function Call** A parameter is sent to a system function that is out of range. Examples of the cause of this error include the following:
- A negative subscript.
- A subscript that is too large.
- A call to a USR function when the starting address for that function had not been given.
- A negative record number used with GET and PUT.
- Trying to list or edit a BASIC program that is protected.
- An argument for a function or statement that is not legal.

6 **Overflow** A number is larger than that allowed by BASIC. If the overflow occurs with an integer, program execution will stop. With non-integers, machine infinity will be returned with the proper sign.

If a number is smaller than that allowed by BASIC, an underflow condition will result. A zero will be returned and execution will continue.

7 **Out of Memory** This error occurs when the program is too large for available memory, or if a program contains too many FOR loops or GOSUB's.

8 **Undefined Line Number**  A reference is made in the program for a line number that does not exist.

9 **Subscript Out of Range**  An array variable contains a subscript that is outside of the range that was given in the DIM statement.

10 **Duplicate Definition**  The same array was defined twice. The following may cause this error:
   1. Two DIM statements were included for the same array.
   2. A DIM statement is used for an array after a default dimension of 10 had been established previously.
   3. An OPTION BASE statement which sets an unacceptable array size was encountered after an array had already been dimensioned by a DIM statement or by default.

11 **Division By Zero**  Either division by zero was attempted, or an attempt was made to raise to a negative power.

12 **Illegal Direct**  An attempt was made to enter a statement in direct mode that can only be entered in indirect.

13 **Type Mismatch**  The data used for a variable does not match that variable's type (ex. numeric data for a string variable).

14 **Out of String Space**  BASIC assigns available free memory to string variables until that memory is depleted. When this occurs, this message will be displayed.

15 **String Too Long**  The user attempted to create a string in excess of 255 characters.

16 **String Formula Too Complex**  The string expression is too long or too complex. Try breaking the expression into smaller, less complex expressions.

17 **Can't Continue**  CONT was used in one of the following situations:

- CONT was used to attempt to start a program that had

stopped because of an error.
- CONT was used to attempt to start a program that had been changed during a temporary halt in execution.
- CONT was used to attempt to start a program that does not exist.

18 **Undefined User Function**  A function was called before it was defined with DEF FN.

19 **No RESUME**  The program branched to an error trapping routine without a RESUME statement.

20 **RESUME Without Error**  A RESUME statement was encountered before an error trapping routine was executed.

22 **Missing Operand**  No operand following an operator such as +, *, AND.

23 **Line Buffer Overflow**  The user tried to enter a line with too many characters.

24 **Device Timeout**  Information was not received from an input or output device within an allotted length of time.

25 **Device Fault**  A hardware error flag was returned by the interface adapter.

26 **FOR without NEXT**  A FOR statement was encountered without a corresponding NEXT.

27 **Out of Paper**  Either the printer has run out of paper or it is not turned on.

29 **WHILE without WEND**  A WHILE statement was encountered without a corresponding WEND.

30 **WEND without WHILE**  A WEND statement was encountered without a corresponding WHILE statement.

50 **FIELD Overflow**  The program contains a FIELD statement in which more bytes are allocated for a random file's record length than were specified for that file in its OPEN statement. Another possibility is a situation where the end of the FIELD buffer was reached while a sequential input/output was being performed to a random file (ex. PRINT#, WRITE#, INPUT#, etc.).

51 **Internal Error**  Some problem is present internally in BASIC. Call IBM or your IBM dealer with a description of the circumstances under which the error occurred.

52 **Bad File Number**  A file number is referenced that is not currently assigned to an open file, or is not within the range of valid file numbers specified during initialization. Another possibility is when an invalid device name is used in a file specification or when the filename is invalid.

53 **File Not Found**  A file is referenced in a LOAD, KILL, FILES, NAME, or OPEN that does not exist on the diskette on the specified drive.

54 **Bad File Mode**  This error occurs when the PUT or GET statement was used with one of the following:
- a sequential file
- a closed file
- to MERGE a non-ASCII file
- to execute an OPEN with a file mode other than input, output, append, or random.

55 **File Already Open**  An attempt was made to open a file that had been previously opened for sequential output or an append. This error also occurs when an attempt is made to kill a file that is open.

57 **Device I/O Error**  An error occurred during a device I/O operation. Error recovery is not possible in DOS.

58 **File Already Exists**  The filename with a NAME statement

duplicates that of a filename already being used on that diskette.

61 **Disk Full**   The entire diskette space is being used. When this error occurs, all files will be closed.

62 **Input Past End**   This error statement indicates that an end of file error occurred. This is caused by an INPUT# statement being executed for a sequential file whose entire data has already been read or for a null file. By using the EOF function, this error can be avoided. Another cause of this error is an attempt to read from a file that had been opened for an append or for output.

63 **Bad Record Number**   The record number used in a GET or PUT statement was either zero or was greater than the allowed maximum (32767). BASIC 2.0 (16,777,215).

64 **Bad Filename**   An invalid form is used for a filename.

66 **Direct Statement in File**   Any ASCII files loaded by LOAD or CHAIN should only contain statements with line numbers. If a direct statement is encountered in a program file being LOAD'ed or CHAIN'ed, the LOAD or CHAIN will be terminated. A common cause of this error is the inclusion of a line feed character.

67 **Too Many Files**   An incorrect file specification was used, or an attempt was made to create a new file when the directory was full.

68 **Device Unavailable**   An attempt was made to open a file to a non-existent device. The device may have been disabled or the hardware may not be present.

69 **Communications Buffer Overflow**   A communications input statement was executed with the input buffer already full. When this error condition occurs, use the ON ERROR statement to attempt input again. When ensuing inputs are attempted, the error condition will be cleared unless charac-

ters are received at a rate faster than the program can process them. In this case, you can try one of the following:
1. Use /C: option when you start BASIC to increase the size of the communications buffer.
2. Use a hand-shaking routine with the other computer to send a message to tell it to stop sending data so that the receiving computer can empty its buffer.
3. Use a lower baud rate for data transmission and reception.

70 **Disk Write Protect**  The user attempted to write to a diskette that was write-protected.

71 **Disk Not Ready**  Either a diskette is not in place or the diskette door is open.

72 **Disk Media Error**  Generally, this is due to a bad diskette, although the cause can be a hardware related problem. The user should copy any existing data to a new diskette and reformat the bad diskette. If the formatting fails, the diskette is unusable and should be discarded.

73 **Advanced Feature**  This error occurs when a program attempts to use an Advanced BASIC feature when Disk BASIC is being used. Load Advanced BASIC and run the program under it.

74 **Rename Across Disks**  During an attempt to rename a file, the wrong disk was used.

75 **Path/File Access Error**  The user used an illegal path or filename during an OPEN, NAME, MKDIR, CHDIR, or RMDIR statement.

76 **Path Not Found**  The specified path cannot be located.

- **Incorrect DOS Version**  The command specified requires a different version of DOS.

— **Unprintable Error**  The error condition does not have a corresponding error message. This message is generally the result of using an ERROR statement with an undefined error code.

Appendix D. 341

## Appendix D. ASCII Character Codes

In the following table, the ASCII codes will be given with any associated characters and control characters (for codes 0-31).

If you wish to display these characters, you can do so by issuing the following statement:

PRINT CHR$(x)

where x is the ASCII code of the character being displayed.

| ASCII Value* | Character | Control Character | ASCII Value | Character | Control Character |
|---|---|---|---|---|---|
| 000 | (null) | NUL | 016 | ▶ | DLE |
| 001 | ☺ | SOH | 017 | ◀ | DC1 |
| 002 | ☻ | STX | 018 | ↕ | DC2 |
| 003 | ♥ | ETX | 019 | ‼ | DC3 |
| 004 | ♦ | EOT | 020 | π | DC4 |
| 005 | ♣ | ENQ | 021 | ə | NAK |
| 006 | ♠ | ACK | 022 | ▬ | SYN |
| 007 | (beep) | BEL | 023 | ↨ | ETB |
| 008 | (backspace) | BS | 024 | ↑ | CAN |
| 009 | (tab) | HT | 025 | ↓ | EM |
| 010 | (line feed) | LF | 026 | → | SUB |
| 011 | (home) | VT | 027 | ← | ESC |
| 012 | (form feed) | FF | 028 | (cursor right) | FS |
| 013 | (carriage return) | CR | 029 | (cursor left) | GS |
| 014 | ♪ | SO | 030 | (cursor right) | RS |
| 015 | ☼ | SI | 031 | (cursor down) | US |

\* Decimal

## 342 IBM BASIC User's Handbook

| ASCII Value | Character | ASCII Value | Character | ASCII Value | Character |
|---|---|---|---|---|---|
| 032 | (space) | 071 | G | 110 | n |
| 033 | ! | 072 | H | 111 | o |
| 034 | " | 073 | I | 112 | p |
| 035 | # | 074 | J | 113 | q |
| 036 | $ | 075 | K | 114 | r |
| 037 | % | 076 | L | 115 | s |
| 038 | & | 077 | M | 116 | t |
| 039 | ' | 078 | N | 117 | u |
| 040 | ( | 079 | O | 118 | v |
| 041 | ) | 080 | P | 119 | w |
| 042 | * | 081 | Q | 120 | x |
| 043 | + | 082 | R | 121 | y |
| 044 | , | 083 | S | 122 | z |
| 045 | - | 084 | T | 123 | { |
| 046 | . | 085 | U | 124 | \| |
| 047 | / | 086 | V | 125 | } |
| 048 | 0 | 087 | W | 126 | ~ |
| 049 | 1 | 088 | X | 127 | ⌂ |
| 050 | 2 | 089 | Y | 128 | Ç |
| 051 | 3 | 090 | Z | 129 | ü |
| 052 | 4 | 091 | [ | 130 | é |
| 053 | 5 | 092 | \ | 131 | â |
| 054 | 6 | 093 | ] | 132 | ä |
| 055 | 7 | 094 | ^ | 133 | à |
| 056 | 8 | 095 | — | 134 | å |
| 057 | 9 | 096 | ` | 135 | ç |
| 058 | : | 097 | a | 136 | ê |
| 059 | ; | 098 | b | 137 | ë |
| 060 | < | 099 | c | 138 | è |
| 061 | = | 100 | d | 139 | ï |
| 062 | > | 101 | e | 140 | î |
| 063 | ? | 102 | f | 141 | ì |
| 064 | @ | 103 | g | 142 | Ä |
| 065 | A | 104 | h | 143 | Å |
| 066 | B | 105 | i | 144 | É |
| 067 | C | 106 | j | 145 | œ |
| 068 | D | 107 | k | 146 | Æ |
| 069 | E | 108 | l | 147 | ô |
| 070 | F | 109 | m | 148 | ö |

Appendix D. 343

| ASCII Value | Character | ASCII Value | Character | ASCII Value | Character |
|---|---|---|---|---|---|
| 149 | ò | 188 | ⹁ | 227 | $\pi$ |
| 150 | û | 189 | ⹁ | 228 | $\Sigma$ |
| 151 | ù | 190 | ⹁ | 229 | $\sigma$ |
| 152 | ÿ | 191 | ┐ | 230 | $\mu$ |
| 153 | Ö | 192 | └ | 231 | $\tau$ |
| 154 | Ü | 193 | ┴ | 232 | $\Phi$ |
| 155 | ¢ | 194 | ┬ | 233 | $\Theta$ |
| 156 | £ | 195 | ├ | 234 | $\Omega$ |
| 157 | ¥ | 196 | ─ | 235 | $\delta$ |
| 158 | Pt | 197 | ┼ | 236 | $\infty$ |
| 159 | $f$ | 198 | ╞ | 237 | $\emptyset$ |
| 160 | á | 199 | ╟ | 238 | $\in$ |
| 161 | í | 200 | ╚ | 239 | $\cap$ |
| 162 | ó | 201 | ╔ | 240 | $\equiv$ |
| 163 | ú | 202 | ╩ | 241 | $\pm$ |
| 164 | ñ | 203 | ╦ | 242 | $\geq$ |
| 165 | Ñ | 204 | ╠ | 243 | $\leq$ |
| 166 | ª | 205 | ═ | 244 | ⌠ |
| 167 | º | 206 | ╬ | 245 | ⌡ |
| 168 | ¿ | 207 | ╧ | 246 | $\div$ |
| 169 | ⌐ | 208 | ╨ | 247 | $\approx$ |
| 170 | ¬ | 209 | ╤ | 248 | ° |
| 171 | ½ | 210 | ╥ | 249 | • |
| 172 | ¼ | 211 | ╙ | 250 | · |
| 173 | ¡ | 212 | ╘ | 251 | $\sqrt{}$ |
| 174 | « | 213 | ╒ | 252 | n |
| 175 | » | 214 | ╓ | 253 | 2 |
| 176 | ░ | 215 | ╫ | 254 | ■ |
| 177 | ▒ | 216 | ╪ | 255 | (blank 'FF') |
| 178 | ▓ | 217 | ┘ | | |
| 179 | │ | 218 | ┌ | | |
| 180 | ┤ | 219 | █ | | |
| 181 | ╡ | 220 | ▄ | | |
| 182 | ╢ | 221 | ▌ | | |
| 183 | ╖ | 222 | ▐ | | |
| 184 | ╕ | 223 | ▀ | | |
| 185 | ╣ | 224 | $\alpha$ | | |
| 186 | ║ | 225 | $\beta$ | | |
| 187 | ╗ | 226 | $\Gamma$ | | |

## Appendix E. Extended Code For Use With INKEY$

Certain keys or key combinations cannot be represented with standard ASCII code. These are represented with extended codes. The INKEY$ variable can be used to read such a code from the keyboard into a variable.

If a two character string is returned via INKEY$, the first character of that string should be the null character (00 hex). Generally, the second character can be used to allow determination of the key that was pressed. The ASCII codes for the second character are given in decimal in the following table with their associated keys.

| Second Code | Meaning |
| --- | --- |
| 3 | (null character) NUL |
| 15 | (shift tab) \| ← |
| 16-25 | ALT Q, W, E, R, T, Y, U, I, O, P |
| 30-38 | ALT Z, X, C, V, B, N, M |
| 44-50 | Function keys F1 through F10 (when disabled as soft keys). |
| 71 | Home |
| 72 | Cursor Up |
| 73 | Pg Up |
| 75 | Cursor Left |
| 77 | Cursor Right |
| 79 | End |
| 80 | Cursor Down |
| 81 | Pg Down |
| 82 | Ins |
| 83 | Del |
| 84-93 | F11 through F20 (Uppercase F1 through F10) |
| 94-103 | F21 through F30 (CTRL F1 through F10) |
| 104-113 | F31 through F40 (ALT F1 through F10) |
| 114 | CTRL PrtSc |
| 115 | CTRL Cursor Left (Previous Word) |
| 116 | CTRL Cursor Right (Next Word) |
| 117 | CTRL End |
| 118 | CTRL Pg Dn |
| 119 | CTRL Home |
| 120-131 | ALT 1, 2, 3, 4, ,5 ,6 ,7 , 8, 9, 0, -, = |
| 132 | CTRL Pg Up |

# Appendix F. Keyboard Diagram and Scan Codes

## Keyboard Scan Codes

| Keyboard Position | Scan Code (Hex) | Keyboard Position | Scan Code (Hex) |
|---|---|---|---|
| 1 | 01 | 43 | 2B |
| 2 | 02 | 44 | 2C |
| 3 | 03 | 45 | 2D |
| 4 | 04 | 46 | 2E |
| 5 | 05 | 47 | 2F |
| 6 | 06 | 48 | 30 |
| 7 | 07 | 49 | 31 |
| 8 | 08 | 50 | 32 |
| 9 | 09 | 51 | 33 |
| 10 | 0A | 52 | 34 |
| 11 | 0B | 53 | 35 |
| 12 | 0C | 54 | 36 |
| 13 | 0D | 55 | 37 |
| 14 | 0E | 56 | 38 |
| 15 | 0F | 57 | 39 |
| 16 | 10 | 58 | 3A |
| 17 | 11 | 59 | 3B |
| 18 | 12 | 60 | 3C |
| 19 | 13 | 61 | 3D |
| 20 | 14 | 62 | 3E |
| 21 | 15 | 63 | 3F |
| 22 | 16 | 64 | 40 |
| 23 | 17 | 65 | 41 |
| 24 | 18 | 66 | 42 |
| 25 | 19 | 67 | 43 |
| 26 | 1A | 68 | 44 |
| 27 | 1B | 69 | 45 |
| 28 | 1C | 70 | 46 |
| 29 | 1D | 71 | 47 |
| 30 | 1E | 72 | 48 |
| 31 | 1F | 73 | 49 |
| 32 | 20 | 74 | 4A |
| 33 | 21 | 75 | 4B |
| 34 | 22 | 76 | 4C |
| 35 | 23 | 77 | 4D |
| 36 | 24 | 78 | 4E |
| 37 | 25 | 79 | 4F |
| 38 | 26 | 80 | 50 |
| 39 | 27 | 81 | 51 |
| 40 | 28 | 82 | 52 |
| 41 | 29 | 83 | 53 |
| 42 | 2A | | |

346 IBM BASIC User's Handbook

## Keyboard Diagram

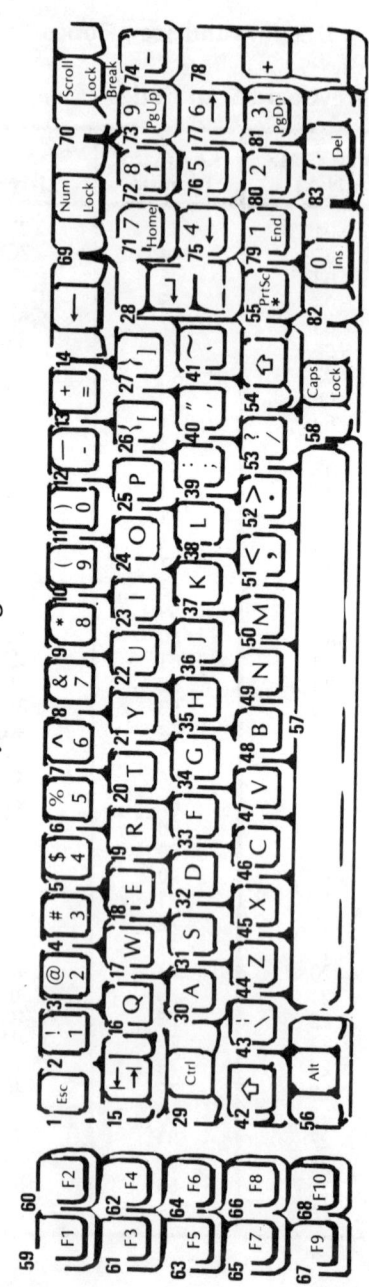

The number in the upper left hand corner of the key indicates the keyboard position.

# INDEX

A Command **179**-180, 183
A Parameter 149, 151
A: 124, 153-154, **334**
ABS 109, 110, **194**
Absolute Form 161
Absolute Value 194
Active Page 205
Addition 52, 62
Advanced BASIC 14-17, 171, 340
Advanced Feature 340
ALL 210
Allen, Paul 11
AND **56**, 58-59, 61-62, 186, 188-189, 295, 324
Animation 184
APPEND 132, 276
Apple 12
Argument 22
Array Variables 97
Arrays 93, 95-96, 100
Arrays, data types 100
Arthmetic Expression **50**-51, 53-54
ASC 116-117, 194
ASCII **39**-40, 155, 202, 305-306, 315
ASCII Code 113, 194, 341-343
Arctangent 195
Aspect Ratio 170, 176-177
Assembly Language 12, 13
Assignment Statements 49
Asynchronous Communications Adapter 19, 209, 269
ATN 20, 108, 195
AUTO 24, 25, 195-196

B 166
B Command 178, 183
B: 124, 153-154, **334**
Backslash 124

Backspace Key 30
Bad File Mode 338
Bad File Number 338
Bad Filename 339
Bad Record Number 338
BASIC 1.0 14
BASIC 1.1 14
BASIC 2.0 **14**-15, 123-124, 245, 247, 302
BASIC Command **17**-20
BASIC, IBM 11
BASIC, advanced 171
BASIC, device names 334
BASIC, error messages 335
BASIC, graphics statements 164
BASIC, Microsoft 11, 12
BASIC, reserved words 333
BASICA 17
Baud Rate 339
BEEP 197
Binary Conversion 59, 60
BLOAD 125, 197
Boolean Operators 50, 56
Branching 88, 90
BSAVE 125, **198**-199
Buffer 19, 130-**131,** 277
Buffer Variable 142
Built-In Function 105, 106

C Command **178**-179, 183
C: 124, 153-154, 334
Calculator Mode 20
CALL 199
Can't Continue 336
Carriage Return Line Feed 67
CAS1: 124, 153-154, 278, 305, **334**
Cassette BASIC 14, 15
CD 279-280
CDBL 109-110, **200**

**Note to Reader:** Please note that for selected topics with several page references, one reference may be in bold type. The page noted in bold denotes the primary reference or definition of that topic.

## 348  IBM BASIC User's Handbook

CHAIN 125, 149, 151-152, **200**-**201**, 210, 339
CHDIR 201-202
CHR$ 40, 116-117, **202**
CINT 109, 110, 203
CIRCLE 168-171, **203**-204, 208
CLEAR 204, 282
Clipping 330
CLOSE 134, 141, **205**
Closing, Random File 141
CLS 205, 324
COBOL 12
Coefficient 41
Color Burst 157
COLOR 159-163, **206**-209
Color Graphics Monitor Adapter **155**, 157, 184, 281
COM STOP 209
COM **209**, 268-269
COM1: 124, 153-154, **334**
COM2: 124, 153-154, **334**
Command **21**, 22
Commodore 12
COMMON 152, 201, **210**
Communication Buffer 279
Communication: Buffer Overflow 339
Communcation Receive Buffer 19
Compiled Code 13, 14
Compiled Language 13, 14
Compiler 13
Compound Expression 52, 53
Concatenation 82, 112, 113
Conditional Branches 87
Conditional Statements 90
CONFIG.SYS 19
Constant 39, 41
CONT **210**, 244, 312-313, 336
Control Key 27
COS 20, 106-108, **211**
Cosecant 107
Cotangent 107
CR/LF **67**, 83, 136-137
CRSLIN 212
CS 279
CSNG 109-110, **211**
CTRL 27
CTS 279
Current Directory 125, 126, 127, 201-202

CVD 146, 212
CVI 146, 212
CVS 146, 212

D 41, 78
D Command 175
D: 124, 153-154, 334
Dartmouth College 11
Data 39
DATA 93, 100-103, **212**-213, 296, 299, 335
Data Conversion 47
Data Files 121
Data Segment 217
Data, inputting 63, 83-85
Data, outputting 63
Data, reading 146
DATE$ 213-214
DEF FN 110-111, **214**-215, 337
DEF SEG 197, 199, **217,** 283, 289
DEF USR 217
Default Directory 126, 128
Default Drive 36
DEFDBL 46, **216**
DEFINT 46, 216
DEFSNG 46, 216
DEFSTR 46, 47, **216**
Del Key 30, 32
DELETE 218
Delimiter 64-65, 68 121
Descriptor **118,** 142
Device Fault 124, 337
Device I/O Error 338
Device Name **123,** 124, 127, 334
Device Timeout 337
Device Unavailable 339
DIM 97-99, 100, **219,** 336
DIR 125
Direct Mode 20
Direct Statement in File 339
Direct Access 129
Directory 124
Directory Path 123-124, **127**
Directory, Current 125-**126,** 201-202
Directory, Default 126
Directory, Parent 128
Directory, Root 125, 126
Directory, Tree-Structured 126
Disk BASIC **14**-**17**

Disk Full 338
Disk Media Error 339
Disk Write Protect 339
Disk Write Ready 339
Division by Zero 336
DOS 14-15, 316
DOS, start-up 16
Double-Precision 42, **43,** 44, 48, 79, 100, 118, 200
DRAW 174-175, 208, **219**-222
DRAW, A Command **179**-180, 183
DRAW, B Command **179,** 183
DRAW, C Command **178**-179, 183
DRAW, D Command **175,** 182
DRAW, E Command **175,** 183
DRAW, F Command **175,** 183
DRAW, G Command **175,** 183
DRAW, GDL Commands **175**-184
DRAW, H Command **175,** 183
DRAW, L Command **175,** 183
DRAW, M Command **177**-178, 183
DRAW, N Command **178,** 183
DRAW, P Command **181,** 183
DRAW, R Command **175,** 183
DRAW, S Command **180**-181, 183
DRAW, TA Command **180,** 183
DRAW, U Command **175,** 182
DRAW, X Command **182,** 183
DRAW, scaling factor 175-176
DS 279-280
DSR 279
Dummy Argument **110,** 111, 118
Duplicate Definition 336

E 41
E Command 175, 183
EDIT 28, 33-34, **222**
Editing **28**-33
Editing Keys 28, **29,** 30
Editor 28
ELSE 88, **236**-237
END 210, 222-223, 312
Entering, Program 23
EOF 139, 146, **223,** 338
EQ 55, 62
EQV **56,** 59, 62
ERASE 98-99, 224
ERL 225

ERR 225
Error Messages, BASIC 335
ERROR 225-226
ESC Key 20
Evaluation, order of 52, 53, 56, 61
EVEN 279
Execute Mode 22
EXP 20, 108, **226**-227
Exponent 41
Exponential Notation 41, 77
Exponentiation 51-52, 62
Expression 50
Expression, compound 52
Expression, simple 52

F Command 175. 183
F1-F10 244, 247
Field 121
FIELD 69, **142**-143, 227-228, 337
Field Overflow 337
Field Variables 142
File Access 128
File Already Exists 338
File Already Open 338
File Buffer 141
File Commands 149
File Not Found 37, 338
File Number 338
File Specification 18, 123, 124
Filename 35, **123,** 127, 153, 339
Filename Extension 35, 123
Files **121**
FILES **19,** 149, 151-**152,** 228-229
Files, opening 130-134
FIX 109, **229**
Fixed Disk 124
Fixed Length Sting Field 78
Fixed Point Numbers 41-42, 44
Floating Point Numbers 41-42, 44
FOR 87, 92-93, 103, **230**-231, 335, 337
For Without Next 337
Format 69
Format String 69
Formatting Characters **69**-80
Formatting, horizontal 80
Formatting, vertical 82
FORTRAN 12
FRE 99, 118-119, **231**-232

## 350 IBM BASIC User's Handbook

Function 105
Function, built-in 105-106
Function, user-defined 105, **110**-111, 214-215
Functions, math 105, 107
Functions, numeric 105
Functions, string handling 113

G Command 175
Gates, William 11
GDL Commands **175**-184
GE 55, 62
GET 145-146, 184-187, 227, **232**-234, 279, 335, 338
GOSUB 87-89, 91, **234**-235, 247, 300-301, 335
GOTO 87-88, 91, **235**-237, 297
GT 55, 62

H Command 175
HEX$ 236
Hexadecimal 236
Hexadecimal Numbers 41, 42
High Level Programming Language **12**, 13
High Resolution Graphics 155-156, **164**
Home Key 29
Home Position 33, **205**
Horizontal Formatting 80
Housekeeping 118-119, 232

I 133
I/O Operations 19
IBM BASIC 39
IBM BASIC, history 11
IBM BASIC, start-up 15-20
IF 87-88, 90, **236**-237
Illegal Direct 336
Illegal Function Call 335
Immediate Mode 20
IMP 56, 59, 62
Incorrected DOS Version 340
Index Variable 93
Indirect Mode 20
INKEY$ **237**, 245
INKEY$ Extended Codes 344
INP 238
INPUT 63, 83-85, 100, 131, **239**-241, 278

INPUT# 136-137, 146, **240**-242, 338
INPUT$ 136, 138, **241**-242
Input Past End 338
Input Prompt 83
INSTR 242-243
INT 109, 229, **243**-244
Integer **41**, 43, 117, 263
Integer Division **52**, 62
Internal Error 337
Interpreted Language 13, 14
Interpreter 15, 21

Joysticks 274-275

Kemeny, John 11
KEY **244**-247, 272
Keyboard Scan Codes 345-346
Keyword 21
KILL 125, 149, 151, **247**-248
Kurtz, Thomas 11
KYBD: 124, 153-154, **334**

L Command 175
LE 55, 62
LEFT$ 113-114, **248**
LEN 248-249
LET 49, 100, 249
LF 279-280
Line Buffer Overflow 337
Line Editor 28
LINE INPUT 63, 83-85, **251**
LINE INPUT# 136, 137, 146, **252**
Line Number 21, **22**, 23, 196, 298
LINE 165-167, 208, **249**-251
LINE, B **166**-167, 250
LINE, BF **166**-167, 250
LIST 25, 27-28, 244, **253**-254
Listing Program 25, 27
Literals 79
LLIST 28, 254
LOAD 36-37, 125, 144, 149-151, 244, **255**-256, 339
Loading, program 36
LOC 139, 140, 146, **256**-257
LOCATE **257**-258
LOF 139-140, 146, **258**-259
LOG 20, 108, 259
Logical Operators **56**-58, 60-61

Loops **92**-94
Loops, nested 93
LPOS 259-260
LPR **156,** 166-168, 177
LPRINT 68, 82, **260,** 310
LPRINT USING 68, **261**
LPT1: 124, 153-154, 244, **334**
LPT2: 124, 153-154, **334**
LPT3: 124, 153-154, **334**
LSET 143, 146, 227, **261**-262
LT 55, 62

M Command **177**-178, 183
Machine Language 12, 13
Machine Language Subroutines 19
Mantissa 41
MARK 279
Math Functions 105, 107
Medium Resolution Graphics 155-156, **161**-162
MERGE 125, 149, 151, 200-201, **262**-263
Microprocessor 12
Microsoft BASIC 11, 12
Microsoft Corp 11
MID$ 113-115, **263**-264
Missing Operand 337
MITS Altair 11
MKD$ 144, 146, 148, 262, **265**-266
MKDIR 125, **265**
MKI$ 144, 146, 148, 262, **265**-266
MKS$ 144, 146, 148, 262, **265**-266
MOD 52, 62, 81, 306
Modulo Arithmetic **52,** 62
Monochrome Display Printer Adapter 155, 160
MOTOR 266
MS-DOS 11
Multiple Statements 37

N Command 178, 183
NAME 125, 149, 151, **266**-267, 338
NE 55, 62
Negation 52, 62
Nested Loop 93
NEW 22, 267
NEXT 87, 92, 93, 103, **230**-231, 337
Next without For 335
NO Resume 337

NONE 279
NOT 56, **58**-59, 62
Null 47
Numeric Constants 41
Numeric Data 40
Numeric Formatting Character 69-78
Numeric Precision **42**-44
Numlock 28

O 133
OCT$ 267-268
Octal 20
Octal Numbers 41-42
ODD 278
OK 17
ON 87-88, **90**-91
ON COM 209, **268**-269
ON ERROR **269**-270, 339
ON...GOSUB 270-271
ON...GOTO 235, **270**-271
ON...KEY 271-272
ON...PEN 273
ON...PLAY 274
ON...STRIG 274-275
ON...TIMER 275-276
OPEN COM 278-280
OPEN 125, 131-134, 141, 146, 205, **276**-278
OPEN, record length parameter 19
Opening, random file 141
Operands 12, 337
Operations 39
Operators **39,** 50-51
OPTION BASE 99-100, **280**-281, 336
OR 56, **58**-59, 61-62, 186, 188-190, 295
Order of Evaluation 52-53, 56, 61-**62**
Out of Data 335
Out of Memory 335
Out of Paper 337
OUT 281
Out of String Space 336
OUTPUT 132, 276
Overflow 335

P Command 181, 183
P Parameter 149
Page 157-158

PAINT 171-174, 208, **281**-282
PAINT, Tiling 172-174, **281**-282
Palette **162**-163, 208
Parameter 22
Parent Directory 128
Parentheses 53
PASCAL 12
Path 123-**125,** 127
Path Not Found 240
Path/File Access Error 340
PEEK 283
PEN 273, **283**-285
Physical Coordinates 327-330
Pixel 155-156
PLAY 274, **285**-287
PMAP 287-288
POINT 288-289
POKE 289
POS 290
PR 279-280
Precision 42
PRESET 164-165, 186, 190, 208, **293**
PRINT 21, 63-68, **290**-291, 310, 337
Print Position 317
PRINT USING 63, 68, **291**-292
Print Zone 64
PRINT# 134-134, **292,** 310
PRINT# USING 134-135, **292**
Program Entry 23
Program Files 121
Program Lines 22-24
Program Listing 25, 27
Program Loading 36
Program Mode 20, 21
Program, running 34
Program, saving 35
Programming Language 12
Prompt 17
PSET 164-165, 186-190, 208, **293**
PUT 145-146, 184-188, 227, 261, 279, **293**-295, 335, 338

R Command 175, 183
R Parameter 150, 151
Radian 106
RAM 14, 22
Random Access 128
Random File 19, 128-130, 293

Random File Access 140, 147-148
Random File Buffer 141, 293
Random File, closing 141
Random File, opening 141
Random File, writing data 143
Random Number Generator 295
RANDOMIZE 295, 303
READ 93, 100-103, 212-213, **296,** 299, 335
Reading Data 146
Reading, record 145
Reading, sequential files 135
Record 121
Record Length 128
Record, reading 145
Record, writing 145
Relational Expression 50
Relational Operators **54**-55, 57
Relative Form 161-162
REM 297
Rename Across Disks 340
RENUM 25-26, **297**-298
Reserved Word **21,** 45-46, 333
RESET 298
RESTORE 101, 296, **299**
RESUME **299**-300, 337
RETURN 89, 234-235, 271, **300**-301, 335
RETURN without GOSUB 335
RIGHT$ 113-114, **301**-302
RMDIR 125, 302
RND 303
ROM 14
Root Directory 125-126
RS-232 14
RSET 143, 227
RTS 279
RUN 22, 34-35, 125, 149, 151, 244, **303**-304
Run-Time Monitor 13
Running, Program 34

S Command 180-181, 183
SAVE 35-36, 125, 149, 244, 255, 263, **304**-205
Saving, Program 35
Scaling Factor 175-176
Screen Buffer 205
Screen Coordinates 161

# Index

SCREEN 157-159, 206, 212, 244, **305**-307, 323
SCRN: 124, 153-154, **334**
Secant 107
Sequential Access 128, 130
Sequential Files 128-140
Sequential Files, reading 135
Sequential Files, writing 135, 135
SGN 109, 308
Simple Expression 52
SIN 20, 106-108, **308**
Single Precision 42, **43,** 44, 48, 79, 100, 117
SOUND 308
Source Code 13, 14
Source File 197-198
SPACE$ 81-82, 279, **309**-310
SPC 80-81, **310**
SQR 20, 109, **311**
Start-Up 15-20
Statement 21
STEP 93, 230
STICK 311-312
STOP 210, 312
Stop Bits 279
STR$ 116, 147, **313**
STRIG **313**-315
String Concatenation 112, 113
String Constant 39
String Formatting Character 78-80
String Formula Too Complex 336
String Handling 112
String Handling Functions 113
String Space 118
String Too Long 336
String Variable 142
String Value 142
STRING$ 315
String Numeric Conversion 116
Strings 39, 40
Sub-Directory 126, 302
Subroutines 89-90
Subscript 95, 335
Subscript Out of Range 336
Subscipted Variable 95
Subtraction 52, 62
SWAP 316
Switch 18

Syntax Error 335
SYSTEM 316

TA Command 180, 183
Tab Key 30, 31
TAB 80-81, **317**
Tables 95-97
TAN 20, 106-108, **317**-318
Tangent 317-318
Text Mode 155, 159
THEN 87-88, 236-237
Tiling 172-174
TIME$ 318-319
TIMER 275-276, 295, **319**
Too Many Files 339
Trace 319-320
Transmit Receive Bits 279
Tree Structured Directory 126
TROFF 244, **319**-320
TRON 244, **319**-320
TRS-80 12
Truncation 22, 229
Two's Complement 59
Two-Dimensional Arrays 96
Type Mismatch 336

U Command 175, 182
Undefined Line Number 336
Undefined User Function 337
Unprintable Error 340
User-Defined Function 105, **110**-111
USR 217, **320**-321, 335

VAL 116, 321
Value, Variable 45, 47
Variable 45, 95
Variable Length String Field 78
Variable Name 45
Variable Table 117, 118
Variable Type Characters 46, 47
Variable Types, mixing 54
Variable Value 45, 47
VARPTR 322
Vertical Formatting 82
VIEW 287, 322-324
Viewports 322-324

WAIT 324

WEND 87, 94, **325**-326, 337
WHILE 87, 94, **325**-326, 337
While without Wend 337
WIDTH 67, 68, 81, 159, **326**-327
WINDOW 287-289, **327**-328
Work Area, BASIC 19
World Coordinates 327-330
WRITE 330-331
WRITE# 134, 135, 331
Writing Data, random files 143
Writing, record 145
Writing, sequential files 134, 135

X Command 182, 183
XOR 56, 58, **61**-62, 186, 188-189, 295, 324

## Special Characters

&H 20
&O 20
/C 339
/C: 18, 19
/D: 18, 20
/F: 18, 19
/M: 18, 19, 20
/S: 18, 19, 141
16 Bit Interger Mask 167
8088 Machine Language 12
< 18
> 18

# ABOUT THE
# WEBER SYSTEMS, INC. STAFF

In 1982, Weber Systems, Inc. began a start-up publishing division specializing in books related to the personal computer field. They initially published three books, and within a year, expanded their list to eighteen machine-specific titles, with fourteen more scheduled for early 1984.

All Weber Systems USER'S HANDBOOKS are created by an in-house editorial staff with extensive backgrounds in computer science and technical writing. The three basic tenets of their publishing philosophy are: quality, timeliness and maintenance (frequent updating).

Weber Systems is located in Cleveland, Ohio.

Other Books in This Series
Published by Ballantine Books

**VIC-20® USER'S HANDBOOK**
**IBM PC® & XT® USER'S HANDBOOK**
**KAYPRO® USER'S HANDBOOK**